the
Reel World

Scoring for Pictures

By Jeff Rona

Miller
Freeman
Books

San Francisco

Published by Miller Freeman Books
An imprint of Music Player Network
www.MusicPlayer.com
Publishers of *Guitar Player, Bass Player, Keyboard, Gig, MC2*, and *EQ* Magazines
600 Harrison Street, San Francisco, CA 94107

Distributed to the book trade in the U.S and Canada by Publisher's Group West, 1700 Fourth Street, Berkeley, CA 94710

Distributed to the music trade in the U.S. and Canada by Hal Leonard Publishing, P.O. Box 13819, Milwaukee, WI 53213

Editor: Richard Henderson
Additional Edits: James Levine, Robyn Lynn
Page Layout and Production by Greene Design
Cover Design: Richard Leeds
Cover Photo of conductor: R. Nesmith/FPG International

"Orchestral Instrument Ranges and Transpositions of Popular Instruments," pgs. 264-266 reproduced from *Inside the Music* © 1999 Dave Stewart, published by Miller Freeman Books

Library of Congress Cataloging-in-Publication Data:
Rona, Jeffrey C. (Jeffrey Carl), 1957-
        The reel world: scoring for pictures: a practical guide to the art, technology, and business of composing for film and television/by Jeff Rona
                p. cm.
        includes index.
        ISBN 0-87930-591-6 (alk. Paper)
        1. Motion picture music—Instruction and study. 2. Television music—Instruction and study. 3. Composition (Music) I. Title.

MT64.M65 R66 2000
781.5'4213—dc21   00-056058
                                                             CIP

Printed in the United States of America
00 01 02 03 04 05   5 4 3 2 1

for
z

Thanks

The author wishes to thank the following: *Keyboard's* Dominic Milano for allowing me the forum in his magazine for my thoughts and words in the first place. To Robert Doerschuk, Tom Darter and Ernie Rideout for performing ongoing grammatical surgery over the years to help people make sense of this all. To Marvin Sanders and all the wonderful people at *Keyboard* who have helped me along the way. To James Levine for keeping it all together. To the many amazing film composers who have shared their craft and wisdom with me—there is no better place to learn how. To Mark Isham for his friendship and wonderful sense of simplicity and ambience. To my dear, dear friend Hans Zimmer for his constant support, advice and nagging. To my compatriots at Media Ventures with whom I've been able to learn, share, criticize, inspire, and take it on the chin. To the directors and producers who have showed me the way to really listen to music. To all the worldclass musicians and artists with whom I've collaborated, and who have made my work so much better in so many ways. To David Low for keeping me from getting into more trouble. A special thanks to Cheryl for helping me to get into more trouble. A heartfelt thanks to my family for letting me hide away from the real world into order to be in a better place (and write about it from time to time).

⊳ Contents

SECTION TWO: Technology

SECTION THREE: Career

INTRODUCTION

Why are virtually no films made without music? Music adds emotional energy to the stories and characters in films in a way that a film can not do on its own. Film music is a unique entity. While every other aspect of a film is designed to give the illusion of reality—from the sets, costumes, lighting, artwork, editing, special effects, right down to the actors performances and the director's vision—music does nothing like that. Music elevates a film's sense of reality and places it into an opera-like level, where the characters and stories are larger than life, yet made more easy for us to relate to our own lives. Music becomes an amplifier of everything that occurs with it. One has only to see a dramatic film with its music removed to get a clear sense of the contribution music makes.

My first real interest in film music came from a friend who was a devoted film music fan with an enormous collection of score recordings. Although I was already a musician and composer, I had not really paid much attention to film music. That all changed quickly when I began to listen to scores on their own. It transformed how I watched (and listened to) movies. Soon enough, I knew that I wanted to get involved in this art form.

A well-written film score leads the audience gently through the emotions and actions on the screen without letting them know just how much they are being helped along. It breathes of musical history while firmly being a highly contemporary style, allowing for so many kinds of musical explorations and experimentation with sound, rhythm, emotion and structure. It differs from conventional musical genres by its basic form as a story-telling device, being an intrinsic component of the story on the screen. It is subordinate to that story, but the best scores almost always speak for themselves to the listener.

Throughout the relatively short time I've been involved in film scoring, it has been my good fortune to meet some wonderful and inspiring people who have contributed a great deal not only to the art of film music but to my own knowledge of the craft. The tremendous amount which I've learned from them I use every day in my scoring work. The same is true for all the fantastic directors I've had the pleasure to work with. Also, I have had a forum, via articles and occasional seminars, to describe to others what I've absorbed. There is a Chinese proverb which says you can not truly know something until you have taught it to another. This is certainly true for me. As I continue through the life-long process of learning and developing my musical craft, I have been aided to a great extent by the people who have listened to me talk or have read my writing. They have helped to crystallize the formless ideas that go into creating my music, and as a result my approach to making music has evolved in new and unexpected ways.

In this book are the observations, ideas, opinions and lessons I have assembled in my head while working as a composer and musician. These will describe to you some of what it means to create music in a very demanding and specific world. As much as possible I have tried to broaden the scope here to include, in addition to my own, the ideas and thoughts of others involved in this field.

Film music is a highly technical artform. First, it must fit the very specific timespan, energy level and transitions created by the director and editor, which requires not only forethought, but precise calculation as well. The performance and recording of a film's music must ultimately be compatible with the highly technical formats of movie theaters, television broadcasts, dubbing stages, and recording studios. A film composer today must know a great deal about the technical process that synchronizes picture and sound in addition to the musical aesthetic at the core of his or her art. Film has always been a highly collaborative medium, bringing together people from a wide range of fields and crafts, but all of their contributions must join together seamlessly. This is especially true of the marriage of sound and music. There is little room for error.

In the process of developing trust and understanding with the people with whom we work, it has become essential for a composer to create mock-ups and demos of each piece of music created for any project. While crude demos were acceptable before, detailed and accurate demos are now required. The personal home studio has become a virtual requirement for the working film composer. I think of my studio as my main instrument, something I have learned to play well. Just as any musician needs viruosity in order to express even the simplest of emotions, so must a composer use technology and technique to translate musical ideas into something that a director or producer can fully grasp and understand in the context of their film, prior to the final recording made with (or without) other musicians. For better or worse, this is the reality of a composer's life, one which requires not only a well-equipped studio, but the knowledge of how to get the most from it.

I don't believe in any absolute rules about what makes a film score good, great, or even merely acceptable. However, there seem to be certain conventions and concepts (and even some sleight-of-hand) which enables music to have an important influence on the dramatic content of a scene.

Each composer that creates a film score brings something new and personal to the craft. Yet some musical ideas and vocabularies seem to work better than others. Entire books have been written on this, and yet they shed little practical light on this. I believe such concepts are for music critics, not music creators. Careful listening in a darkened movie theater can probably teach you as much about what makes music work within a film as can any book or amount of academic film music theory. I've written my thoughts about what elements contribute to a successful film score from a musical perspective, but these are my personal perspective and observations, and are not intended as defining statements. I have collected my observations in this book, and additionally have enlisted the help of some of today's most influential film composers to describe their own outlook on the esthetics and craftsmanship essential to scoring motion pictures.

A life in this field of endeavor is based on talent, hard work, relationships and luck. Positive energy put toward any of these (except for luck, which you can't do much about) will help to move you forward toward the goals which you've set for yourself. Hopefully, the ideas, examples, problems and solutions presented here will prove helpful as you forge a path toward your own career goals in the world of film music.

>The Creative Process

Introduction

Nearly every aspect of movie making, from the scripts to the sets, the acting to the picture and sound editing, is designed to fool an audience into believing they are seeing something real. That reality can be the sort of everyday existence we all experience as the backdrop to a story, or it can be a fantastic, alternate reality, like science fiction, that we can believe in just the same. Movies create new realities by careful creation and manipulation of images and sounds. Music is the only exception to this. We all know there is no symphonic music floating around in the world, or in outer space for that matter. When two people in love kiss each other, there is no swell of music in real life, yet without music, a kiss is just a kiss (and a sigh is just a sigh). We know this, yet we readily and often unknowingly accept music in those scenes where no music could naturally exist.

Music elevates everything in film. It is an emotional amplifier that makes funny things funnier and sad things sadder. In film, music takes ordinary stories and raises them to a higher level, in which everything is larger than life.

Music is a truly intangible art. It has an undeniable emotional effect on the human species for reasons that no one can really explain. Music can make us cry, smile, conjure up mental pictures, bring up unexpected memories, and make us more receptive to everything else we see and hear. Music is almost pure emotion with no physical connections. These are the qualities making music so perfect as companion to the pictures and stories in the movies.

So what distinguishes "film music" from other forms of music? Is there in fact such a thing as "film music," unique from other musical styles and forms? Undeniably yes, though defining it is very difficult. Many styles and kinds of music function well within a film to enhance an audience's experience of the story, characters and events. There are some musical concepts and conventions that find their way into scores more frequently because they work—over and over again.

Classic film scores are almost always melodic, simple, and have a structure and flow that closely matches the pictures going by on the screen. Unlike songs, which have a specific structure (verse, chorus, verse, chorus, bridge, etc.), film music has what composer Leonard Rosenman calls "literary form." In other words, film music is phrased not based on traditional musical forms, but by what appears on the screen. And while that may seem awkward and unmusical, there are methods which allow music to be supportive while still retaining its artistic integrity.

All of music's traditional organic elements—melody, harmony, rhythm, and even structure—have a vital role in film score. Film music can and often does remain musically satisfying, even on its own. But it is carefully fitted to its matching images and actions so the connection is clear and direct. As flows one, so flows the other in time as the story is told. That is the challenge of film composition. Here then, are some of the peculiarities of film music.

CHAPTER ONE

⊜ Music for Film

The Door

Shaping the Overall Character of a Film Score

Every film score needs a primary thematic element that makes it unique, identifiable, and memorable. In most cases, that thematic element is the main melody used to introduce the score. There are many well-known film scores that are identified by their main musical theme. That theme can be a full blown, melodic idea, like the scores of John Williams, a consummate melodist. Some melodic themes can be small fragments, such as the famous shower scene from Bernard Herrman's score to *Psycho* (arguably the most famous film theme in history), or William's *Jaws*.

Themes can be more ephemeral as well. Many films have been scored with music in which the actual melody is not remembered, but the rhythms, harmonies or sound design are. Call it "vibe." If you can find a compelling musical idea that can be adapted and used throughout a score to make your musical point, then you have the makings of a good theme, even if it is not strictly a melodic one.

Every film score needs a "door," a single, unique way in to help give it focus and identity. And each composer will approach this entry way differently. Some composers will slave over a basic theme, because that theme (or themes) will often go a very long way to creating the score, reappearing as often as desired to function as a connecting element. The musical term for this is a "leitmotif." This can be classical or pop but will in some way give something unique to the film. Other composers will come up with a sound or a chord sequence to be played by a particular instrument or synthesizer. For instance, many of Thomas Newman's scores are identifiable by a rhythmic figure that becomes the major thematic motif for the score, rather than a memorable melody.

Successful pop songs have "hooks" that become their main identifying point. A hook usually comes down to just a few notes or a phrase. That is the art of pop music, to quickly become memorable through a simple, brief, catchy phrase. Successful film scores are no different, though they often add a layer of complexity to the musical style in order to make it work well in a number of programmatic or dramatic situations.

Hitting the Spot
Putting Music Cues in Their Place

Nearly as important as the style of music you may choose for a particular film is where the music will go into the film—the starts and stops of each musical cue. This is called *spotting*. This is one of the first opportunities to make compositional errors, by not choosing the best places for the music to come and go. It's also the time for a director and composer to discuss thematic ideas on a scene by scene basis. Similar to weaving a tapestry, the spotting session starts to build the relationship between the music and the picture, and the story and its characters: some colour here, a jolt of energy there, and a sense of romance in another spot.

Spotting is a significant part of the art and craft of scoring, having a profound effect on the feel of the score. Most often, you want the music to enter and exit without drawing too much attention to itself. Once a cue is going, then you can push it to the desired level of energy and complexity. Starting a cue at an awkward moment is a common mistake made by less experienced composers. It's an easy mistake to make. The unwritten rule says that music should come in response to the actions or words on the screen, and shouldn't foreshadow it. This is especially true for scenes that are heavy in dialogue. Watch for facial expressions that show how the characters are feeling, and use those as a guide for beginning a cue. Conversations often have pauses in them which are good times to begin a cue. Once the music has begun, be very careful about hitting notes at the same time as a word. Try to put most of the notes of the melody between the words. Think of it as musical counterpoint. Music must never get in the way of dialogue. They can coexist nicely, and even with some real energy if you write the notes to fall more or less in between the words. There's room for looseness in scenes where there is no real action.

Making a Subtle Entrance
Beginning a Cue

When spotting a scene, I think about the moment when I want the music to be well established, then look backwards from there to find the right spot to bring in the music. I may start with even a single tone, or something equally simple. If done right, the audience won't notice the cue starting or stopping, but they'll get the music's full impact when it is really needed. Some cues aren't going to sneak in, such as a percussion-oriented piece. In those cases you need to be even more careful of where the music begins. If someone in the scene says something of importance that triggers the music, wait for a moment after the line for the audience to take it in and understand its impact. After that brief moment (called a *beat* in the film and theatre worlds) the music can begin. Always give the audience that beat to take in the information on the screen, then allow the music to respond.

But not all cues are meant to be subtle. Some cues are more about energy, shock and surprise than emotions or dialogue. They can start with a bang, sometimes starting on an edit or other very noticeable moment. Again, its like musical counterpoint—finding the perfect moment in the scene to be the launch point for the music. With a fast-paced action scene, music that hits edits or significant moments (such as something or someone hitting the ground, a door flying open, a gun going off, and other exciting and important moments) tends to add greatly to the excitement. It synchronizes the aural and the visual experience for the audience, which is part of the satisfaction of the genre. These moments where the action and music hit together are called, appropriately enough, *hits*. All of the information that goes by in a fast-paced scene can sometimes give the audience too much information, and they can't process it as quickly enough. But music can help lead the audience along, showing them what's happening as the scene unfolds moment by moment. It elevates a scene into being more operatic and exciting. Think of an exciting chase sequence: the music as it careens and hits with the action, propelling images right off the screen. Is good about to triumph over evil? Is the good guy about to get killed? Is someone committing an act of true heroism? The music speaks far better than the images alone.

The Hit
Underscoring Crucial Moments

However, there needs to be limitations in regards to hitting too many things in a cue. Too many hits can sometimes make a score feel "cartoonish." The old classic cartoon scores would hit every piece of action, which made them far funnier. The same applies to any film score. It takes practice to find the right balance of hits and non-hit moments in a scene. They can always be added or taken out later as you refine a cue. Some scenes feel the need for lots of hitting, but with others you can reserve musical hits for just those major moments that need more attention brought to them. Part of spotting a scene includes defining the truly important moments in the film, as decided by both composer and director, and then choosing the best way to accentuate them. In addition to starting and stopping music, important moments can be accentuated by a modulation to another key, or a change of tempo. Anything that causes people to take notice of the music will cause them to associate that moment in the scene as important. Other ways to hit a moment in a scene are starting a new melody, recapitulating an important theme, bringing in an instrument or section, introducing a rhythm or variation, hitting a chord or note with some energy, or making any significant musical change.

Continuity and Contrast
Sustaining Interest with Variations in Tone

An important part of effective scoring is learning how to create music with continuity and contrast. Musical changes at specific times in a cue will have a great deal of impact on the emotional content of the scene. Music really is the glue that holds a scene together. Angles and perspectives change within a scene, but if your music remains constant the result is a more cohesive dramatic experience. Conversely, when a piece of music changes tone, it signals a shift within the story itself. For example, during a scene a character may undergo an emotional change. Nothing necessarily happens visually to show this, but by modulating the music in some way—bringing back a theme or taking one out, changing key, introducing a new melody—the scene shifts for the audience. With even a subtle contrast in the music, you help propel a scene to a more dramatic conclusion.

A composer can make an error with continuity by sustaining a single note for too long, assuming that it will give tension or cohesion. Sustained bass notes (or drones) are usually not as much a problem. Many a cue has consisted of a long low drone. The problem is more when high notes are held bar after bar after bar. Any sustained sound that is near to or above the vocal register of anyone speaking on screen is going to start to stick out after a while.

In noisier scenes, especially on TV, it is when the notes *change* that the audience will hear the music as music. When a note is simply sustained, it tends to wear on the listener and gets annoying. I've found that by keeping upper lines moving, even very slowly, music blends with a scene far better than when simply holding a sustain single-note "pad."

Economy
When Less Means More

While good film music can, and often is, filled with complex, interesting dissonant harmonies and melodies, it also keeps the overall soundscape relatively simple. It is easier to overwrite than to underwrite a film score, and some of the most well-crafted scores have an economy to them that allows each idea to be heard without causing significant distraction. As with so many things in life, the simpler the better. Every time I've bogged down a cue with loads of musical elements—layers of different rhythms or counterlines—the end results bog down the scene (until the sound mixers start to make the music softer and softer) or all my "subtle touches" simply vanish before making it to the screen. Given the need to stand clear of dialogue and effects, some elements of a multilayered score will simply not be heard. The best scores invariably do just one or two things at any one moment, and allow the scope of the sound to lend power. A well-chosen string chord can be more moving than those same strings accompanied by generous amounts of additional musical "stuff." Musical economy means getting the most impact with the least amount of sonic material, and is one of the main keys to most good score writing. Composing music in which each part truly counts is one of the real challenges of any genre.

Transition

The Composer's Response to Changes

Music helps to tell a film's story. Movies use plot, dialogue, and montage to convey that story. The music, when it is part of a scene, must in some way shadow those changes that occur in the film, be they emotional, or kinetic. Films make jumps in time and story, and need the music to support those transitions. If a film's story shifts from night to the next morning, the score may need to convey that shift as well. These musical shifts can be subtle, like adding a new instrumental color (or taking one away), or more overt, such as beginning a theme, ending a theme, going to a new section of the theme, changing key, or changing tempo. Any of these basic music elements will say to the audience, "now something is different," and the audience will then look at the screen and assume that what they are seeing is now different than it was before the musical transition. Transitions become an important tool for creating a score that locks with the feel and essence of a film.

Music that moves and alters with the cuts and fades within a scene imparts energy to the story. The more you create musical transitions that align with edits and actions of the picture, the more energy you impart. However, it is also possible to overuse transition, a phenomenon sometimes referred to as "cartooning" because too many transitions, or musical hits make a scene start to resemble old-style cartoon scores, such as those of Carl Stalling.

A more subtle approach to transition is also musically valid. You can score through picture transitions without making any changes at all, if the effect is desirable. A good example is when pop songs are used over a scene with many changes, yet there is no tip in the music that those edits exist. It creates a greater sense of montage—that the cuts are all part of a greater whole, and should not be taken as separate elements.

Transitions can successfully occur on, just before, or just after an edit. Transitions that are frame accurate to a cut will feel most closely tied to the picture. Transitions that occur prior to the edit, by a few frames or a few seconds, have the effect of drawing us into the next scene, which can be a very effective form of narrative transition. A scene of violence transitions to a scene of quiet aftermath, but the music makes that transition earlier by a few seconds. The audience can begin to feel the emotions of that aftermath while still steeped in the images that led to the final emotional resolution. Likewise, a cue can bleed over a transition before resolving, thus tying the current scene with the one previous. This can be done by simply putting something like a cymbal roll into the final part of a section that leads right up to the cut, or a swell in the music that peaks on the cut. As a general rule, transitions are best executed on or slightly before a cut or hit. Those placed even a fraction of a second afterward tend to look and sound late.

In most films the vast majority of edits are "hard cuts," with no optical transitions. Some scenes crossfade from one to the next over a period ranging from a second to several seconds. If, in your estimation, the music needs to make a transition over a crossfade, then you should use the very beginning of the fade as your pivot point. The audience is very quick to pick up on the fact that a crossfade has begun. They may not know what is about to come dramatically—typically crossfades are used to indicate a jump in time—but they instantly know the cinematic transition has occurred from about the first frame of the crossfade (also called a "dissolve"). That is the place to make or begin your musical transition.

In a fast-paced scene, such as a high-energy chase or action sequence, there will be dozens of transitions. The picture may cut between the good guys and the bad guys, to close-ups of faces or weapons, possibly to another location of people unaware of the dire goings-on in the main scenario. Musical underscore will nearly always want to reflect many of these cuts. Shifts can be simple, but a composer need not be afraid to make significant transitions on the moment by moment changes. Changing to various themes or keys will make the whole thing feel more complex, interesting, and compelling to the audience. It is up to the composer to choose just how much contrast to put into a scene via transitions on edits.

However varied a cue will be, or how strong the transitions between scenes, cues still need to maintain some continuity. That is, a cue can't simply be like a group of short cues glued together. Transitions should be handled in a way that still gives a sense of unity to the cue as a whole. Think of how a pop song goes from chorus to bridge to verse.

Perhaps a transition will be very contrasting, but the tempo remains constant or near constant. That will tie the cue together while still allowing a successful transition. Perhaps a percussion part remains through a number of transitions, then a string line (or note) carries through a few, etc. Themes which go and then return will also help to link the various sections of a cue together. You don't need a single musical device to make the cue unified. One of the prime skills of successful film composers is the ability to score through a scene, drawing out the emotions and energy of the scene moment by moment without bringing too much attention to the music, while still creating a sense of flow and continuity to the score as a whole.

Tempo

The Pacing of the Score

Perhaps more important than any other musical choice you make in writing a cue is the tempo, or tempos (*tempi* for all you musical literates and Italians). Much of what a cue will do emotionally to a scene is right in the music's tempo. Most film composers spend time carefully choosing the pace of each cue. Some scenes suggest a tempo by rhythmic occurrences in the picture—somebody walking boldly into the scene, fast paced edits, a train moving on its tracks. Film music can have an enormous range of tempos, from barely moving, to blistering fast.

Writing a cue with lots of hits and transitions becomes easier as the tempo rises, since the beats keep getting closer and closer together in time. Thus, the likelihood that a beat will hit on or near a key frame goes up. If it gets close, then one only has to adjust the tempo slightly (which is oftentimes imperceptible) in order to get the beat to hit right on the appropriate frame. Here's an example:

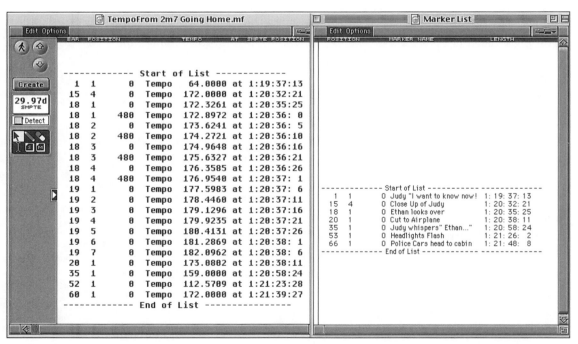

Figure 1.1 A sequencer's tempo map allows specific beats to line up with chosen frames.

The tempo of music can also be more fluid than just a single tempo or quick tempo change that delineates cinematic transitions. Tempos can slow down and speed up gradually, just as they do throughout classical music literature, and yet, gain more expressivity. A slow build in tempo can add tension and energy to a scene in which something is gradually becoming more significant, such as danger. A cue can slow down as a sign of winding things up, or to simply give the music a sense of phrasing.

On a somewhat more technical note, it is important to be very familiar with the tempo calculating tools of your musical sequencer. Most all provide the ability to create tempos and tempo changes that will land any desired beat directly on any desired frame. They can also create accelerandos and ritardandos for greater musical expression. Knowing how to work with your sequencer's tempo functions will help you to create a score that is more flowing and agile.

Most sequencers have the ability to create a tempo track by a moving MIDI controller. Using this feature can make your sequences feel much more alive and human, even if you quantize (process all the notes to fall exactly on rhythmic divisions of the beat) all your parts. This may not be a desired effect all the time, but very useful for the more *esspressivo* moments.

If you plan to record your music with a live ensemble, you must be careful about how you change tempo during a cue. An ensemble cannot be expected to make a sudden radical shift of tempo while maintaining any dense rhythms such as constant eighth or sixteenth notes. Gradual tempo changes are usually not a problem, nor are subtle changes. You need to anticipate any significant change in tempo. One way is to end a section of one tempo with a held note, and begin the new tempo during that note.

Figure 1.2 Example of a tempo change during a held note

No one listening will know that the tempo changed during a note, and the musicians will be able to prepare for the next section at the new tempo. A subtle variation of this is to begin a new tempo with a briefly held note or slow rhythm. In either case, the objective is to make it as easy as possible for the players to stay with the new clicks.

If the tempo of a cue (or section) is very slow, then it is advisable to create a double-time click, one that ticks eighths instead of quarter notes. This makes playing rhythmic passages at slow tempos far easier for everyone and usually makes for a more accurate performance. Some sequencers have the ability to do this automatically. For those who use sequencers that can't, it may require creating a click track by hand on a track of the sequence. It also helps to switch to an eighth click on meters such as 3/8 or 5/8. Clicks can be accented on the downbeats of bars if you are deriving your click from one of your MIDI instruments, or even from your computer itself. Musicians and conductors seem somewhat divided on the preference for this. Some enjoy it while others find it distracting.

Style

Is Film Music Different from Other Kinds of Music?

There is no single style of music that can be defined as "film music". Film scores draw from every type of music known. Early film scores were more consistent in their style—they were based predominantly on 19th and early 20th century classical symphonic literature, with some early American pop and jazz thrown in. Now, anything goes. Many film composers become well versed in their ability to write in a number of styles in order to create scores that will best fit a particular film. It also allows them the opportunity to work on a broader range of films.

Style is, however, a very personal thing and should not be confused with genre. There are certainly musical genres that will work better for, say, a western or a science fiction film. Once a genre has been determined, be it symphonic, jazz, ethnic, techno, or some hybrid, then a composer should take and apply it to their own aesthetic sensibilities. Make it their own. In the case of westerns, many composers have looked to the music of Aaron Copeland for inspiration. Some will simply imitate, while others will look at the essence of what makes a piece of music "Copeland-esque" and adapt that into a score that also allows them to make a personal musical statement. The same applies to all other musical forms.

It becomes a composer's mission at the outset of a film to help seek out the best musical approach that will work itself into the soundtrack, and then adapt it into something unique and vital. Once a style or approach has been determined, possibly by experimentation and possibly by directorial choice, then careful listening to recordings by the masters of that genre can be tremendously inspiring and educational.

Graceful Exit

When to End a Cue

Once you've begun a cue and gotten to the end, you need to exit as gracefully as you started. This often means a sustained note, chord or riff (called a *vamp*).

I often hold the last note of a cue overly long, so that the sound mixers at the final dub session (where the music, dialogue, and sound effects are mixed for the final soundtrack) can fade it. They like having that control, and that's fine with me. Be careful not to end a cue too early. You don't want to give away the fact that a cue is about to end too soon. It lets the audience off the hook dramatically. They shouldn't know that a situation is about to end just because the music has gotten to the last chord. You end up with a cue that just sits there for too long.

Music for pictures is an art and a craft. For each unwritten rule, there is an example disproving it perfectly. But these rules work far more often than not. None of them prevent each of us from working within our own unique and personal styles. And each of us can learn how to adopt and adapt these rules in our own way, which is important if we are to continue to write music from a personal perspective. The best way to learn about the unwritten rules of scoring is to just go out and watch, and listen, to good films and good film scores, and listen for the ways in which the composer gets their music to connect with the story and pictures on the screen. It's the best school there is. A growing list of such score recordings can be found at the companion site.

⊗ Visit online at www. reelworld-online.com

As Henry Mancini once said: "God, it's an empty feeling watching a movie without any music!"

Case Study

White Squall

One of the more ambitious film scores I've done was for the Ridley Scott film, *White Squall* (1996). While not a major commercial success, it was an excellent musical (and educational) opportunity. It was the first large budget feature I had ever done on my own.

I was never supposed to do it. The film had already been scored, but the score was thrown out by the director because of conceptual differences between he and the original composer, and thus a new score was needed pronto because the film's release date would not be changed. Scott had worked with composer Hans Zimmer and first asked him if he was available in a pinch. He wasn't, but he recommended me. Scott hired me based on that recommendation and from some of my scores that he knew. The next day, work started.

Ridley Scott, probably best known as the director of *Blade Runner, Gladiator* and *Alien*, is a brilliant director, and this film was a significant departure from his previous works. *White Squall* was an adventure film and a coming-of-age story. A meeting was arranged the next night to watch a rough cut of the film, complete with *temp score*, which is music put into the film while it's being edited to give the director a sense of how the film looks with different kinds of music. Temp scores, typically made from bits and pieces of other suitable film scores, are removed when a composer is hired to compose the actual score. At this point the film was over two and a half hours long and still being edited. The temp score was an eclectic mix ranging from electronic music, such as Maurice Jarre's *Witness* score and some Vangelis, to sweeping grand orchestral scores such as John Barry's *Out Of Africa*.

So why was the first composer's score thrown out? It's more common than most people think. I've known composers to be 'taken off' a film because they wouldn't stick closely enough to the director's temp score. But the original composer of *White Squall* was fired for just the opposite reason; he stuck too closely with the temp score. The director expected to be more surprised. It is rather amazing that the score got all the way to the orchestral recording session without anyone having heard it. Faith, I suppose. While I never heard any of the first score (little of it was recorded, and none of it was mixed), if it was anything like the wondrous temp score, it was great music—but simply not what the director wanted. Still, I was standing in a very imposing shadow. And I had just three weeks to write what seemed like a near epic score. This wasn't how I pictured getting into bigger projects.

Over dinner with Scott that night I played it as cool as I could, made a few jokes, and started trying to figure out how in the world I was going to pull this off without getting myself fired. I felt I was in way over my head here. Could I write this much music in this amount of time? I never had before. After I stopped hyperventilating, I got to it. It was time to write some music.

Zimmer, who wrote the scores for Scott's *Black Rain, Thelma & Louise*, and subsequently *Gladiator*, gave me two useful bits of advice based on his own experiences with Scott. The first was to be very melodic and to come up with a theme that Scott might find memorable and hummable; the second was simply to be myself and not try to write music in a style that wasn't my own. That requires a good deal of confidence, which I wasn't quite feeling right then. As cool as I was attempting to be on the outside with director Scott, I was just a touch terrified inside.

The story of the movie followed a group of American boys aboard a large 3-

masted ship in 1961. I didn't want my score to simply reflect the film's era, the boys' nationality, or their Caribbean destinations. I wanted the music to be about the boys themselves, about their voyage of discovery, about the beauty they saw, and about the dangers they encounter during their trip. I saw it as a voyage of self-discovery more than anything else. And the film's great cinematography of the sea and the islands they visited became inspirations for the score.

Incidentally, money was the last thing on my mind. It wasn't important to me whether I made a financial profit from this project. The music had to sound great and very large. I decided immediately to take some of the first money I got and use it to buy some more gear for my studio. I have a pretty insatiable appetite for gear, and in this case I felt completely justified—I had more samples that I wanted to use than my samplers could hold. I ended up buying several more Akai and Emu samplers. This allowed me to have a greater palette of sounds up, all at once, for demos. Scott wasn't going to let another composer write anything without his hearing every note and approving it before the recording sessions. I wanted to give him as big a sound as I could get.

I didn't touch the video of the film for a few days. I sat at my computer and sketched themes with a piano sound. I tossed out a lot of thematic ideas over those first days.

In trying to write something sweeping in scope, the first themes didn't feel enough like my own music. Finally though, I started into doing something personal, and it started with these four simple chords:

Not particularly earth shattering. It's your basic I-V-IV-I (with a tonic pedal, of course).

I put this melody over them at first:

As much as I liked that, it was too syncopated and not simple enough. I toyed with it some more and came up with my first theme:

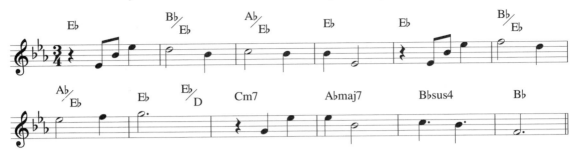

Some *White Squall* theme demos can be heard online at www. reelworld-online.com

This theme, with a number of variations, shows up throughout the film. Sometimes it's in 3/4, sometimes in 4/4. The 3/4 version comes across a little more jaunty, while the 4/4 is for the more serious moments.

With this theme, and some subthemes for other parts of the film, I began the process of scoring the film to picture. For my first real cue I chose a spot near the beginning of the film, right after the (still nonexistent) opening titles, a great place to begin a musical voyage. Though it was a short, simple cue, it also gave me a chance to experiment with some of the more interesting sounds I wanted to use in the film. It was important to me to make the score feel exotic and "worldly" but not be identifiable as being from any one place or culture. I used gamelon, pennywhistle, considerable amounts of sampled percussion instruments from around the world (including India, Hawaii, Indonesia, Africa, Europe, and North and South America), steel drums, male choir, Tibetan harmonic singing, and I programmed a number of odd synth sounds. This may seem like a big mess, but the key was always to keep things simple and colourful.

As this film takes place mostly at sea, I needed something special that would be a "call to the sea" to use throughout the score. I chose the sound of blown conch shells, which sound something like a wild horn. A friend with an extensive collection of conch shells spent several hours sampling different notes and phrases which I used a great deal. They gave the score a primitive and evocative flavour. This served as an important reoccurring thematic element for the score.

After writing a few more cues I had the first meeting with the director to play him material. This was the big moment. He sat quietly and watched the video monitor while I played him the first cue. I knew he liked things loud so I wasn't bashful with the volume. At a spot in the film where we see a magnificent tropical panorama with a wonderful old propeller airplane landing at a small airport, the music crescendoed into some big low frequency synths, gamelon and strings. I am keeping my eyes on the director's face to gauge where he is happy or not. At the spot where all the big sounds came in, I could see the smile on his face. So far, so good.

In that same first cue there came a spot where an Irish pennywhistle entered, representing a certain purity and innocence. I recorded myself playing pennywhistle onto an audio track in the sequencer and he lit up. Pennywhistle, it turned out, is one of his favorite instruments! The cue, which was a model for many parts of the score, was a success. He liked the theme, the textures, and the instrumentation. We were off to a flying start.

All that was left was to write the other 98 percent of the score, get it orchestrated, recorded, and mixed, and I was done. After getting the first few cues approved by the director, I worked nearly around the clock, seven days a week to write the score. When the director returned to my studio about a week or so later, I was able to get another batch of cues "signed off" (meaning he approved them), either as they were or with minimal and simple fixes. Then they were ready to be sent to the orchestrator with no further approval from anyone else. The demos of the cues could be recorded both for the orchestrator as well as for the orchestral sessions.

As I am a flute player, I played all the solo woodwind parts myself straight into the sequencer. Even just adding a real pennywhistle to a sequence brought it to life (and thus increased the chances of it getting approved). I know the difference between how a sample and a real musician sound, but the same is not true for most film producers or directors. This process helps it all go much smoother. I played a number of the instruments on that score, including flutes, ocarinas, and one called a Da-ban-di (a Chinese oboe-like instrument).

As I was scoring the picture, the director and editor were continuously recutting it, and rendering cue after cue unusable. Unfortunately, this is a fact of life in the film world. Even when you are promised the final cut of a project, word comes that some "minor changes" are coming. Some of those minor changes can make a cue meaningless, especially if the overall structure or basic emotion of the scene changes. One of the hardest parts of film scoring is adapting cues for scenes that are recut. They rarely come out as good as the original cue. As I receive new cuts, I go into the sequence and remove beats or bars, putting in gaps. Then I begin writing the bridging material, sometimes simply changing the tempos in order to accommodate the revisions so all the hits that I so carefully composed still line up with the picture. Some revisions take only a few minutes, while some can take the better part of a day—a day that would be better spent writing new music. But the changes have to be done. It is not unheard of for a scene that has been altered to be restored to its original version, so I never throw away a sequence when I revise it, it may come back.

Some scenes changed more than once. One of my favorite cues was one that the director also liked very much. The next set of video tapes had the scene almost destroyed. A composer's job is to support the film as best as possible, and changes are an inevitable part of the process. But in this particular case, since the scene was very music-oriented, I decided to ask that the scene be put back as it was when I originally scored it. Such requests are a touchy thing, and sometimes it comes down to choosing one's battles. But as we got more comfortable with each other, Ridley Scott agreed that it was worth restoring the scene in order to save a cue we both preferred in its original form. This was a well picked battle. The victory didn't last too long because, as I later learned, the editor didn't keep a log of the version I scored, so I ended up having to make changes to shorten the cue anyway.

When working on a large scale project, staying organized is an important aspect of the job as it is with any job. As a film is being edited, it is divided up into smaller sections called reels. Each reel is anywhere from about 10 to 20 minutes long, depending on the editor's work methods. As videos of revised reels arrive, I label them with a version letter. The first batch is labeled A, the next B, and so on. Some versions may only be a reel or two, not the entire film. It is important to keep a log of which version of the cut was used for each cue. Some cues may be B, some D, some F, etc. I mark the version letter in the sequence itself. If a new version of a scene arrives, I update it in the sequencer.

While I compose, I am in contact with the people making all the necessary arrangements for the orchestral recording. I need to specify: what instruments I want and how many of each (keeping within a budget); recording dates; availability of certain soloists, orchestrator, and copyists; travel dates if needed; shipping of gear; tape or hard disk formats; rental of other gear; engineer's availability; studio availability (very difficult on relatively short notice); mixing dates and video format. This is the part of the job in which I am now a music producer. Since film dubs will often last for several days or even weeks, you can arrange to deliver final music mixes to the dub stage in parts, as long as the mixers have the music they need on the day they are mixing that reel. You are in one studio mixing music while they are elsewhere mixing the whole film. Some dubs begin with a day or more of dialogue and effects mixing, called a *pre-dub*, and they don't even listen to music on those days. You need only stay ahead of the stage by a day's worth of mixes.

With this film, I knew the date by which they needed the music, so I worked backward from there to determine the last possible day to leave LA and do the orchestral recordings in London, where the film was being finished, and where the director was. That in turn told me exactly how much time I had left to sit and write, and that was getting shorter every day. Even though the film's production company was against it, I insisted on bringing certain things from my studio in LA. I wanted my computer and some synths with me in case there were mistakes or if the director wanted changes. Ridley Scott is known for coming up with many last minute ideas that could change the music's direction. I also wanted to use my orchestrator and have him present at the recordings in case of any last second changes to the score at the recordings. I wanted my music editor with me, since he knew every note of the music very well. He's very good at cutting scores on Digidesign's ProTools (a popular digital audio editing system used by music editors) when needed, and would be important for the final editing and help on the dub stage in case anything changed in the picture. In fact, he became invaluable because when we got to London we discovered there were an incredible number of last minute changes to the film's cut. For some reason, they had no problem making changes to the film and letting us discover it on our own.

As I was getting cues approved (still in LA), I would make a recording of my demos and give that and MIDI Files (a standard computer file that allow the sharing of musical sequences between different brands of sequencers or computers) on a disk to my orchestrator. He also asked for a copy of the video because he wanted to see what was going on in both sound and picture during the music. He showed me his work along the way, and occasionally we would discuss possible options. As he finished cues and I signed off on them, he would fax them to London where the copyists were preparing for the session. Everything on that end went as smoothly as possible.

As my deadline approached, I was sending demos on video to Ridley in England and he would phone me back with comments and ideas. A few times he would disappear for a weekend getaway, leaving me twisting in the wind while waiting for his reply on a critical cue. The last piece I wrote was the film's main title. I was never given anything to look at, and they had no idea how long the piece needed to be. My time was about up, and I couldn't wait any longer. I just wrote something that I thought would work. It was a vocal piece so I had a friend come and sing on it, layering six tracks of vocals for the background textures. I sent it off to Ridley, who liked the feel but didn't like some of the percussion, which he thought made it sound too Eastern. Easily fixed, and the score was done.

As cues were finished and approved, the process of putting the metronome click and synth parts (important for the musicians to have in their earphones while they play) to tape started. Toward the last days of writing, I would stop composing around 10 or 11PM, and my engineer and assistant would begin to work on the multitrack recording, going until dawn. We decided for various reasons not to record or mix the score strictly with a hard disk audio system. So tracks were printed to 32 channels of digital tape. We also made "slave tapes" on a second 32 track tape. Slave tapes are rough mixes of the music, the metronome clicks, and demos of the solos and other parts to be recorded by the musicians. We used eight tracks of the 32 track tape, leaving ample tracks for the musicians at the orchestra sessions. Then for the final mix, we would lock the two tape machines together, one with all synths and one with all musicians. At the time, access to enough tracks of hard disk recorder was too difficult. This would be one of the last projects I would do exclusively on tape.

Finally, with one day to spare before getting on the plane, I finished. I wrote the last cue and made the last changes. "Phase One" was done. I rested for half a day and then packed to go. I hadn't gotten a full night's sleep in three weeks, and hadn't had a single day off to do anything else. But it was done. Now comes the fun part: new city, new goals, new people, new musicians. Tired but happy, I got on the plane and took off.

CHAPTER TWO

→ Music for Television

Doing TV

Music for the Small Screen

Film and television music are close cousins. The musical challenges are in essence the same. But the details of the business are quite different. I've scored a number of television shows, some very successful, some not so well known. There are some differences between the media of TV and film. The differences are small and tend to be more logistic than aesthetic. With TV you are usually on a tighter budget and shorter deadlines, so you must use your resources differently. You also don't have the pleasure of that big theatrical sound in the home theatre as you do in movie theatres (though I've been in movie theatres that were worse than my old cassette deck).

Relationships are slightly skewed from the film world as well. On a film project you typically answer to the director before all others. In television you rarely if ever meet the director. They are hired on an episode by episode basis. They direct the actors and help with a rough cut of the picture. Then they are dismissed. The producers handle the rest. One producer is typically put in charge of spotting and approving music, though sometimes that task is spread around to more than one person. Let's take a look at the small screen.

A Case of *Homicide*

Scoring a Network Cop Show (on Short Notice)

As do so many things in our modern world, it began with a phone call. "Could you come down here? We need to talk to you about a homicide." Not a good way to begin a day. I dressed, got in my car and drove through the rain. I held my breath as I entered the building. I was lead to a small, smoky room and found myself seated face-to-face with The Director.

"Have a seat," he said. I sat.

"I want you to look at an episode of this new show we're doing called *Homicide: Life On the Street* and see what you think about putting in a few sounds. We're thinking about doing the entire show without music, but there are a few scenes that need 'something'."

I had first met director Barry Levinson when I worked on *Toys*, for which I had written a few cues that were rather quirky and sound design-oriented. Levinson remembered my work and asked me to come and look at this show to possibly do some abstract type of musical sound design. The show was a drama set in Baltimore that followed the lives of a group of detectives as they solve some of the city's nastier crimes and deal with their own human foibles along the way. There were no chases, gun fights, killings or graphic violence depicted in the show. Unlike other types of "cop shows" the catch here is that a homicide officer is only called upon after a crime has been committed. It's about unraveling the mystery of what has so obviously happened—someone killed someone else, an interesting premise for a program. It was shot mainly with a hand held 16mm camera that gave the show an urgent, unpolished look and feel. It had an experimental feel in many ways, from the photography to the direction, the editing, and now, hopefully, the music and sound design.

There were just three scenes in that first episode that appeared to be in need of some added tension that might be provided by a soundtrack. Levinson was unsure that anything was needed but was interested in hearing something, as long as it wasn't (heaven forbid) music. This was strictly an experiment for a television show trying to do things a bit differently. If he liked it, maybe it would only be for that one episode, or maybe there would be a few other stops to add a few more "somethings." We scheduled another meeting for two days hence, and I took a copy of the video home to ponder and play with.

The first scene I looked at was of a rain-drenched night. The camera hovers over the lifeless and bloodied body of an eleven year old girl, illuminated only by a flashlight. We see a young, rookie detective looking at her for clues, as if she might speak to him. In the background we see and hear some of his comrades talking in an inappropriately jovial manner about sports and financial plans—it was a strange and macabre juxtaposition. And an excellent opportunity for unusual sound and atmosphere.

I started by creating an atmospheric sound montage with some gritty and organic samples. I sampled several bits of police radio, cars, and traffic. I sequenced a performance of those sounds and then ran them through a harmonizer to pitch them down a fourth (five semitones). When blended, this interval gives sounds a very strange and musical quality, even when there is no outright pitched material in the original sound. I also filtered these sounds to make them less and less recognizable.

I then added some very gentle, low sweeping drones with some older synths to add a little more drama to the sonic mix. The end result felt far more like a sound effects track than music, but a very strange and ambient one. It gave the scene a surrealistic mood without intruding, which seemed to be exactly what Levinson was looking for as best as I could tell.

I played the scene for him the next day, and thankfully, he was very happy. While I was playing back the montage, I accidently leaned on a synth keyboard, emitting a sound much like a wine glass being rubbed. Suddenly Levinson's eyes lit up. He loved the combination of complex, strange sounds coupled with the simplest and sparsest of musical material. With this added inspiration I went to put together a revised demo with this approach, made to fit the scene and dialogue.

I rescored the scene again, but this time locked to picture using a video tape with SMPTE *timecode* (more about timecode in Section 2). The synths had to stay away from the dialogue at very precise moments and return on certain cuts. I took the sound montage I made originally and recorded it into my digital audio sequencer on my Macintosh, then composed the other tracks around it using just three synthesizer sounds (low, mid, and high).

⊗ This first sketch can be heard online at www. reelworld-online.com

When I returned for the next meeting I brought a video tape with the scene scored and mixed the way I thought the final mix should sound. This is a useful demo method I used throughout the project, which is described in detail in Section Two, Technology.

The experiment was successful enough to have me take a look at all the episodes that had been shot and were being edited. And so began several weeks of unrelenting work to grind out my first episodic television efforts. For many years I didn't even own a TV, but this was a great opportunity to work with a great director on an interesting, well-crafted project. It was a lot of hard work, but it was a chance to create a sound and a unique approach to scoring for television.

From the very beginning of the project, the goal was to work counter to TV music conventions by working with musical texture and sound as abstractly as possible, but still approached as composition. I am not a sound designer in the usual sense. I am a composer. So even working with nonmusical elements, I would manipulate and organize them as I would with any instrumentation. Over the first weeks of the show, the music I wrote underwent a metamorphosis by adding more and more traditional musical elements of rhythm, melody, harmony, and instrumentation, though I never strayed fully from my initial themes and sonic textures. In order to make a score cohesive throughout a television series, it's essential to maintain a set pallet of sounds and motives. In a word, style. More on that later.

As my first experience in network series television, I had to learn what was expected of me by simply jumping in and doing it. I knew nothing about the process and conventions of producing a weekly show. I think my naivete helped me. Had I known what I was getting myself into I probably would have abandoned half my ideas and approaches before the first episode. I didn't know the first thing about how a TV score was put together or delivered. Each episode must be planned, composed, recorded, mixed and delivered in a timely and technically perfect way. I didn't know how others were doing them, because I simply didn't know anybody in that line of work, yet. But fortunately for me I learned quickly. Here's the process I went through each week working on the series.

TUESDAY—I would receive a video tape copy of the episode from the editing house in New York, where *Homicide* was being produced and mixed.

I would carefully watch it and make notes where I felt the need for score. Moments of anger, action, suspense, and odd moods were the obvious prime candidates. Occasionally I would do a quick sketch on the spot if I felt inspired by certain scenes, knowing full well that the scene might end up not being scored if the producer wanted it left empty.

WEDNESDAY—I would meet with Barry Levinson to go over the episode and spot it. Having already watched it a couple of times, I could go into the meetings with my spotting ideas already firm in my head. By being prepared, the meetings usually went very smoothly and quickly. Often we wouldn't even watch the episode all the way through, and could forward to the likely scenes I had already chosen. Homework helps.

WEDNESDAY NIGHT to FRIDAY—Go to my studio and WRITE, WRITE, WRITE. This is perspiration time. The goal with this music was subtlety, ambience, and a street sensibility. I used some of my sampled ambience sounds in place of any kind of synthesizer pad. This kept the music sparse while still making it unusual and interesting. I used a number of drum styles, including some samples of vintage analogue drum machines like the TR808, as well as some more standard drums. I usually dropped the pitch of the samples to make the drums darker and weirder. Though I am not a jazz musician, nor was the focus of the score jazz, I frequently incorporated some jazz elements for colour. I was fond of trumpet, both muted and unmuted, blended with the other elements of the score.

The score would be entirely sequenced, with the aforementioned samples and ambient synthesizers being the primary tools. I used a few live musicians on each episode. When I came up with something I liked I would go ahead and do a quick mix on the spot in case it got approved. For some reason sometimes a rough mix created while composing is the best a piece of music will ever sound, so I made sure to grab those spontaneous mixes.

SATURDAY or SUNDAY—Get the music approved by Levinson. I would record my demos not only to DAT, but also onto a videotape along with the picture and dialogue. I would take this video back with me to Levinson's house in order to show him what I was doing for each scene. He either would approve a piece, ask me to make specific changes, have me do it again from scratch differently, or decide that the scene really didn't need music after all. His word was final. On *Homicide*, as is true of most episodic television, it is the producer and not the director who wields the clout.

As the show progressed, I became better at knowing what Barry liked, and the process became more streamlined. Barry had a high standard for the music, and sometimes, just when I thought I had nailed a cue, he would ask me to change the approach. As disappointing as that could be, I have always enjoyed the challenge that he put on my work. Being so close to deadline, I would usually have a new demo video sent over to him by messenger so I could keep writing. If I could, I'd go in person, but by early Monday it was time to press the ol' record button for the final recordings and mixes.

MONDAY—Mix the music and get the tape to the Federal Express office near me in Los Angeles in time to send it back to New York for their Tuesday morning dubbing session. It was typically an adrenaline-filled, heart pounding race to beat the 6 PM deadline. Last minute changes, difficult mixes or other logistic problems guaranteed a heart-stopping ride for those four long miles from my house.

TUESDAY—Do it again (see above).

I used the timecode from the VCR to drive my sequencer as I was mixing to the master tape. On this project, and this is unusual, they only wanted the music in stereo, never split out onto multiple tracks. I used a Sony timecoded DAT machine for the mixes. Since then I've never delivered music on less than eight tracks for a television mix. Timecoded DATs are not a very standard format, which concerned me. At the time, very few production facilities wanted music on hard drive, though this was among the first productions using digital audio workstations for postproduction. In the event there might ever be problems with the timecode on the master DAT tape I sent to the dub, I put a click (with a drum machine) exactly two seconds before the first note of the music. This is called a sync pop or two pop. I noted the timecode number for the click (2 seconds prior to the SMPTE offset in my sequence) as a reference for the editors in New York, and included it on the tape label. If the timecode failed, they could simply use the click to align the music to the proper start frame. Eventually, I gave up on using timecode at all, and just used the sync pop for reference. For some of the denser cues that I felt needed to be mixed at the dub, I would mix the music in two passes, one percussive and the other textural. That way, in case there was an element of my score that interfered with the dialogue, they could lower the level of that element without dropping the music altogether. It was very handy on several occasions.

I was not a very fast composer at the time. I worked carefully and intuitively, as I still do. The point of the music in *Homicide* was to bend the conventions of typical television music. As much as possible, I tried to make the music for all the episodes as "genre bending" as possible, while still doing the basic thing that all good film (or television) music does—enhance a scene emotionally without drawing undo attention to itself. In *Homicide*, I tried to fulfill the producer's wish to have the music blur the line between score, sound effects, and source music (music which comes from the scene itself, like a radio or television in the scene). Alternating between ambient and pounding, the music often integrated with scenes in surprising ways.

Though most episodes didn't have a great deal of music, it still took a commitment of virtually all my time, including many long, late, and lonely nights. I found a new respect for the composers doing these shows with 30 or even 45 minutes of music every single week for months. And I should know, because I've done that as well. I had a great time, and by the end of the first season I felt that I had developed a 'sound' for the show.

Many of the sounds I created for the show reoccurred regularly in several episodes as sonic audio "signatures." Though I would come up with new sounds for many episodes, by halfway through the series I probably had about 90% of all the unusual sounds I used. One of my favorites was a diverse collection of about 20 kick drum samples I pulled together from various kits. They were bright and punchy enough to come through a small TV speaker. I created odd rhythms with nothing but different types of kick drums to add just a little propulsion to a cue without saying "Hey, here's the drums now!" There were scenes where I used more percussion, though never a standard drum kit. I included sampled metallic hits, 2x4 boards banged together, wrenches banged together, a rain stick slowed down several octaves, telephones, radios, and various odds and ends. I almost always would run these sounds through the harmonizer pitched down a forth and mixed with the dry signal.

Another odd approach to percussion I did a few times was with sampled hip-hop loops. However, instead of leaving them alone (we can't have that now, can we?) I would process them. One quickie is to simply play them back with the sampler's filter turned down so far that they begin to resemble heartbeats (though very funky ones), a very cool effect. The other trick I did with a drum loop is a bit more complicated. There is a patch on the Eventide Harmonizer called "BACKWARDS." It takes the incoming sound, chops it into small bits (of programmable length, usually 300 to 700 milliseconds) and plays each bit backwards. The result sounds like music being played backwards, but the material is really forward. It also makes things rather jerky and weird. I would take a drum loop, flip it backwards in the sampler and then play the backwards loop through BACKWARDS (…with me so far?). The result is the drum sounds— coming out forwards—but the rhythm is still reversed, though somewhat spazzed out, yielding a most odd and wonderful sound. This may all seem a bit dry and technical, but the idea was entirely part of my creative process. I wanted a score that had a very interesting, but subtle sound. All these techniques brought about a score that could not be created with off the shelf sounds or tonal concepts.

I learned to shy away from anything that was a deep low bass with few harmonics. Those types of sounds don't come across on 90% of the television sets. No long sustained synth pedals, no low pads, no deep mellow percussion. They simply are not heard that well. The sounds that come across best are not static or stationary, but ones which evolve and change in time. In fact, it's only the changes in timbre (or pitch) that really come through. Sounds need to move, and so does the music.

There was also room for musical diversity in the project, which kept the work lively and interesting. I wrote a number of instrumental jazz pieces (though do not consider myself at all a jazz composer), some Italian folk music, and some pop songs as source material. I worked with several talented musicians who added greatly to several of the episodes with percussion, guitar, vocals, winds, and trumpet. Once I had defined what the series sounded like, I wanted to explore that sonic space in new ways that still retained the essence I had created.

Film and television music is not always a subtle art. It can be like painting with a wide, wide brush. Fine musical details are often lost by the time they make it past the dialogue, overly loud sound effects, ambiance, compression, and the transmission of the television signal into the homes of people watching while talking, eating, or cooking something in the microwave. Much of the music in *Homicide* was created to be played softly, so adding too many little details or intricacies was a waste of time. I learned to capture to the most direct idea that would best express the scene without getting too complex or multi-layered.

So much television relies on all-electronic scores. However, I really believe in the power of live musicians for the more emotional parts of a score. I always use real players to achieve that. When the budget allows for more musicians, and the music warrants it, I get more. I've gone as large as a full orchestra a few times and, sometimes, as small as a single player. It depends on the circumstance along with your commitment to making the music sound as great as possible.

Changing Channels

Chicago Hope

After two seasons of *Homicide: Life On The Street*, it was time to do something very different. I had done a few small films, but another opportunity to score a quality television show came up. *Chicago Hope* was practically a study in stylistic and production contrasts compared to the schedule, musical style, and creative process of scoring *Homicide*. And while the show was, at first, constantly compared to the more popular ER, the shows were very different in style and emotional tone.

The main concern of the show's producers was for the emotional aspects of the story to come across very clearly in the music. Aside from the life-and-death moments in the operating and emergency rooms, much of *Chicago Hope* concerns the relationships of the main characters and how they deal with the pressures and ethical dilemmas they face in each story. This was important to remember in devising my approach to the music. For the sake of consistency, the style and instrumentation of the main title (which I did not write, but worked on very closely with composer Mark Isham) was an important factor. Finally, there were conversations with the show's producers who, though not able to speak in specific musical terms ("I think I hear an oboe here"), had some very definite ideas of what they wanted the music to do. My job was to give the producers what they want emotionally, while using my musicianship to show them the best way to achieve it.

For *Chicago Hope*, that meant very little use of electronic keyboards. This show was, for the most part, "unplugged." Samples and synths simply cannot convey the same type or depth of emotion as live instruments, at least not to the makers of the show, who were very familiar with MIDI studios and were very wary of anything sounding remotely "electronic." While I could certainly take a stand to the contrary, there is no point in it. Good musicians playing traditional instruments have a feel that is unique and valuable. Which is not to say I didn't use my MIDI gear to its full advantage. I just did so with a light and restrained touch. The blend, about 80 percent live players, worked well for everybody. The instrumental lineup varied from show to show depending on what I wrote, but the basics of the ensemble were strings, anywhere from 1 to 12, nylon string "classical" guitar, trumpet, oboe (or soprano sax) and piano. I used woodwinds and vocals on a few episodes as well. I used synths and samplers for bass, percussion, pads, some analogue-esque arpeggios, and the occasional odd tension and angst-filled weirdo sound. Because I needed to demo each cue I wrote for the producers approval, I sequenced all the parts, including those that would eventually be played live. So I also had samples of strings, guitar, trumpet, piano, and voices. My approach to percussion is pretty eclectic. I created some percussion sounds on analogue synthesizers and sampled the results to build kits. They were subtle enough to not trigger any bad reactions from the producers, while satisfying my need to have some unusual sounds in my scores. I also have timpani and other orchestral percussion (gongs, cymbals, gran casse, snares, triangle), marimba, trash percussion (big hits made by banging things together and slamming car doors in an underground parking garage), shakers, some ethnic drums, jazz brushes, and a few other miscellaneous noises. I like percussion, but I don't use it all at the same time.

Due to schedule demands, I would hire an orchestrator to take my sequences, and transcribe them for the ensemble each week. I'd have done it myself, but the weekly schedule doesn't allow me the luxury. I create every note on the computer. My sequencer prints out imperfect but useful scores that the orchestrator used to create the final score by hand. I also gave her a tape of my demos so she could hear my articulations and dynamics, which do not get transcribed by the computer. She came to each recording session with the scores from which I conducted and parts for all the musicians. I would give her some free rein, so occasionally she devised some lines of her own, based on the piano or other part on the tape, (and gave it to the string section). These touches were often wonderful and added some spice to the arrangements. There is nothing like collaboration with talented people.

I sometimes think that the music software industry is trying too hard to convince us that, with the right hardware and software, we can do everyone's job, from editing picture, printing score and parts, performing every part, right down to mixing the final soundtrack in surround sound. But there is usually no time for this in the reel world. And it doesn't allow for the wonderful symbiosis and fun of working with other talented people who do their jobs better than you might anyway. There are exceptions to this of course—there are artists who can do amazing things on their own with enough time and resources. Some art is best when left as a personal statement by one person. Other types (and I use the word "art" here a bit more loosely), such as films and television, work because of the collaboration between a group of gifted craftspeople who do their respective jobs together. The best use of technology is to assist in the collaboration process itself, so that we may exchange ideas and materials easily, regardless of our choice of tools or working practices. But I digress.

The *Chicago Hope* process went something like this: On Saturday or Monday morning, I go to the producer's office to spot each new episode. Present were the show's two producers, my music editor, the show's post production supervisor and myself. Occasionally, if they were behind in their schedule, the sound effects editor would sit in on the meeting and take notes for sound and dialogue, which slowed things down considerably. Usually I'd been given a cut of the show prior to the meeting, but occasionally this will be the first time I see it. We watch, we pause, we talk, we try to imagine if music will help or hinder a scene. Unlike the starkness of the music in *Homicide*, this show was very melodic and thematic, and it really made the spotting a different process. The meetings would also include discussions concerning how we wanted the audience to respond to specific characters and situations and how we would accomplish that thematically.

When we decided on a spot for music, the music editor would make a note of the approximate start and end times (from the SMPTE timecode on the screen) and any notes about what the music's intent should be based on the conversation at the meeting. While a music editor isn't a necessity, it's so much better for a composer to not be a note taker at a spotting session. It's distracting, and takes your attention away from the important elements of the spotting, which is creating a flowing score for the film (or episode). Thinking about numbers makes that much harder. After a few episodes, we usually agreed about where music would go. If I saw a place for score that the producer didn't, he'd say to "go ahead and try something," which meant I could score it, as long as I didn't mind it not being used in the show.

After each spotting session, the music editor would go back to her computer and type up the notes from the meeting using a special program called Cue. She included more details, including precise start and end times, and descriptions of significant events within the scene. The computer adds up all the timings, and also generates a Standard MIDI File (SMF) with all the cue points. The editor faxed the notes to me and e-mailed the SMF. I put the printed notes into a notebook and imported the MIDI Files into my sequencer, thus putting all the major hit points right in my sequence file as needed for reference. I had all the info I needed to get started right in front of me.

Now I write.

I needed to have the music written no later than the end of the day Thursday. As is so often the case, it's not what you can do in this business, it's what

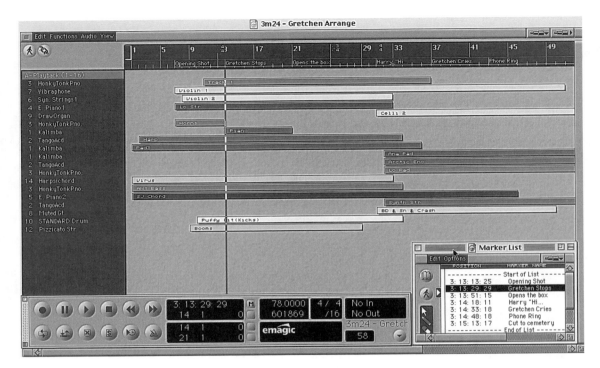

Figure 1.4 A sequence with markers for reference (lower right)

you can do in a small time allotted by people with no sense of how long it takes to write music. I tried to finish a bit before my deadline whenever possible. We scheduled a meeting for the producers to listen and approve (hopefully) all the music. They would come to my studio each week, and I would play each cue to picture, one at a time. When I first started doing this, I didn't have digital video in my MIDI sequencer which would bring up the video instantly. No forwarding and rewinding to find the right spot. I would have to lock the sequencer to a video tape and shuttle to each cue. In either case, when I play a cue for a director or producer, I start about ten seconds or so before the music comes in to give them a sense of the scene prior and how the music comes into each scene. I would say which scene was about to come, but say little or nothing about the music. It's best to let producers and directors make up their own minds about the music's intent and success. Afterward I would explain what I was trying to accomplish if they weren't sold on it. If they did like it, there was nothing to say. I'd put a check mark on the spotting notes and move on.

I used a small monitoring mixer to blend the music demos with the dialogue at a fairly realistic level. This really helps a lot. Usually the fixes they requested were pretty simple—make a cue go for a little longer, or start a little sooner. Sometimes they were not so simple, like "what the hell were you thinking??" In some cases we talked about what I wrote. I might sometimes take the opportunity to explain and defend some of my ideas. Sometimes I won, sometimes I lost. It doesn't really matter that much, my job is to make everybody happy (if they want to tamper with brilliant gems of inspired musical genius, hey, that's their business!). Actually, most of the changes requested made perfect sense. It's easy to get caught up in musical minutiae, but the producers are able to hang on to the big picture and see things in a broader perspective.

It usually took no more than a few hours to make the changes requested. There was no time to re-audition the music, so they simply trusted that the changes would achieve the desired effect (namely, good music). It was then time to record.

On Thursday afternoon I printed out musical transcriptions of the parts to be played live at the recording session the next day. I called my orchestrator to take my sequences and create the final score and parts.

Friday morning, 10AM. Downbeat. With the nature of the music I wrote for *Chicago Hope*, I preferred to record the musicians a few at a time, instead of all together. I did my string section first, with me conducting, and then came the rest of the parts in assembly line fashion. Trumpet at 11AM, guitar at 11:30, piano at 12:30. I played flutes and pennywhistles, which I recorded on my own in my writing room, playing straight into the sequencer. By 2PM, we're done recording all the musicians, and we jumped into mixing.

Mixing always took longer than I wanted. We mixed to six tracks on digital tape. We separated out the orchestral elements from the percussive elements and kept the bass and solos on their own tracks as well. We striped continuous timecode on the tape for the entire duration of the show (from 01:00:00:00 to 01:50:00:00) and laid each cue down in the correct point in time it played during the show. The music editor watched over everything to be sure we didn't miss anything and everything lined up to the picture properly. We used a fair amount of compression on the master recording, which enhances its intelligibility at low playback levels. I use more compression in TV than in film. I also boost a bit of the high and low end as well with an EQ. When the mix is finished, we made a "safety copy" which we kept at the studio in the event that anything happened to the master tape on its way to or at the dub stage. The master tape got whisked away so the music editor could prepare for the dub sessions Monday morning.

As with all episodic television, here is where the repeat marks are inserted; time to do it again. The schedule averaged three shows a month. Some weeks were brutal, while others flowed like water, and I actually got some sleep. It depended on the amount of music for an episode and the nature of the music needed. I tried never to slide by, preferring to challenge myself every week and learn something new in the process.

I did that show for four seasons, during which I only missed about three episodes while working on a film. (I got a friend to cover for me with the approval of the show's producers.) Over time, and scoring many more episodes of the series, I streamlined the process in ways that didn't detract from the quality of the score. As I got more episodes under my wing I became quicker at delivering my scores. Some could be written in a day or two, and only a few took more. Since I'd grown familiar with the desires and tastes of the producers, I could watch a scene and instinctively know where to take it emotionally. This made the writing process far less experimental and more productive. I was not repeating myself—every episode had fresh themes and ideas—but I could get the right answer much faster. The music had over time matured into something more meaningful for the show.

Once I had gotten the producers to begin coming to my studio, instead of me sending them a video tape demo and waiting for a response, I was able to get notes right on the spot and begin fixes. There simply is no replacement for having your producer or director sitting with you during playback of cues for approval. The process moves much faster, and your presence makes a difference in their approving the music.

Eventually I began to streamline the recording process as well. I abandoned tape in favor of recording onto the digital audio tracks of my sequencer. I began recording more of the players in my personal studio and not in another studio. I purchased a digital mixing board with memories that made the mixes go many times faster. These may seem like small things, but they added up to the ability to get much more sleep at night. On a few occasions the producers came to me with special musical requests. One episode was done with full orchestra, and no synths at all. A few involved my arranging and recording vocals, some to be played back on the set for the actors to lip sync with. It kept the show interesting and fun for the long while I did it.

Examples of music from *Chicago Hope* and the soundtrack CD are available online at www. reelworld-online.com

Titles

Intro Music for TV Shows

Television shows use main title music at the beginning of each episode to create an aural logo that helps give the show an identity. The music is played either at the very start of the program, or comes after some sort of opening prologue, called a *cold opening*. The same theme music is used all season. These themes can be anywhere from a few seconds to a minute or so in length. Some shows also have an end title cue used every week as well. The producers will determine the overall length of these two segments.

In some cases the visuals will be created to the music, but more likely you will be asked to score a picture, often one still in progress. The main title sequence will be set at a specific length and it cannot be violated. If the music has a final note that rings out into reverb, even the reverb must be cut in order to not allow the music to exceed the length of the titles.

End titles are typically much simpler. There is no picture to be concerned with, just a mood and an overall length. Additionally, many television series require one or more short musical pieces called "bumpers." Some programs will have a 3 to 5 second logo somewhere toward the middle of the program, during a commercial break, to entice people to watch the rest of the show ("Stay tuned, we'll be back"). Again, timings must be very accurate and can never go over.

The Main Theme

Is There a Doctor in the House?

I had scored a number of television series before having the chance to compose a main title for one. My first endeavor went poorly—the producers were mainly interested in me copying an existing piece of music and not having me do something of my own; not much fun in that. Fortunately (for my artistic self-respect) that show vanished quickly without much of a trace. My second experience was much the opposite; I had a chance to be as creative as I wanted. My approach was somewhat different this time around.

I was contacted by a producer of a new drama series for CBS called *LA Doctors*, having been recommended by a colleague. At first the producer was wary of my credentials, hoping for someone who had done less TV and more film, which shows the bias in the film industry against composers with any amount of TV work on their resumes. So I played a dirty trick. I submitted a demo of my music to the producer anonymously though my friend. With a more open mind he liked what he heard, and I got the job. Now on to actual composing!

I chatted with all the producers of the series (three of them) and got their take on what they liked and didn't like musically. They sent me the storyboards, which are sketches of each scene of the title sequence drawn much like an over-sized comic book, from the graphics company doing the title graphics. I knew the theme would be allotted 45 seconds, and that might get cut down to just 40. I also had only a few days to come up with a theme, as they had waited until the last possible moment to start on this aspect of the series (hmmm, why not score it months ahead of time, and then cast it just before it airs!!). A few months earlier I had done some sketches for a series pilot that did not get picked up, and a couple of the themes seemed like possible springboards here. As frustrating as it is to write music that doesn't get heard, its great to know that when you need to come up with something in a short amount of time, you might have some ideas in the bank.

One of those sketches had a driving acoustic guitar rhythm that I had recorded into my sequencer and that became the launching point of the theme. I used the guitars as well as some processed drum loops I had created. I dropped the original melody and started working on a new idea. I came up with the rather simple theme in fig 1.6a.

Figure 1.6a Melody 1

With that in place, I fleshed the theme out with more rhythms, guitars, and textures. I wanted it to have a definite vibe. While the melody itself (and perhaps even having a strong melodic approach at all) was not particularly cutting edge, I like my music to sound creative and fresh. I also chose not to go full throttle energy-wise, which goes against the current trend in TV themes to be a bit over the top sometimes. The sketch was more subtle and textural than most main title music, and I liked that.

I spent a day or two finishing it up, but didn't want to present only one idea to the producers. So I created a second demo as well, in order to give them some options. It was a little less melodic, leaning more towards groove. I brought a guitar player in to help with the demos. Both themes used guitar extensively, and I didn't want to rely on samples.

The show's producers came to my studio to listen to the first theme ideas. The moment of truth—playing music for near perfect strangers and hoping they will like it (which I still often equate with liking me!). Happily it went quite well, though we didn't quite hit the ball out of the park. They definitely preferred my first theme idea to my second, which was fine with me. But they wanted a different feel: More energy, of course. Why fight it? Everyone and everything is clamoring for attention, which is hard to come by these days.

⊗ All the demos can be heard at www. reelworld-online.com

So I reworked the first theme quite a bit. I brought my guitar player back in to refine the melody and give it more bite. An important synth line that the producers thought sounded too much like another television series had to be taken out. I could have argued that such a line did not exist in that theme at all, but it doesn't matter—if they want it out, it's out. Nothing to be gained by arguing about musical technicalities. If a director says they want you to take the horns out of a piece that has none, you don't explain what horns sound like or tell them how mistaken they are. You try to figure out what they thought were horns, remove them, and then see if the arrangement still works. Sometimes it does, and sometimes you need to find ways to plug the holes left by these simple but damaging comments.

In all, I went through five versions of the theme before they started to be really pleased. By now, my guitarist was getting pretty tired of my calls to come and do one more demo, but I had to make each version of the theme better than the last, so I couldn't go back to using samples. To get the desired energy

Figure 1.6b Bass line

into the theme, I switched to a techno-style bass line ala fig 1.6b, using the Yamaha ANx1 synthesizer and adding a great deal of compression. I used a drum loop from a popular sampling CD, but compressed and distorted it heavily. I added two other loops from my collection to get the groove to burn hotter. When I layer loops, I prefer to have a main loop that is pushed up in the mix and any other loops pushed back, just to add bite and feel. This works very well for me.

The offending synth was the basis of the theme's intro and hook, so I needed to come up with something to replace it that would draw your attention right away. Hooks are very important in most styles of music. Hooks can be almost anything, a few notes of a melody, a repeating figure somewhere in a tune, a signature sound or even a beat. The more distinctive, the better. But finding a hook is essential to making something memorable. It needs to be simple and to happen many times during the song. While my melody seemed catchy enough, it was not a hook, because in :45 it only gets to happen once; not a good hook candidate.

Figure 1.6c String part for the theme's hook

I had avoided an orchestral approach in this piece because I wanted it to sound more contemporary and unique. But something inspired me to try adding a punchy string line to the theme that would serve as the first thing we would hear at the beginning of the theme and would run throughout the tune. I came up with the line in fig 1.6c, at around version three or four of the theme, which took it in a whole new direction. I now had a decent hook, enough so that I decided not to use samples, and brought in 12 string players to record the line (6 violins, 2 violas, and 4 celli).

While the producers were pleased with the new feel of the theme, I wasn't yet happy starting off with just the string line. They had always said that the very beginning of it should pull people in to want to listen. I recorded the string players in a recording studio direct to hard disk. I mixed them to stereo and put that into my original MIDI sequence back in my own studio. I took the first two bars of the string line and utilized an audio processing program on my Macintosh to create a cool filter sweep effect that would cross-fade into the normal string sound. It came out great but sounded a bit too much like a fade-in. It needed more impact. So I took the same two bar string line and processed it again, this time using another audio plug-in, a very deep flange effect that made it almost piercing in quality. By itself it sounded wrong, but blended with my filter sweep version, it was a strange effect—a tweaky high sound coming down on top of a low rumbly sound coming up and meeting in the middle to become a string line that runs through the whole piece. I now had a very cool intro for the theme both thematically and sonically.

After getting the final sketch approved, my engineer came in for the final mix. We mixed it onto 8-track digital tape, splitting out the bass line, solo line, and percussion from the synths and strings. The show was going to premiere in only 3 days! Sure enough, I was threatened with the possibility that the theme would have to be cut down to :40. I put up a bit of a fuss. It would have gotten ruined to cut 5 seconds from the arrangement, which was very concise. I said it would take me a couple of days (not exactly true) and after a flurry of phone calls, it stayed at :45.

The series also needed an end title theme. Instead of just rearranging the opening theme, I used the second theme I had written, the one that wasn't used. It was a good complement to the opening theme, and they liked it—just not as much as the theme that they chose. I arranged and recorded it as well. Lastly, I had to create a five second bumper used during the show about half way through as underscore for "we'll be right back." It's standard in most hour long dramas. I gave them two ideas based on the opening theme. With that, I was done. The show itself lasted but one season, but I got a number of good compliments on that theme. I felt that the hard work for those 45 seconds were very worthwhile.

CHAPTER THREE

> Developing A Style

Critique
Learning by Doing

With something as unfathomable as music, which is nearly impossible to describe with words (with all due respect to music critics and academics), describing things that don't work sometimes helps to narrow our focus on the more successful options, while leaving the widest range of musical possibilities. Most successful film composers learn their craft from a combination of intuition, talent, observation, and practice. While formal academic training in music is never a bad thing, there doesn't seem to be a lot of highly schooled composers working in the field.

Those composers who are just trying their hand at scoring for the first time often make certain common mistakes that can be of value to others trying to improve their craft. I've met a number of interesting and promising new composers at the occasional film music seminars and workshops I've spoken at. I come away from these encounters with a greater sense of how wonderfully important music is in the world of visual media, and how dramatically our craft enhances the emotional experiences of those who watch and listen. Music can speak reams of information that no other sensory element can, even if a particular piece is in someway flawed. And through a musical "failure" can come an inspiration of how to do it right next time. I look at elements of some of my music as sorts of "glorious failures" that, while still accomplishing a goal for the project, leave me wanting to try it again and see how I can improve upon it. Art and evolution can be soul mates.

At one workshop I attended there was one film in particular which brought up for me a number of important issues about what can and does go into a successful score. The music was well written, but its relationship to the film caused some significant problems. Film music never stands alone. It can only be judged by how well it serves and supports the scene it accompanies. The film was short, only about 30 minutes long, and there were perhaps ten cues. While each cue was good in one way or another, they all sounded completely different from one another. A single composer had written the whole score, but it sounded like a different person had done each piece. There was no sense of stylistic cohesion to the score as a whole.

If you listen carefully to any good film score (trying not to get too distracted by those annoying plots or characters!) you will usually notice a strong sense of stylistic cohesion. For now, forget about songs and other source elements of the score, and just focus on the dramatic underscore.

While a score may cover a wide amount of ground to support all the action and moods of the film, there is virtually always a strong bond that links all the music together into a cohesive whole. The main bond is usually *theme*. Theme can have more than one definition. It is traditionally a melody or phrase— though it can also be a unique sound or instrument, a certain beat, a riff, or a small set of chords—that link the parts of a film together. The most memorable film scores are those with strong melodic themes. The theme in Jaws was only two notes, but everyone remembers it because of how well, and often, they were used throughout the film.

Themes are sometimes linked to characters, with each major character getting a theme of his or her own. This way, as the people in the film interact, so do their themes. A character's theme tells the audience more about them than can be seen on the screen. You can suggest the nearby presence of a character even if they aren't in the scene, just by reprising their theme. When a well-liked character dies, playing their theme is almost a sure-fire tearjerker. Hearing their familiar theme makes us miss them that much more. If a film is driven primarily on the strength of the characters, then a strong theme for the main roles can be very enriching. If a film is less character-oriented, then a main title theme that reprises throughout the film will lend continuity to the story as a whole. It says, "This is an important moment" in a more subtle way. Themes can be used to reinforce bravery, heroism, romance, tension, humor, or danger without attachment to any specific character. This too helps make a film a more cohesive whole. Even an emotionally complex film with many characters may come down to just a handful of themes at best. Too many themes become too complicated for an audience to recognize.

Beyond the score's main theme or themes, there is room for less important, simpler music for those moments that are of lower prominence in the plot. Most scores go back and forth between thematic and nonthematic moments, often within the same cue. It certainly is possible to overuse a theme. As with all things, the success is in finding the balance. Most good scores make repeated use of a small handful of themes, and repeat them at the key moments in the story. Beyond the main themes are a consistent use of style and harmonic vocabulary, which also keep a score feeling like a single entity, as opposed to many small moments.

Getting back to that film's score, scored by a student composer, another problem I noticed was in the score's sonic palette, something to which I always pay close attention. In addition to not having any strong, memorable (or even noticeable) themes for the film, every cue felt like it had its own set of sounds. This only added to the sense that every cue could have been created by a different member of the "composer committee". Whether you score a film with orchestra, synths, guitars, or scratching nails on a chalkboard in waltz tempo, keeping some sonic cohesion throughout the score allows the music to keep a stronger bond with the audience. It also enhances the sense of style to the score. There can be exceptions to make a point—don't bring in the crunchy guitars until the main battle, or save the violin solo until the boy and girl meet. But the majority of any one score should keep to a limited number of instruments and sounds. With the astonishing number of sounds available with electronic music gear, it is easy to want to try out all the ones we like in the same score.

Every film score needs to have its own personality. The best film composers have learned not to try and say everything in a single score. The best way to do that, I believe, is by imposing some strong limits on yourself in choosing instruments, sounds, rhythms, tonalities, or melodies. A good score stands out because of one or two things that it does that people will remember. Throw too many ideas at an audience at once, and they will all start to sound the same after a while. It's the same with art. Too many colors on a canvas start to come out as just muddy grey. This is the concept of *economy*, getting the most from a limited number of resources, both thematic and sonic.

Over the Top

Melodramatic Music

Another of the films I saw at that screening had a much more cohesive score, and seemed to get a lot from a simple theme and instrumentation; so far so good to my ear. But the composer broke another of the unwritten "rules" of scoring (no one knows where these "rules" came from, but most people notice when they are broken). It was, in a word, overly melodramatic, it was just too over the top. One scene that stood out had a woman we didn't know yet walking down a street, turning the corner and walking into a dark alley. Without more information about the woman or the possibly treacherous alley, we the audience still can know that this might be a somewhat dangerous situation, and she could be getting into jeopardy. As composers, we can express some concern for the situation or the character in the music. Tension works that way—nothing is really happening on the screen, yet we must convey some sense of danger or foreboding. Without more information from the story itself, such as seeing the bad guys waiting in the alley or driving up in a car, we want to be careful of going overboard and scoring the scene into the ground with heavy, ominous, scary music that shrieks at us saying "Oh no! Get out of that alley now! There's a murderer there!! Run for your life!!!" Even a very well-made film has a hard time building tension without the use of music.

There are moments when a whisper can speak to us louder than a scream. This is especially true if a scene is just getting under way. It's not our job to tell the audience something that they may wish to figure out on their own. There is a word for this in the scoring world—it's called *telegraphing*. It's when you tell the audience with music what is going to happen before it does. It is to be avoided unless it is for a very specific effect. It is usually best to start slow and wind things up as they go along in the story. We try to stay in the moment and not jump ahead. Build musical tension slowly as a scene unfolds. Certainly there are times when you really want to go for it, nothing held back. But don't tip your hat by getting the message across too quickly or too early. It's annoying when movies bludgeon the audience with music that just speaks to the obvious—"They are SO in love!" "He's a real HERO!"—that sort of thing. Sure, it works for some films, and in some scenes, but sometimes it just goes way over the top. I for one do not like to feel that I am being manipulated or told the obvious, even when that is exactly what is being done. Movies really are about manipulating emotions. But it can't be done too overtly, or it just turns into a soap opera. By keeping the music within certain bounds, and not building the audience's expectations too much or too early, we enhance and lead the audience's experience without their awareness. This is when music works best. When it is time to really hit things—the murder, the chase, the pinnacle moment of the story, then the music can go for it without having already exhausted the audience.

If you ever notice some of these musical transgressions in film scores, don't be too quick to automatically blame the composer. Often these things come from the wishes of the director or producer. On those occasions that I hear something in a score that rankles me, which is pretty rare I must admit, I remind myself that each of those cues was approved by the director and/or producer. I've been in situations where a director is not happy with a scene and tries to mask what they see as dramatic weakness with a layer of musical goo. I try to help find the best level for each moment that balances the score with the needs of that specific scene. No composer gets to just go off and score a film; a film score is the product of a collaboration. Maybe the composer argued against it and lost. Maybe the composer argued for it and won. Either way it comes down to what the filmmakers want for their film. But by being sensitive to the potential pitfalls of these "musical errors" you can more easily steer clear of situations that may come back to haunt you.

The CD Is in the Mail

Analysis of a Problematic Demo

I've heard quite a few demo CDs by composers trying to get started in film scoring, asking for feedback and advice, which I don't dispense so much anymore. My opinions are my opinions; who am I to tell someone if their music is good enough or not? I've written lots of music that I loved and other people hated, and vice versa. I like what I like, and don't like what I don't like. Some types of music are more enjoyable to me than others.

One demo that I heard made me think for a while. The composer/demo sender wrote to me of his deep interest in scoring film, and listed some of his influences and film score heroes. It was a great list of composers, including several of my own favorites. I looked forward to listening to the music. During a break from my work, I listened for a while.

The music was good. In fact, it was very good. Some of it was orchestral, played by what I assumed was a university student orchestra. Other pieces were electronically realized, but were in a similar musical style. The harmonies were sophisticated and interesting, the orchestration was sophisticated, and generally the pieces came across as well conceived and executed. It was very well done contemporary orchestral music.

However, there was a problem. And the problem put me in a bind. I couldn't decide how to respond to this composer. While I really liked what I heard on the tape, it seemed obvious (to me anyway) that this simply was not music for film. It was music in a very different genre, created for a very different purpose. There is something to the kinds of music that work well to picture. It is a vastly wide category, but it does have boundaries. This music fell well outside of even broad limits. Film music has a marvelous history that has shaped and defined what we expect to hear and are expected to compose today for film and television. Innovation does not ignore its predecessors.

This starts to touch closely to the nature of art and art history. In the study of one's art (be it aural, visual, or literary), the basic lessons are to look at, and study, what has come before, then use that as inspiration for our own work. Music students may study the works of Bach or Mozart (or, God help us, Palestrina) to come to some kind of understanding of how (and perhaps why) these exemplary artists did what they did. Studying the art of the past helps to see the art and artists of the present in a more clear light. For those who desire to become artists or composers, studying the art and artists of the past also helps to avoid reinventing the wheel (or its close cousin, plagiarism). Fortunately, for the nonacademics among you interested in the art of film scoring, you don't even need a library card—just go to the nearest video rental store and check out what's there, or go to any record store and look in the soundtrack bins.

The state of any art—music, visual or literature—is defined by the major figures currently engaged in creating works for the public. In film scoring that would include (but not be limited by) such established people as John Williams, Jerry Goldsmith, Ennio Morricone, Danny Elfman, Hans Zimmer, and the many others in the prime of their careers. If you look at the entire field of working film composers, you see a huge range of stylistic and dramatic approaches. Today's major films have scores that range from serious symphonic music to jazz, electronica, ethnic, techno, and other influences—not to mention the growing reliance on songs to create a score. No one style or composer defines film music today. Yet each artist comes from a perspective or awareness of the music of past films and applies that to his or her own, and hopefully unique, musical sensibility.

Though there is tremendous diversity in today's film music—certainly compared to the scores of the past—some musical elements don't seem to fit into the film music genre. Contemporary avant-garde music shares many facets with film scores: they both can be very abstract and textural. But where "art" music can be as demanding, dense, and difficult as the composer wishes, film music cannot go too far in any direction that takes the listener's attention away from the rest of what is happening in the film. Few avant-garde composers have made a significant inroad into film score. One composer whose music has been successfully adapted to film is Georgi Ligeti, whose music is textural and evocative, and relies on a great deal of economy and focus. Composers such as John Corigliano, Tan Dun, Elliot Goldenthal, and Philip Glass have all had success as composers of serious concert music as well as film scores. But much of their music, while adventurous, contains those elements of economy and focus that are so important in film music.

The vast majority of successful film scores leave room in the audience's attention for the picture up on the screen. They are highly linear, often emotional, and often unabashedly melodic. Film music flows in rhythmic waves that blend with the action of the story and the editing of the picture. A good score supports the picture and makes it look better than it really is by not making extra demands on the listener's already engaged attention. Though there are some fantastic exceptions, most film scores reside within a somewhat narrow range of colors and themes in order to lend cohesion to the film, while they explore whatever new territory the composer wishes.

It comes back to this once again: theme is the most important element. Theme is the basis and foundation for a film score. If you listen carefully to a soundtrack, try counting how often a particular theme is stated in whole, in part, or in variation. You may be very surprised. There is an approach of contemporary avant-garde composition, often taught in universities and conservatories, that steps away from this view of music. I studied it myself when I went to school. The contemporary music taught in these institutions is often dense, complex, intellectual, fragmented, and nonthematic. This is a generalization, but one borne from experience and observation. And it is this style of academic music that has the hardest time fitting into the context of most film scores. What I heard on that composer's demo fell exactly into this category.

Well done in its own right, but not the kind of music that a director would listen to and conjure cinematic images in their head.

To become proficient in composing music for films, it is critical to listen to the music of the past and present before making the decision to ignore it and go your own way. Music is a language—and film music is a common language used to help tell the story of the picture. It is far less about making a personal musical statement, and in that respect it differs greatly from other "fine" arts. Film music is not created to stand as great music, though the best film music does just that. It is one part of the collaboration that goes into making a movie.

Workshop
More Thoughts on Demos, Plagiarism, and Conservative Choices

Each year the American Society of Composers and Publishers (ASCAP) sponsors a very highly regarded workshop on film scoring. Admission is by audition, and only about 20 students per year are invited to participate. It is typically taught by a veteran composer, and is geared toward traditional, orchestral-style film music. I know several people who have attended the workshop and raved about it. I know that many people have started long term working relationships and friendships from the workshop.

One year I was asked to help listen to some of the demos that had been submitted by potential workshop attendees in order to select that year's participants. I'm not a music critic, but I agreed to listen to a few of the CDs in order to help, and out of curiosity. I was asked to listen to seven demos and rate them on a scale of 1 to 10, based on whether I thought the composer had a shot at a career in film scoring. I groaned at the idea of making such a delicate decision. I imagine that anyone who listens to my music might give me any one of those ratings if they happened to like my particular slant to scoring. It's all about personal taste really, isn't it?

Disappointingly, of the demos I listened to (from over 100 they had received) only one stood out as real film score material, and even that was marginal to me. Before you condemn me as being overly harsh and judgemental let me explain that there are a few basic notions that can be more obvious than others when it comes to film scoring.

I must first say that the level of technical musical proficiency on most of the demos was amazing. There are some very well-trained and talented musicians out there interested in scoring films. My guess is that most of these people were serious students of classical composition and orchestration, and were staying awake in class. Several demos had live orchestra and were very well orchestrated and performed. There was a very high degree of musical sophistication in terms of harmony and harmonic development. Some were musically very "old school" and others explored some newer types of orchestral compositional techniques. These were not musical slouches in any way. I could see that there was a uniform amount of emphasis placed on technique and musicianship, and I was impressed. However, there were some fundamental problems from the point of view of film music that I noticed right away.

First of all, if you ever send music to a composer, music supervisor, director, producer, or anyone else in the film business, never ever think you can fool them by ripping off any existing scores or classical pieces and claiming the themes are yours. They will know, and not appreciate the attempt at subterfuge. In the demos I heard (five or six pieces per composer), at least three were obvious rip-offs of scores or composers with which I was familiar. Some were truly well done, but other were simply poor versions of their models. Remember: it is all right to steal ideas, but not notes. Use anything and everything you hear for inspiration, but find a new way to use it. As do most of my musical colleagues. I'll take the essence of an existing composition that turns me on, and I will begin to see where I can take it in order to make it into something new and more "mine." Change the chords but use the rhythm. Grab a melodic shape but find some new twists and turns. Try a completely new orchestration to colour the music in a new way. Then do it again. By the time you are done, you should be able to have something that sounds unique and personal.

The world has enough music by John Williams. Don't write another *ET* or *Indiana Jones* cue and call it "your" music. Those Williams-esque lydian scales are acceptable, and very charming, but look for a new way to use them. No one is going to hire a composer because of how well they rip-off John Williams. If you want to write a John Williams cue as a technical exercise, that's great. He is one of the best, and we can all learn a lot from emulating him. But don't play them for anyone else who is evaluating you for a possible project unless they specifically say "Hey, you got any John Williams rip-offs?" Then sure, whip one out. Otherwise you will be much better served by bringing something different and more personal. You will be so much more admired for failing at something original than succeeding at something trite.

The use of themes and melodies seems to be highly underrated by student composers. I think this harkens back to what I was saying earlier about the nature of academic compositional training. We must remember that pop music works because of its musical phrases that are so simple and obvious, and are used numerous times, that they have the tendency to stick in the mind. It can be a three note phrase (ala Beethoven's 5th), a repeating rhythm (Ravel's Bolero for instance), a unique solo instrument repeating a phrase or anything else that stands out quickly. Of the composers' demos I listened to, almost none had any real melodies—all were caught up in orchestral fluff and technique. You can blend ambience, nontraditional approaches of sound and style, and still have room for a musical hook.

Perhaps the most surprising thing to me about all the ASCAP demos I heard was the level of stylistic conservatism. I knew that the emphasis of the workshop is orchestral, but they all sounded as though they had been written 20 years earlier. Film scores usually reflect some of the musical aspects popular at the time in which they were written, with exceptions for period-style films and a few others. Early film music began in a romantic classical tradition. Jazz scores came when jazz was what was on the radio. Rock scores came when rock had established itself as the predominant popular style. As ethnic music made inroads into pop music via artists such as Peter Gabriel, it started to find its way into film soundtracks more (there are exceptions, such as the score to *The Third Man*, which used ethnic instruments a few decades earlier). All art must continuously reinvent itself, and producers and directors look for that in their choice of music. If not the style, then the use or placement of music needs to be unique or fresh (think of the sublime use of Strauss's "Blue Danube" in *2001: A Space Odyssey* or the haunting Barber's "Adagio for Strings" against the carnage of *Platoon*).

Perhaps the prospective workshop attendees thought that such conservatism was expected of them, but I was surprised at how little synthesizers and other interesting colors or even percussion instruments were used. It's not that film scores must have weird electronics or unconventional instrumentation to be contemporary or more relevant to their subject, but they certainly have taken their place alongside the orchestra. Most prominent composers working today who use orchestra in their scores often use synths as well—including people like John Williams, Basil Poledouris, Jerry Goldsmith, Mark Isham and on down the line. The film *Titanic* was drowning (no pun) in gooey, anachronistic synth colours alongside the lavish orchestra and Celtic vocals. And the electric guitar has certainly become a major part of music in the latter half of the 20th century and beyond. For whatever reason, none of these "young composers" trying out for the workshop took advantage of all the cool possible sounds available to create interesting or new sounding music, regardless of the use of orchestra or other traditional timbres and thematic approaches. One's approach to film scoring is a personal thing, but there are good reasons to use contemporary aesthetics and approaches when writing even a very traditional style film score.

House of Style
Cultivating a Unique, Identifiable Sound

I want to tell you the greatest compliment anyone has given me about my music. I also want to tell you about a very important lesson I got once about writing music that probably applies to just about every facet of our lives.

I often like to play scores I'm working on to friends and colleagues to get their reactions and criticisms. It's about the closest thing to music school I have in my life. I'm always looking for the unexpected response that tells me something new about what my music communicates to other people, especially people who aren't seeing the pictures for which my music was written. And as I'm scoring a project, I'm always bugging the people around me to come and listen to a new cue and tell me what they think. Fortunately for me, I'm surrounded by some great ears, ready to listen and give (sometimes brutally) honest feedback.

Probably the best thing anyone can say to me is "it sounds like you." Oddly enough, I usually don't have any idea what they mean. After all, not only am I called upon to write music in a variety of styles and approaches, but I feel that my music is continuing to grow and change over time, hopefully for the better. The music I write today feels quite different than what I was doing even a few years ago. Yet people tell me that they hear common threads and consistency in my work. I believe what they are talking about is style, which is something I've been thinking about lately.

A great number of people in the entertainment industry (Isn't it great to think about your creativity, talent, and passions as being some part of an "industry"?) read *Daily Variety*, a strangely named trade publication that caters to the people in film, television, and other media. For many it's the bible of what is happening in Hollywood and around the world in "the biz." Variety reviews virtually every new film, television show, play and live concert that comes along. Because it is a financially oriented publication, they often look at a project in terms of its money-making potential. Music is typically allotted about one sentence, if at all, within most of its reviews. Something on the order of "The lush score by **<name of composer here>** successfully underlined the major dramatic points in the film." That would constitute a lot of attention for the music in their pages.

I had noticed a review of a movie in *Variety*, that stood out at me. First because it spent the better part of a paragraph talking about the music, and second because the composer under scrutiny was a friend. To get right down to it, the review was pretty vicious, both to the show and the music. In essence, it described the music as being both overly generic, overblown, and a distraction from the rest of the show. Ouch! These were unusually strong words, especially for a composer who is one of the more talented, experienced, musical, and technically adroit people I know.

Apparently, the composer, after having spent a lot of time doing small-scale work, had embarked on a mission to do more serious, larger-scale dramatic projects. He had begun musical studies that included some classic and influential film scores and major composers. But I believe, if I accept what the reviewer said, that the composer possibly took those lessons too closely to heart. He let go of whom he was as a composer in order to create what he believed others wanted to hear from him. He let go of what is most important to a composer's career: a unique and unmistakable personal style. I must add though, that I believe behind every questionable film score is a director who said "Yes, that's what I want!" Where does style fit in to film music?

Pop stars have it easy. We hear a famous voice and can recognize it immediately. If Sting sings a Kurt Weill song, you still know it's Sting within a few words. Most instrumental composers have it a bit harder. Others are playing your music for you, or you are using the same synthesizers or sample libraries as the rest of them. How do you make your music your own and able to stand out from the rest? It's not that easy. I can usually identify a score as being by a few composers by the style, but most I cannot.

There is probably no greater asset in one's musical career than having a unique and identifiable "sound" that sets you apart from others. No matter how

⊗ For information on *Daily Variety* and other entertainment trade publications, go to www. reelworld-online.com

eclectic or versatile you are or want to be in your music, it usually comes down to "Why should we hire this composer over any others?" The answer is "Because we like his (or her) sound and approach, and we can get it by hiring them."

Some composers are far more versatile than others, but even the least versatile ones who maintain a very distinct style are more in demand. Look at Ry Cooder for example: He only really does one thing, but he does it better than anyone else around. He probably gets about as many films as he wants (if not, he's greedy!). Style is what it's all about. A composer needs technique, of course, as well as savvy about the business of film scoring. But on top of all that is style—what makes each of us unique and therefore of value to others, especially the others who might hire us. By developing a strong, unique style you become a more rare thing, and rare things, like diamonds, are always of greater value.

Jerry Goldsmith describes himself as being a "musical chameleon." You certainly need to have some of that if you want to score a wide range of films. Goldsmith has done pretty much every genre of film and has adapted himself accordingly. Yet he never loses touch with his "Goldsmithness" in any of them. He is a very versatile composer. Carter Burwell is a far less versatile composer. Like Cooder, he only accepts projects that allow him to do what he wants and match his unique and quirky style.

I've always tried to find projects for which my style of writing is a good match. And as I do more films I continue to experiment with new ideas and approaches. I've turned down films that I thought I wasn't suited for, because there is no point in taking on a project and not doing a good job, or writing something that doesn't feel at all personal.

One film I did felt like it needed a score that was grand in scope and needed a "big" score, something I hadn't really done before. I finally came up with a theme that I was proud of. It sounded like a "big" movie theme to me, and I thought it would fit the film well. I sat at a piano and played it for a friend. I was eager for his opinion, since he knew the director and his tastes pretty well. When I was done I looked up and saw this rather blank look on his face, which I knew well when he didn't like something. He said to me, "They hired you for this project so you'd write something in your style. What's this?" I understood immediately. I mistakenly thought that what I had done was better than my own style, but that's impossible. Style is not subjective. I nearly blew it trying to be something other than myself, which defeats the whole reason for being a composer in the first place. It was a crisis of confidence.

I started again, this time looking inside myself for the ideas that felt most personal and right for me. And it worked. Within a day or two I had a theme that worked for the film and was approved by the director that felt like my own musical style. Which is not to say it was going to be an easy project, but it beat trying to figure out how to write like someone else. I continued trying new ideas and ways to get the score to sound as big as possible, which is what the film really needed. I got the sound I wanted, but I did it from my unique perspective. I guess people who know me would say it sounds like me. For better or worse.

The Art Film
(aka Working For Peanuts)

One of my very first scores was for a small, independently produced film called *The Lipstick Camera.* The film was a who-done-it murder mystery with a few twists, made on a very modest budget by a first time director. Though quite well made, it seemed a longshot that it would ever be released, since it lacked the box office appeal of any big name stars or major studio backing. Still, it was a worthwhile endeavor, and I got to write some fun, dark, adventurous, and textural music.

One of the great challenges that film composers have is working with first time directors. They can be nervous, error prone, and highly opinionated at the same time. Picture a deer staring into the headlights of a Mack truck, with the driver explaining how good a driver he is. It is your job to serve the directors you work with, and yet gently guide them at the same time with your own experience and musical sense. Unlike the other technical aspects of movie-making, such as lighting, photography, or editing, few directors have a grasp of the technicalities or craft of musical scoring, and that often frustrates them. They can't tell you in specific musical terms how to do what they want ("Wouldn't an A♭ minor 7 be better when we see her face?") when they want something changed. It's your job to realize their vision in a way that lets them feel like they are at least partially in control.

Lipstick Camera started with a phone call from one of the film's three producers. I had been recommended to them; they wanted to know if I could submit some music immediately. I did, they liked it, and asked me to score the film. However, the film's director was still interested in one other possible composer.

Could I meet the director, see some of the film, and play him some of my music? Sure! I met the director a day later at the loft where the film was in the midst of editing. I watched a ten minute excerpt from the film that, in my opinion, required little or no music.

"So, what would you put in this film, musically?" he asked. Tough question, from what I had just seen. I really had no immediate response, yet the job offer hinged on my answer. "I don't know that I'd put any music on that scene; it works great just the way it is." A blank stare. Followed by a thoughtful look. He knew I didn't bluff. "Well, I'll listen to your music and we'll be in touch." The meeting had ended.

A few days later, the producer called me again and asked me to score the film. She also indicated that I was chosen against the wishes of the director, who wanted to hire a composer friend of his. Not a good start to what is a very important relationship between a composer and director. It got a bit more complex. The producer told me that I was to answer only to her on all decisions concerning music, and that she, not the director, would approve the score. It is very unusual for the director of a feature film, unless he or she has been fired, to not be the main person working with the composer. This was the first, but not the last movie in which this was to be asked of me.

The next day I got a call from the less-than-enthusiastic director. He wanted to meet to discuss the music for the score. He then went on to tell me that I was to answer only to him on all decisions concerning music, and that he, not the producer, would approve the score. This was also not the last movie in which this was asked of me by the director.

This situation, where there is a power play between producer and director, is the recipe for Trouble (with a capital "T" which rhymes with "C" and that stands for "Chain of Command"). I've seen this happen to other composers, and it's come up for me on other occasions, and it can be a big problem, requiring needless and counterproductive meetings and musical rewrites. However, it's by no means the norm. When everyone is professional, it goes smoothly virtually all the time. But it's these projects that test what we are made of.

In any collaborative effort as large as a feature film, there really needs to be a clear, well-defined pecking order. Everyone should answer to one person, and one person only. When that isn't established from the start, things can get out of control quickly. The producer was asking for a very dark, ambient score in the mold of Steven Soderbergh's *sex, lies & videotape*. The director wanted to hear "the melody that everyone will be humming as they leave the theatre." "Like

Andrew Lloyd Webber?" I asked, jokingly. "Exactly," he replied. Oh boy—from Eno to Evita in a single meeting. The two directions just didn't connect, I could do one or the other, but not both at the same time. This spelled, as mentioned earlier, Trouble.

The next day I spoke with the producer again, and told her I was getting a conflicting message from the director, and I really wanted to know who my "boss" was before starting to work. She assured me that she was the only person I need answer to, and she would clear things up with the director. Within a few minutes after that call ended, I got another one, this time from the director. "This has been my film from the start, and I don't plan to have that change now, do you understand?" Of course I understood. Diplomacy.

I figured that this situation would work its way out soon enough, and I had best get started with writing. As is so often the case, they were up against an impending postproduction deadline and needed the music done relatively fast. They promised to deliver the final cut of the film to me about three and a half weeks before the first day of dubbing. Three weeks is not a lot of time to compose, record and mix an entire film score, but in this business it's not what you can do, it's what you can do quickly (and under budget)! It was already a week past their promised delivery date and there was still no film and no music. I was given the message, though, that the dates for the final dub were not going to change.

And so, I began. I sequenced a first sketch for a theme and sent copies to the producer and the director. She liked it, he hated it. To convince me that he wasn't just being subjective, he told me that both his wife and his wife's sister didn't like it either. We certainly can't have that! So I wrote two more themes. Same results. I was getting nowhere thus far, so I asked the producer to talk with the director and try to reach a consensus about the overall approach for the music. I wrote a few more ideas for themes in contrasting moods and sent them to the director.

I must tell you, at this point I was starting to fray around the edges a bit. Time was ticking and I had nothing yet that everyone could approve. The producer had become my only ally, really liking my music and fighting for me with the director. However, the director still needed to be convinced that I had the right approach for the score. At one point, I offered to step aside if the director wanted his first pick composer to step in. In the back of my mind I was praying for them to let me go just so I could stop spinning my wheels. No, we'll work it out, they said.

Finally, a meeting was called. The director and all three producers came to my studio to listen to everything I had written thus far and try to get the project unstuck. Before I could play a note, the director pulls out a tape and says "After listening to a lot of music, I found a piece that I think works perfectly for the main theme of the picture." The last thing I needed at that point was to be given another composer's music to imitate. He put the tape into the machine and hit Play. To my utter surprise, it was one of the first pieces I had written, but abandoned long ago after getting a less than enthusiastic response. The producers didn't know that he was playing my music and asked me what I thought of it. We were playing a little game, and I had to play along. In fact, it was my least favorite choice—I knew it was wrong for the film and I told them so. I then played every other theme I had written for the movie, five or six in all. Each theme was shot down, for one reason or another, by one mogul or another. The last piece I had was the first one I had written, and still my favorite theme. They listened. It ended. The executive producer turned to his colleagues and said "That's a pretty good theme, what's wrong with that one?" Another one said "I like it, we could use it." The producers turned to the director and waited for a response. I knew he didn't like it, and we were getting nowhere.

"I think I can live with that" he said.

It wasn't exactly the most enthusiastic answer I could have thought of, but we finally had a theme! This was a relief. The producers arose as if a single entity and began to leave. The meeting was over. I had a direction for the score that was approved by all, and it was one I felt I could do well with.

With theme in hand, I began scoring in earnest. Over the course of the project, the producers became less and less involved, while the director and I got on very friendly terms. He turned out to be a great person, and he even started to like my weird, "ambient-yet-highly-melodic" music. We had a number of meetings in order to play him bits of the score. His enthusiasm grew as the score did.

After I completed composing and having the score approved by all, I recorded for a few days with a prominent rock guitarist. I also had my friend Mark Isham play some trumpet in a few spots. I mixed each cue with the director present in the studio. This is the only way to be sure that each piece was acceptable to him, and there would be no big surprises at the final mix. He made a lot of last minute changes, but he was very happy with the final results. Also, by having a hand in the music mixing process, the director had a sense of involvement that helped him like the music better. It's very worthwhile, even if it slows the process a bit.

As this was a very low budget film, I was instructed to provide no more than stereo mixes for everything, a practice fraught with potential trouble. This will be discuss more thoroughly in Section 2. With only a stereo mix, if a melody line or percussion instrument conflicts with any of the dialogue, the level of the entire cue must be lowered. When they are delivered separately, there is control up to the last moment. Since the dub stage mixer was already full with just the dialogue and effects, this compromise was made to avoid bringing in more gear (too expensive) and so the sound effects editors would not need to be organized to use fewer tracks (too much work for them).

You should always accompany your mixed score to the *dub session* where the film is going through its final mix. It is essential to go with the open mind-edness to admit when a piece of your music simply isn't working in a scene, even if it felt right at the spotting and as you wrote it. You may also want to listen for volume changes that allow the score to work as best as possible. It's not only good, but rather essential for the composer (or someone intimately familiar with the score) to be present to assist in the event of a conflict with the music. This is also the role of the music editor. As music is usually delivered on a digital audio workstation, it is quite common now for changes to be made to the music right at the dub. Perhaps a cue that is felt to be starting too early can be brought in midway or end earlier while still remaining musical. This can be done by simply fading the cue up or down at the right moment, or might involve some editing to move parts of the music around to keep it sounding all right.

The issue of overall volume is always hanging over the dub. Composers usually want to hear their music louder, while other may want it softer. The people on the dub session hearing the music for the first time may not understand what parts are possibly being drowned out. Sometimes the score needs a real advocate who will say, "The music should really be louder here for maximum emotional impact on the scene." At the same time a composer must also be willing to say "I envisioned this cue being a bit more gentle right here, it is now too distracting." But a composer's comments should only be given to the director, who is in charge of the dub. Composers should neither tell the mixing engineers directly nor touch the console to make changes, unless that is agreed to by all. If you hear something wrong, tell the director. If he or she agrees, they will speak with the mixers. If the director doesn't agree, then drop it and move on.

The rule in film dubbing is this: "Dialog über alles"—Dialogue over everything. Nothing can conflict with or distract from what the characters on the screen are saying. What becomes more subjective is the use of sound effects, ambiance and music relative to the dialogue and each other.

Which brings me to a somewhat disturbing trend in film sound today. Sound effects have become so much larger than life in so many of today's films that music is getting squeezed out more and more. Many recent action-oriented films feature bone-crushing door slams, gargantuan car screeches, massive footsteps and other everyday effects raised to the threshold of pain. Don't get me wrong, I recognize and appreciate the essential role that sound plays in providing important psychological impact for a film. A well-crafted soundtrack can make a movie what it is (listen to David Lynch's *Eraserhead* as a brilliant example). The answer is: Perspective. Each element in a film should happen either to help further the plot, develop the characters, or set an overall mood to a scene. The ancillary elements should be insignificant or not in conflict with the main element. Musical scores play a fascinating role in film, since they are the only part of any film that does not attempt to recreate reality; it is cinematic poetry. Good sound effects can approach that level too, but since they come so much closer to reality, sonic perspective becomes that much more important.

The dub on *Lipstick Camera* was supervised by the sound effects editor and not, as is typically the case, by the dialogue mixer. It became clear early on that my music would be competing with voluminous crickets, traffic noise, distant TVs, and the like (these overall sonic ambiences are referred to as "walla"). I made it a point to sit as close as possible to the director throughout the days of dubbing, so as to have his ear when I thought there was a real problem in sound balance. I did this for the scenes with music, since I had a strong sense of how the music was to fit. For certain scenes where the ambience and other sound effects had gotten totally out of hand (these sound guys really loved their noises!), I felt compelled to speak up to the director, and I did so. Before we got started, I asked for his express permission to add my input. Movie dubs are highly political affairs. Too many cooks will spoil the soup, and there is no going back after this. If it's a "fix in the mix" problem, then now is the time, because this is the mix. If your input is desired and requested, then give it; if it is not, then keep your mouth shut and take deep breaths. Everybody has an opinion, and between three sound people you're likely to get four of them. Defer to those in command, even if you know they are making a mistake. It's their movie and they can do whatever they want to ruin it, they don't need your help. In our dub, the director was in charge, but this being his first feature he knew little about sound mixing, and believed everything the sound editors were telling him, which wasn't always the whole truth. I spoke up when I thought it was to the film's benefit, and the director was glad for my input most of the time. Added to all this was the fact that the time allotted for dubbing this film was roughly half of what was needed.

Fortunately, for the most part, common sense prevailed, and the effects didn't eat up the entire soundtrack. The music ended up well mixed to the perspective of the film, and I left feeling that the film sounded surprisingly good. Many of my suggestions were used and seemed to be helpful. The director was pleased with the music, and only one cue ended up not being used, of which I was in complete agreement. All in all a success, and now it was over. Enjoying the prospect of my first free afternoon in over a month, I weighed my options and decided to go to a movie. It was an action film loaded to the gills with chases, crashes, sound effects galore, and an over-the-top score. Everything the opposite of the film I had just finished work on. I loved it.

Remember: a camel is just a horse designed by committee.

⊗ The video of *Lipstick Camera* as well as musical examples is available online at www. reelworld-online.com

CHAPTER FOUR

> New Directions in Scores

Found Sound
Improvising and Misfit Sounds

One composer friend of mine refers to electronic music making as "accidental music." I think he means that many of the really good things that emerge from these musical black boxes with which we share our studios are often the result of turning the wrong knob at the right time. When I'm programming my synthesizers I don't often end up with the sound I was thinking of when I started. Not because I can't make the sounds I want, but because something will lead me on a tangent of discovery that I find more interesting than what I originally had in mind. I think it's good to spend "unstructured time" with an electronic instrument, just goofing off with it to see if something wonderful happens. Such tangents are no less true compositionally. That great sound designer Igor Stravinsky once called musical composition "frozen improvisation." Taking a cue from ol' Igor, I think it behooves us to occasionally "improvise" with our synths and signal processors in order to stumble upon fresh sounds that aren't rooted in a specific sonic objective. When you hear something you like, SAVE IT, and then continue to see where it takes you. You may be able to come up with lots of variations from a single experiment. Later, write something that specifically showcases those new timbres. This is a process that can bring about music that is not only very inspired, but very personal as well. You can do the same thing with samples as well, if you learn the basics of how your sampler and/or audio editing software works. Take a sample, tune or transpose it way out of its original range, apply filters and other digital effects, and see what you come up with. For those of you using a MIDI/audio sequencer there is a world of sonic possibilities using the various audio manipulation capabilities and plug-ins of your system. Programming, performing, and composing are not so far apart from each other. All art should come from inspired and inspiring places.

For resources on audio processors and plug-ins, go to www. reelworld-online.com

I collect the misfit sounds that I like and see if I can find uses for them in my music. On some occasions I've used them on projects with other composers as well. I spent quite a lot of time working on a film called *Kafka*, working closely for several weeks with composer Cliff Martinez to come up with some unusual, foreboding, and dark textures. The film's director, Steven Soderburgh (of *sex, lies & videotape* fame) hates anything that sounds electronic, so it was important to stay clear of obviously synthesized sounds. The budget was low, so there was scarcely room for hiring players. In fact, the entire all-electronic score has only one synthesized (as opposed to sampled) sound in it. The way to make an electronic score sound more organic is to take ordinary sounds, sample them, and then warp them in a variety of ways. There is an amazing psychological response to hearing "worldly" sounds played back at slow speeds, harmonized, time stretched or played backwards. It's very disorienting, and perfect for setting a strange mood. Some of my choices for *Kafka* were:

- Birds and crickets slowed down many, many octaves. Eventually they become rhythms.

- Rubbed wineglasses lowered three or four octaves.

- Feeding *a capella* choral music into a digital reverb set to "infinite" sustain, then sampling the result from the reverb's output. Loop it and use it as a pitched instrument.

- Music from horror film scores sampled, filtered and played very slow or backwards (technically this is not legal, but our results were completely unrecognizable from the original sources leading me to feel completely OK about it).

- Sample a metal plate being struck, copy the sample, flip the original backwards, and append it to the end of the copy using an audio editing program to create a crescendo-decrescendo effect. This is also great with dissonant piano and guitar chords.

Examples from *Kafka* can be heard online at www. reelworld-online.com

• Loud exhalations sampled and slowed down are very creepy without being too "horror film"-ish.

I once stumbled onto a cool sound that I've used in numerous projects in various ways. I will layer three similar but different sustained sounds (strings, vocals, synth pads, etc.) all to the same MIDI channel, with their pitch bend ranges all set differently. One is set at two semitones, one at five or seven semitones, and one set to no pitch bend at all. I move the pitch wheel all the way up and then play a simple interval of a fourth or fifth while slowly moving the pitch wheel down to center. The result is a huge complex chord that microtonally merges and becomes a simple sound. A variation of this is to start with the pitch wheel at normal and slowly bend it up or down to create a simple to complex sound. I also like to fade-in the whole thing with MIDI volume to make it feel like "it" is coming toward you.

I'm a big fan of harmonizers, something I picked up from performing with composer/trumpeter Jon Hassell, whose signature sound was based on the use of these pitch-shifting devices. Most any sound becomes far more interesting when run through a harmonizer. Drums and percussion become bigger and slightly odder. A harmonizer programmed to pitch sounds down a fourth or a major seventh is one especially intriguing effect. Used as an auxiliary send on your mixer, which allows you to blend the transformed sound with the original, a harmonizer is a great sonic tool. I also use various devices to add distortion to my sounds to get a more aggressive feel.

An important component in many of the sounds I create (or simply take a liking to) are their fluidity in time. Samplers and synthesizers often give themselves away by becoming static at some point in the sound. But when a sound is continuously evolving in time, the ear never gets a chance to become bored. No acoustic instruments or sounds of nature are static, so we can learn an important lesson from this—sweeping filters, crossfading timbres, bending pitch, adding elements or taking them away during the course of a sound can breathe needed life into the colors we create. Many synthesizers and samplers are very adept at creating such sounds when programmed to do so. Some of this can also be done in the sequencer as well. Sure, it is also possible to go too far and create sounds that are too complex, overwhelming or do not blend with what is happening in the music or on screen for a score. That's where taste comes in, something not discussed in instrument manuals or harmony books.

Netforce

The Electronic Score

I've done a number of scores that provided the chance to bring closer together the worlds of dramatic film underscore and synthesizer-oriented "electronica," While I've used synthesized and sampled elements in virtually every score I've done, some projects give me the opportunity to be a little more blatant about it. One project was a major television miniseries called *Tom Clancy's NetForce*. Scoring a 4 hour suspense/action movie project with a schedule that left me barely 4 weeks was a daunting task, to say the least. But a combination of factors made it happen successfully, both stylistically and schedule-wise.

Before I can write even a single note of a score, I always want to know just how much music I need to write in total. It's how I know what I'm up against and gives me a mental picture of how I must pace myself. The total on this one was a little high: 110 minutes. If I needed some perspective on how my time would be spent for the next month, I got it there! It meant that I would need to compose between five and six minutes a day. That is a brutal pace. One thing that gave me some comfort was the nature of the temp score that they had put into the rough cut of the film. To my surprise when I first saw the film, the temp was almost entirely my music. Well, I knew I could do that! Of course the temp score was made up of pieces I had spent the better part of a year creating, but that's beside the point. I wasn't about to just go and recreate the temp. Actually, that would take longer than just doing it from scratch, and the results would most likely feel contrived. But there were some sounds, rhythms, effects, and a general compositional approach they really liked. I knew I could reuse some of them in a new way for this score. With so little time, this would help me a lot.

The parts of the temp score that worked the best were the more overtly electronic elements. Beats and grooves underneath some more traditional film elements of melody and texture, with occasional flashes of orchestral sound. The approach would be less about hitting every part of the action than creating an intense musical ambience to support the action and make it feel more exciting. Synths are great for that, and it would also mean I could lay out some interesting grooves that could go on for longer periods of time. That would save me time as well.

It was a good concept for the film, but concepts cannot take you all the way through a score. As I got into the actual writing process, I knew I would need to lean a little more on those more traditional cinematic elements as opposed to simply going with techno music in order to make the music serve the film the best way possible. There have been some very cool scores written with more of a groove orientation. DJs such as Propellerheads, David Holmes, Moby, BT, and the Dust Brothers have gotten involved in film scores with really great results. It has to be the right fit, though. A drama like this one needed attention to the details of dialogue, transition, and action that required more than just a groove. Some films may work well with a purer, simpler form of electronic groove and less use of transition and contrast. This film's pacing felt more complex, and I wanted other musical elements as well. Was I being too much of a traditionalist to just go techno? I don't think so. I have done other projects that were more ori-ented toward that style (such as *In Crowd*). I was trying to be realistic, and not just hip-for-hipness sake. There's room for everything in the right places.

Still, I decided that some of the key action sequences could be supported with a vibe that would just grow and develop, instead of hitting all the action. In my approach, I didn't want standard drum loops as the basis for the rhythms. Some rhythms were sequenced using African drums, junk metal, prepared piano and other found sounds I'd created over time. Others were run through a distortion unit. I love distorting sounds to make them less identifiable. Why should guitar players have all the fun? I used various kinds of loops as well, but staying away from traditional, obvious drum kits. I got some from a few of the more esoteric sample CDs available, and some I created by use of sound design software.

For links to distor-tion devices and sound design software, go to the www.reelworld-online.com site

I spent a few days designing loops at some different tempos to use through-out the score. I supplemented as I went along with new ideas and variations. I found the Formant Shift in my MIDI sequencer to be a great way to take a sound and quickly subvert it into something similar but new.

One element that will always make a project go more smoothly is a strong theme. A strong melody is a fantastic thing. Hard to come up with at first, but indispensable at times when you might not be sure what to write next (hey, let's quote the theme!) I wrote a few thematic ideas for the film. The primary theme (Fig 1.8) was simple and short:

Figure 1.8 Main Theme to Netforce.

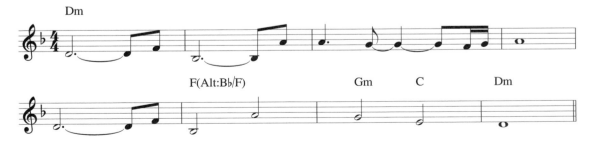

This theme, in numerous incarnations and voicings is repeated throughout the score. There were also sonic and textural themes. One villain was accompanied by African balophone through delays. Why? I don't know—it was just a cool sound.

I used the loops and rhythms as a bed to create the basis for some of the action scenes, some lasting more than 7 minutes (one cue in the film ran nearly 15 minutes). I always worked to picture. At important moments in a scene I would either add or subtract an element of the groove. If the vibe felt entirely wrong, that would be the time to switch to the more traditional type of scoring by going to a different theme, tempo, or key. I would look for a spot in the scene where I felt the original groove could come back. Everything in a score must service the story as it unfolds on the screen, but within that directive there is still room for an aesthetic such as techno or ambient electronica that provides a reliable, steady groove sustaining for periods of time. It becomes somewhat tribal in a way, and gives a scene a different feel than if the score were, more traditionally, varying with each change.

I probably got as much rhythmic juice from synthesizers as I did from drum loops and samples. I employed all of my analogue fury for this. I created percussive sounds with my modular synth, as well as some punchy sounds from my collection of older synths (like the trusty Roland Super Jupiter) and some of the newer "analogue modeling" instruments. Both are great for this sort of thing. I got to know and really liked using the Access Virus. You are able to alter sounds from its front panel and record those changes into the sequencer. I do that as well from the Yamaha AN1x. I have other synths that can do that, but I can't reach them from my seat by the sequencer. I almost always create synth patches and sampler programs that modify their filters in response to MIDI controllers I send from my sequencer. This gives each sound a much greater range of colour, and has become a popular part of contemporary electronic music.

⊗ For a list of available analogue and modeling synths, go to www. reelworld-online.com

Music has such a strong impact on how a scene plays. It changes all of the audience's perceptions of the characters and the situations. One thing I added to this score was a near constant pulse of one sort or another in all but the quietest moments. I wanted even the slower paced scenes to have an edginess. It takes a little finesse, because you can also overwrite a scene, especially a dialogue heavy one. And with so little time, the last thing on my mind was writing too much. I used some odd little synth percussion sounds through a digital delay mixed with some low gamelan samples a lot as an underpinning rhythm. On top of that was some texture or slow simple melody. I would stop myself sometimes to be certain that I was giving the film what it needed while still pleasing the director and keeping up with the furious schedule.

I had the good fortune of a director who enjoyed my music and a supportive producer who wanted the director to be happy. Playback sessions went smoothly, and fixes were simple and minimal. I finished just in time, and it all went as well as could be expected. I got very little sleep during that time working 12 to 16 hour days. That's not so unusual for a project like this. I did ask myself along the way just how the people on this film came up with a schedule that only included three and a half weeks to create 110 minutes of music. Unfortunately, that question will never be answered.

The *Netforce* soundtrack album and video are available online at www. reelworld-online.com

The Art of Documentary

Scoring a Nonfiction Film

The typical documentary film is a labour of love. With little money for production and few venues for showings, the people who make these films are owed our gratitude. Some of the most engaging films made are nonfiction. Harlan and Randi Steinberger were new to the field of the documentary film. Neither had produced a film, but both share a delight and keen interest in the people who inhabit the Venice, California boardwalk. This area, which runs for a mile or so by the Pacific Ocean in Southern California, is home to a great number of local artists, musicians, artisans, performers, and performing "street philosophers." These artists have formed a strong community and play their talents for the thousands of visitors who come to Venice each warm day. Many of them live from their usually meager earnings on the boardwalk, and many are homeless.

Producer Harlan Steinberger once brought several of the boardwalk musicians (many who were in fact homeless) into a recording studio and produced an astonishing album of their songs and words. The cover of the album was a painting made by another of the boardwalk's frequent inhabitants, a 90 year-old Hungarian expatriate artist named Tibor Jankay. His amazing life story, covering nearly the entire 20th century, became the basis of the Steinbergers' first feature documentary film, and through an interesting connection they asked me to compose the score, which I was eager to do.

Twelve hours of footage were shot, and the results were transferred to video tape and then to the Avid video editing system. I got to see a couple of rough cuts while they were still working on the film, and I was immediately moved by the story and their approach to the man's unique life. The first version was about an hour, but by the time the film was completed, it clocked in at just around 45 minutes, a much more TV friendly length. My first decision for the score was that the music would be nearly continuous throughout the film, similar to the approach used in Godfrey Reggio's haunting films *Koyaanisqatsi* and *Powaqqatsi* (the latter of which I worked on extensively). I didn't want to have the distraction of music starting or stopping. Instead I wanted a seamless tapestry of music, words and visuals, much of which was the artist's beautiful paintings and sculptures. There were three basic sections within the film: the artist's philosophies of life, his biographical history, and the story of his personal experiences with the Nazis during the Jewish Holocaust of World War II. The latter section documented his time spent in some of Germany's most notorious concentration camps before committing a bold and dangerous escape. I created an initial musical theme for each of the three main sections.

I decided that except for the sections about the Holocaust, I wanted the score to be simple, organic, and have some flavor of eastern European music without becoming a gypsy score. As is my modus operandi, I began my sketches on my sequencer. Artist Jankay had a great love of African art and music, though his own personal upbringing was steeped in the music of the gypsies and villages of Hungary, Romania, and Transylvania. I devised a synthesis of the two styles, using the rhythms and drums of Africa with the melodies and harmonies of Eastern Europe, along with my own personal musical touch. This was an art project, and I had few if any of the musical restrictions that are part of commercial film and television scoring. Starting in on a project that requires 45 minutes of wall-to-wall music would be daunting to me at first, but I was thrilled to start this.

I had a budget of right around zero to do this score. I wrote with a small ensemble of very unique musicians in mind, all people I had worked with on previous projects, all of them used to me coming to them on bended knee asking for favours. I used a fantastic African drummer and percussionist, and another friend who is a multi-instrumentalist with a deep knowledge of European music. He played some marvelous instruments, such as the duduk, talinka, gadulka, and gypsy-style violin. I added a singer, clarinetist, and myself playing various flutes, pennywhistles (slightly off course, conceptually speaking, but a lovely timbre) and some sampled instrumental sounds that rounded out my musical palette.

I composed all the music in about 3 weeks, and then played my synth demos for the director. The music was written in segments that lasted between five and ten minutes. This made it easier to record and mix. I left several spots open for improvisations by the players. It would be hard to explain this to most producers or directors, but fortunately Harlan is a musician as well and knew what I was going for. With the music approved, it was time to begin recording.

I recorded most of the players and singers in my studio directly into my digital audio sequencer (something that was pretty new at the time). I really do take full advantage of hard disk recording by getting many takes of each player, and then cutting and pasting together the final performance from that, a process called *comping*. It cuts my recording time in half and allows the musicians to be far more spontaneous and creative.

For the percussion, I decided to record the performance in the percussionist's own studio. I used a portable multitrack digital recorder with a built-in timecode synchronizer. I took that, a VCR, a mini-TV, some rented mics and a preamp, and a little portable mixer to the percussionist's studio. I had prestriped the digital tape with timecode, click, and a mono scratch recording of the score with the drums omitted. We could watch the video and listen to the music while he played onto the remaining empty tracks. All I had to do was shuttle the video, and the multitrack would chase along. I filled the tracks with his drumming, which I would then use to replace and enhance my sampled percussion.

Finally I was done recording the score. I played the new tracks for the filmmakers, and with their approval, began mixing. I brought my engineer in to help me with the mix. Having never heard the music, his fresh ears were very helpful. The sequencer, with its digital audio tracks, and the digital multitrack with all the percussion were both slaved to the VCR's timecode, and we began. Since the producers only wanted a stereo mix, I recorded to a DAT tape, with a programmed click two seconds before the beginning of each musical section. I later fed the final mixes back to my digital audio workstation, lined the music up with their original SMPTE timecode start times, and took the disk to the post production facility where the film was being dubbed. I used four tracks in order to have smooth transitions between sections. I also did some digital editing on a piece of music performed by one of the Venice beach musicians for a scene that took place at the Venice boardwalk.

Completing *The Art of Survival* became very emotional for me. Not because of how enjoyable it was to compose and record, but because Tibor Jankay, the remarkable subject of the film, was my uncle, and was one of the main reasons I became a musician and composer in the first place. He lived very close to my family when I was growing up, and I was with him, constantly watching him paint and sculpt, and tell fantastic stories not even in the film. His tremendous love of life and art, and the lack of distinction he made between the two was the basis of my own views of art and the world. He died, 94 years young, just a couple of weeks before I finished recording the score. He loved hearing my music, but he never got to hear the music I wrote for his life story, for which I will always feel sorry. He judged no one and loved everyone. For him, there was no such thing as good or bad art. The joy was in the making. His was never a judgemental response to the products of creation. He would say "I even love what I do not love," meaning that he loved the fact that art exists at all. That's all that mattered—just being an artist and being true to oneself. I miss him, and the film is only the tiniest sliver of who he was and what he meant to me. But I know that every time someone will watch this film, he'll be dancing.

The Art Of Survival is available online at www. reelworld-online.com

Looking Forward
Film Music in the 21st Century

So what about music for the 21st century? Are we ready to make a leap into something absolutely new and fresh? Does the dawn of a new millennium hold a key to a new style, approach, process, or technology? The answer is yes, of course, but we're going to have to wait for it just a little bit longer.

There are a growing number of people experimenting with new forms of entertainment that exist on the web, on computers, or designed for hardware that does not yet exist. I've seen demonstrations of new platforms that have the promise of creating new interactive artforms which we cannot begin to see yet, There are classes and workshops going on around the world on art, music, sound, and technology for "new media." Who of us will be left behind when the "new" or "interactive" media kicks in and becomes the predominant form of entertainment?

At the heart of people's desire to be entertained is the insatiable appetite we all have for stories. Stories told in words, in songs, in melodies, in paintings, in films, in television, in talking, or even gossiping on the phone (or e-mail, or chat rooms, or graffiti). This is basic to human nature, and we, as creative artists, are doing little more than satisfying that primary urge. Even the most emotionally repressed among us gets pleasure out of feeling things, both physically and emotionally. Those pleasures can come from a love story as well as a bloody, violent good guys/bads guys story. It doesn't matter. Those of us who have a difficult time being intimate with other real people still are interested to know about the emotions and feelings of others by way of stories told through some kind of artistic medium.

As music makers we bring something special and unique to the world. Even here in the 21st century no one really understands what it is about music that makes it the most emotional of all arts. What is it about making air vibrate (the composer's and musician's canvas) that can make people laugh or cry so easily? We all know it is true, but no one yet can say why. It plays such a pivotal role in giving films their emotional kick. Ultimately it makes little or no difference why. An empirical, or scientific understanding of the power of music will not help to create a single note more beautiful than the ones we have had up until now.

The creators of new entertainment technologies have, amongst their goals, the desire to create art forms that are more immersive than any that have existed previously. Stories that people will experience by being within them, instead of merely observing them. Ultra high-speed computing will allow audio-visual (and eventually tactile) worlds to be created in real time that not only provide images and sound for us, but will respond to our actions in ways that only the real world does. When we watch a scene in a movie we cannot get up out of our seats and go into the next room of that scene, no matter how curious we are about it. With sufficient technology, we could walk around inside a movie and learn more about what is going on around the characters and plot elements. Video games come close to this in concept (especially if you want to kill the person in the next room), yet they are not that engaging as story tellers. I think this is important to remember.

Masterfully told stories, whether literary, verbal, or cinematic, must be told a very certain way. The listener, not yet aware of what will happen next, cannot improve upon the story in any way, and in fact shouldn't.

Stories, much like the way we experience our lives, are linear—not random access. Music is the same. A song or symphony is revealed to the listener one note at a time, and at the tempo the composer has chosen. Each note can be savored, and the listener is never bothered with deciding when the next note should come.

For composers interested in becoming involved in the immersive and interactive media now emerging, the challenges will be in how to create music that can change as the listener wishes while still maintaining some amount of melodic and emotional cohesion and integrity. It takes a great deal of talent and practice to know how to write a piece of music that brings the listener a satisfying and moving experience. You learn to pace yourself just so, to start out slowly (or not) and build upon that step by step until you reach the peak moment of the music, then return back down.

Frankly, good music has more in common with good sex than any other art form. It's no wonder that people often like to have music playing when they are in bed. Music is sexy because of the way it tells its story over time.

How much of that power will get lost when listeners can decide to jump around in your music any way they want—skip one part, jump to the end, invent a new section here and there. While there may be some enjoyment for listeners to tinker with the art (or the story) they are currently experiencing, ultimately they will probably lose out on the greatest experience they could have had, which is to listen to music as the composer intended. Actually, I believe strongly that those experiences will never go away, people will always want to experience art and music passively and appreciatively. New forms will come, but they will add to the landscape of available entertainment. I don't think interactive entertainment will surpass traditional forms for a very, very long time.

In terms of new technology directly, things are moving fast, but no faster than they were several years ago. MIDI and digital audio were radical new ideas and tools for composers and musicians to use in making music. Few current trends have the same power to change how composers work, but there are developments which are improving our creative experiences all the time.

Better sequencers, more DSP functions, easier to use and more powerful instruments, and the move to more computer-based processing are all great, but the dawn of the 21st century doesn't seem to have anything totally profound up its sleeve quite yet. I'm sure that will change soon; life would be a bit boring otherwise.

In the meantime we continue to make stories. We score films (the greatest advance in story-telling technology history, even over the invention of the printed book), we write songs, jazz tunes, musicals, operas, and symphonies.

We look for better technology with which to make our music, and for ways to send that music out into the world for people to hear, and hopefully pay for. As new forums for our music come along, some of us will adapt into those methods. Others will not. As someone once said, the song remains the same.

Conclusion

In this section we've taken a look at the process of film scoring. Little has been said of notes, harmony, instrumentation, and the other elements of music because those are for you to fill in yourself. We've looked at those things that help or hinder a score from working. We've looked at examples of both to see how music is shaped to work with pictures. We've also had a look at the work schedule that composers go through on most film and television projects.

No two films go the same. Some go smoothly, some are more difficult. We put the bad experiences behind us and look forward to the next task. Hopefully, those less-than-perfect experiences each teach us something important that we carry with us in our careers. In Section Two we will look more closely at the tools that we use to make our scores and see how important they are and how they can help us achieve the best possible musical results.

Perspectives

John Williams

Films include: *Star Wars, The Empire Strikes Back, Schindler's List, Raiders Of The Lost Ark, Jaws*

JR: What do you feel makes a great film score? For that matter, what makes a musically successful composer?

John Williams: A great film score could be defined as being one that supports the film in a way that aids the drama, atmosphere and story of the film, and the characters within it. If, in addition to aiding the structure, the score can also develop melodic identification for the characters, or for the locale of the story, it can make a significant contribution. I think a film composer would be deemed successful if he or she can serve the musical needs of the film, and also enjoy the benefit of being able to take the music out of the film and have it stand on its own merit. Obviously not all film music can accomplish this, since much of it is "accompanimental" in nature, but I think the greatest film scores are the ones that, in addition to serving the film well, can have a musical life of their own.

JR: What kind of advice have you received along the way?

JW: I obviously have been the beneficiary of a lot of advice from many wonderful people. One of my earliest mentors was Stanley Wilson, who was the music director at Universal studio. During a very heated and rushed schedule, his advice to me was "Get hold of a good tune and develop it throughout the film." This may sound a bit crude, but it's actually good solid advice.

JR: What are the mistakes you have learned the most from?

JW: Fortunately, we all make mistakes! It is from our mistakes that we learn, by developing and applying a keen and objective sense of self-criticism.

JR: What words of advice do you have for a composer just starting out or interested in becoming a film composer?

JW: My advice to beginners would be to develop craft. I think one should, if at all possible write something everyday, even if it's only a few bars. Another suggestion would be to examine and study the great works in the concert repertoire.

The business associated with film composition is something that I believe is attached to the rewards of success. This field can offer a very gratifying career.

The essential key to success is being able to do the work well. And, I would go back to my basic advice to composers (beginners and advanced alike), which is to make composing a daily habit. Discipline in the craft is what pays off.

Carter Burwell

Films include: *Three Kings, Being John Malkovich, Fargo, Rob Roy, Raising Arizona*

JR: What did you do before you were scoring film?

Carter Burwell: I did a variety of things. Immediately upon leaving college I was an animator, I worked at a biology laboratory, and I was playing in a band. It was playing in a band (not

the animation nor the laboratory) that got me into film scoring. The band was called The Same and we played around all of the usual clubs in New York from the late '70s to the early '80s.

JR: What were you studying in school?

CB: I began in mathematics and ended up in fine art. In my last year of school I was avidly doing hand drawn animations, but developing an interest in music. If I had been in school for another year I probably would have taken some music classes. Every year my interest changed fairly dramatically.

JR: What in all your background has contributed most to your musical style?

CB: Well it might well be naivete—lack of musical education. So that, compared to many of the things I've done which are cognitive functions, music is by far the most intuitive thing that I do.

JR: Do you think that functioning from a "naive" perspective has helped your process and your style or do you get frustrated?

CB: Well I've always known that I could go off and take courses in music theory or orchestration if I wanted to, and I have made an informed decision not to. That decision has been informed by the fact that I've been well educated in other things. So I know what education is, and I feel that it's got pluses and minuses. Twenty years ago I made an arbitrary decision not to let education impinge on this one area of my life. At that time I had no idea that this one area of my life would become a career. At the time I was just keeping it safe from educational harm and it just so happened that it became a lot of my lifetime.

JR: Tell me your process of scoring for film.

CB: I'll try to describe it in as chronological an order as I can. The first step is usually reading the script in order to decide whether or not the film is worth pursuing. If I decide to pursue it, and I do get the job, the next step is to actually watch a cut of the film, sometimes with the director and sometimes on my own. I'll discuss it with the director in entirely verbal terms, what I think the score could lend to the film, and what the director wants the score to do, which are often very different things.

JR: Do you hear music when you're reading a script?

CB: Never…almost never…(laughs)

JR: Do you hear music when you watch the film's rough cut?

CB: I don't hear music no, but I often have an immediate reaction in terms of the contribution that the music could make to the film. I don't hear notes when I watch a film; that never happens. But I often have a strong feeling that there's something the music could bring to the film that's not already there. Usu-ally then I sit at the piano and start investigat-ing themes. The piano is where I do most of my melodic/harmonic work. I'm also doing sound design work, in terms of putting together a palette of sounds in my synthesiz-ers and samplers that will be appropriate for the film.

Those two efforts go on simultaneously because, of course, they inform each other. Sometimes the writing is more traditional and it really can be done just at a piano. But some-times you really need to be coming up with sounds, and out of those sounds comes har-monic structure or something suggesting melody. So I try to do both of those things at the same time. And I develop sketches of indi-vidual cues based on what I come up with in terms of compositions and sounds, and play those sketches for the director.

JR: Is any of this done to picture at this point?

CB: That last stage is done to picture when I say "individual cues" I'm doing it to picture. I will do all of this "free association" at the piano by myself. But when I play things for the direc-tor I find that its best for it to be sync'ed to pic-ture. That's what really interests the director, they want to hear the music sync'ed to picture. They're not really interested in music just for music's sake, they have to hear to picture. So before I play anything for the director, I will have it put it in some sort of sync to picture.

JR: And what typically happens from there for you?

CB: Either I'm fired, or we talk about what is or isn't working with those sketches and try to zero in on the things that the director and I agree on. Then I broaden out so I'm writing more different parts for the film. There are a couple of possible ways I choose that first cue. There is usually one scene in the movie that sets the tone for the whole film musically. So I'll write that one first. Sometimes I just tackle the most difficult area first, and think that if I've got a piece of music that works there I know it's going to work everywhere else. Sometimes I'll just start with the opening title because its easier and I can go to town in terms of developing a full arrangement and a theme and variation. It gives me more latitude in terms of tapping in to the picture.

JR: Do you feel that you work in a way that you work in a way that is counter to that of other mainstream composers?

CB: In terms of working process, I have no idea, because I don't know what other people do. I wouldn't think that it would be that different, but I really don't know. In terms of how I approach the score and the function of the score, I think that it's different than that of some composers. I've sort of narrowed down that difference to my interest in having music contribute something that is not already present in the picture, as opposed to an interest in music supporting what is already present in the picture. These are two perfectly valid approaches, and of course different movies will require different things. Sometimes I've worked on a film in which the subject matter is so sincere and so free of irony that sometimes the music does need to simply support what is being said. But generally speaking I don't choose to work on those pictures because that's just not what interests me. So I think that's the distinction between what I choose to do in film and what some other people decide to do, but I'm certainly not alone in looking at it that way.

JR: Over the years that you've been scoring films, has your process or approach changed? What have you learned "on the job"?

CB: Well, this is actually very much like the question of education we discussed earlier, and my feeling about it is very similar. I think it's terribly important for me to be aware of

what I don't want to learn on the job. It's easily as important as the things I do learn, because there's a lot of aspects of this business and this work that defeat imagination, innovation and experimentation. These are just not qualities that are valued in a huge business like this where the budget can grow so large. The costs of many feature films demand a certain conservatism from the people making them. "Demand" maybe isn't the right word, but they certainly create a conservative and sometimes fearful environment.

JR: And I'm sure you've scared a certain number of people over the years?

CB: I sure have! And they scare me back! I think it's very important if you work on a film and you have a disaster, like someone throwing your music out, or firing you half way through and rewriting your music, or taking your music and cutting it up and completely rearranging it. All these things have happened to me, by the way, though fortunately not often. These are all obviously disasters, and they hurt a lot. To know what lessons should and shouldn't be learned from them is very valuable. You could easily take away the lesson that one must always listen to the directors and producers and always do what they tell you to do. But that would be the wrong lesson. You must try really hard to not learn that because, after all, what's the real point in trying to do what we try to do as composers. When I hear a film score that I don't like, it is almost always because the music is predictable—it's not telling me anything I wouldn't have known anyway. It's just rote film score that does nothing more than support every moment of the film, and that's not interesting to me as a viewer, listener or composer. So I choose not to learn all the technical and musical lessons that make film score turn out that way. That's not to say they're not valid lessons. They're just not lessons I want to learn.

JR: Do you ever find film scores that are inspiring?

CB: Yes.

JR: What do you think makes a great film score?

CB: For me there are two things. One is when you can sense that you're in the presence of imagination. That's exciting in any situation; it can be true if you walk into a great building, read a book, or use a piece of well-written software. It's very exciting to just know that someone's really made the effort of imagination. The other thing that's exciting to me is when a score is also musically stimulating. That's much harder. Lets face it, they're both diffuse concepts and they're both very personal. I hear pieces that are musically stimulating to me and someone else wouldn't find them so. But those are the things that excite me about a film score, and that's what we should all be aspiring toward - to make efforts of imagination, and at the same time, write great new music.

JR: What's your relationship with technology?

CB: I actually come to music from technology. I don't think that I'd be doing this if it weren't for the technology. If I had had to write music with pencil on paper right from my first score, I doubt I'd be doing it today. It would have been so slow, and the resulting work would have been so half-done, I just wouldn't be doing this. I had much more of a background in computers and electronics than I had in music. When I decided to do music, I came to it from a technological point of view. I started by studying electronic music, computer music, and so I find technology to be an essential part of this process. Now I also love just sitting and playing the piano. I did that before I got involved in technology. I played piano when I was in high school and I play piano pretty much every day, as I have done all my life. When I play the piano

I don't play sheet music, I just sit and play. That is low-tech! It's still a technology of course, but its important for me to have somewhere I can go and not have to turn a switch to make music. To do film scoring the technology is absolutely essential to me because of the schedules involved, the logistics and the orchestra. There's no way I could write charts for a large orchestra without technology and without the kind of tools that we have now. So it's absolutely at the heart of what I do.

JR: What advice do you ever give to composers or musicians—people interested in getting involved in film music?

CB: The first question people usually ask when they're looking for advice is: How do they get work? And the first piece of advice I give them is that I'm a very poor source for that information because I did not aspire to be a film composer. I had no particular interest in it. I was asked to do my first film, *Blood Simple*, and when it was released people called and asked me to do other films. So, unfortunately, I'm not a good source of information on how to get into the business, although my story is similar to a lot of the other successful feature film composers that I know. This is sad, because it suggests that the very notion of wanting to be a film composer may somehow even handicap you. That sounds a little absurd, and yet it may actually be true. It relates to what we were speaking of earlier, as to what should you learn and what should you refuse to learn.

I think that if you want to be a film composer because you've heard all these great film scores and you love them or because you like working in the "Hollywood" milieu with big stars and producers and directors - if those things attract you to it, that may prevent you from writing interesting film scores. Because you're being drawn to a tradition rather than being drawn to a musical aspiration of finding your own individual artistic voice and sound as a musician and composer. So while I tell young composers that I am not able to help them get a job, the one thing that may be learned from my example is this: I was out there making music regardless of having a commission or having a job. I was out there making music because I just enjoyed making music, I enjoyed playing in bands, and it was the fact that I was performing my music that allowed people to hear it and then ultimately offer me this type of work in film.

I think that people who wait for a commission or wait for the film industry to call are perhaps making a big mistake. The opportunity is to just go out and play, put together your own ensemble or work on student films, but those will always be the best choices. We are so lucky to be able to be musicians. It's something we can do by ourselves. We're not directors who need a crew and millions of dollars. Musicians and performers can just write and perform themselves. When I first came to New York that's what people were doing, that's what guys like Philip Glass, Steve Reich, and all the bands I knew were doing. They were just putting together their own ensembles, doing their work, and not waiting for an industry to take notice.

James Newton Howard

Films include: *Snow Falling On Cedars, Runaway Bride, My Best Friend's Wedding, The Fugitive, Pretty Woman*

Jeff Rona: What were you doing before you started scoring films?

James Newton Howard: I was doing a lot of sessions as a keyboard player and arranger. I was also doing a lot of string arrangements for records with artists like Earth Wind and Fire, Toto and Barbara Streisand…lots of people. In the '70s I toured with people like Elton John, Crosby, Stills and Nash and then started doing session work in the 80's and producing records. I produced an album with Ricky Lee Jones called *The Magazine*. I produced things with the Brothers Johnson, Chaka Kahn and Cher. And though I was producing records, my leaning was decidedly more esoteric and not very mainstream.

JR: Are you formally schooled? Did you study?

JNH: I started with classic piano when I was four. Did a couple of years at the Music Academy of the West in Santa Barbara. I was a piano performance major at University of Southern California. A couple of years after leaving U.S.C., I was in rock 'n' roll bands. That's where I was for a long time until '85 when I started doing films.

JR: How do you see your pre-film experience helping you with your first scores musically?

JNH: Well, I think my time in the record industry was hugely valuable. First of all, learning studio technique, recording technique, which has a lot to do with the way I write. I started off as a synthesist very early on. I own an Ionic monophonic synthesizer from '73 and an ARP 2600. I was really into synthesizers early in their development. At one point I visited Robert Moog in New York and he was going to build me a big modular system, but that fell through. I learned synthesis recording techniques, and then when I joined Elton I had my first opportunity to work with orchestras. It was a wonderful experience, melding orchestral components with rhythm tracks. It was a style I used for a long time that I don't use so much now; I've gotten a little bored with it. So I learned just a lot of the aspects of the [composing] trade.

JR: That's interesting, because you're describing the role of a music producer as much as you're describing the role of a composer as part of what you do. Just the way a producer works on an album, part of what you do is to compose, but part of what you do is to actually produce the score as well.

JNH: Absolutely. I tend to approach these things as a record producer, especially the multi-layered arrangements with a lot of synths and rhythm tracks and choral and orchestral stuff. My ears are kind of tuned to it on that level. I like to approach it that way as far as details are concerned. A lot of times the magic for me (I suppose I shouldn't say magic because I don't know if there's any magic in

it), the best part that has intrigued me over the years is the attention to detail and how all those different elements are related to each other. That has a lot to do with production.

JR: Absolutely. Having been a studio musician and arranger for so many years, what did your first film feel like?

JNH: It felt terrifying! I had no sense of the technology involved in terms of synchronizing from music to picture. I didn't know tempo, spotting or what anything was. I had written quite a bit of instrumental music at that point, but I didn't know whether I could write any more or whether it would be good or write it with time constraints. I was talking to a friend of mine who used to be a keyboard player. This was 1985, and he was doing a movie at the time. I was just getting ready to start my first picture, a silly little movie called *Head Office*. I was talking to him, and he was using this thing called the SPX 80. He was working with George Massenberg at The Complex recording studio here in L.A.. I saw him using the SPX 80 for synchronizing and it was just overwhelming. I didn't know what they were doing and he said "James, remember that there is a finite amount of technology in the world, and once you get that, it's just about the writing." So I kind of just charged in! I went into it very nervously, but my first experience was very, very good.

JR: How has your relationship been with technology since then?

JNH: Very comfortable, very happy. I think it's clearly defined the way I compose to a large extent. I think it's very valid in this day and age to be employing technology. It seems like an obvious part of the creative process. Had it been around a long time ago, I'm sure the composers of that era would have used it.

You write the way you're comfortable writing. John Williams writes with pen and paper and a big scorebook. I came up this way, and so I write the way I'm most comfortable.

JR: What do you think makes a great score?

JNH: First of all, supporting the movie: the right feeling music in the right scenes. It sounds like an obvious thing, but it's not that easy. Even if you disagree with somebody's melody or you don't like a particular theme, if the music is resonating correctly in the scene I give somebody a lot of credit for that. I think that spotting makes a great score, choosing where the music is not makes a great score. I think dynamics make a great score as do melody and rhythm. But essentially supporting the narrative of the movie, helping expanding the experience on a subtextual level, and helping to dictate and enhance the tempo and pace of the film.

JR: How do you think your own musical style and working approach in film has changed over the span of your career to now?

JNH: Well I think the most obvious thing for me is that I write much less pianistically. When I first started out I was a pianist, so I would write orchestra parts that I could play on the piano. I don't do that nearly as much anymore. Also, I was writing very string heavy for about the first 30 movies I did. I'm still working on that. It's something that Marti Page, my first orchestration teacher, used to tell me; he said that strings are the backbone of the orchestra and he was absolutely right. It's become more of a color issue for me now and not something that is at the heart and soul of my writing style. I've written for a string orchestra exclusively, but that's a creative

choice. I think less from a pianistic viewpoint now. My music is more evolved, more complicated in terms of the timbral selections, more varied, with better orchestration and somewhat more tonal. My music is a little more subjective, not quite so specific, not quite so "on the nose."

JR: That's a good point. Can you elaborate on that?

JNH: Well, I think the thing I do most naturally is to write a string line melodically. And I think anytime you write a melody, you're making a strong point, one which is reduced to a specific thought. So I've tried to be less melodically driven except when I make a conscious decision to do it. Most of the time I try to be a little more vague about the implications.

JR: How would you describe the way you work with directors?

JNH: Very comfortably. Most of the directors I work with now are friends. I work with a lot of the same guys over and over again. But I also try to add a new relationship every now and then. I feel I can get along with just about everybody. There have been a few problems, but only with a few. I understand the director's dilemma. By the time they come along to the music they're pretty beat and wiped out. I try and empathize with their state of mind and emotional state. I try to help them through the process as much as I can. I try to translate their less-than-articulate musical direction to something that sounds like a response to their notes, so that we end up with a score that reflects what they were hoping to hear, but couldn't articulate. That's my goal.

⊘ Technology

Introduction

Anyone who has picked up a musical instrument knows the learning and practice required to become technically proficient. It takes time and dedication to master any instrument well enough to be facile and expressive. The same is true for composing. It takes practice and technical skills to express a range of emotion with clarity and ease, and to be able to write for various instruments. The goal in making music is to make it expressive, well performed, and well recorded.

Previously, it was sufficient for a composer scoring a film to compose using paper and pencil, and play sketches on piano to show the director something of what the music would sound like with the orchestra. Those times, for better or worse, are behind us now. What is required of composers now is to provide a detailed demo of what a score will sound like. In some cases these demos become some or all of the final score. Composers have more options now than ever before, but at a price. That price is that composers must now take on the role of music producer. And what fuels this new model of film composer is technology. The technology of the home studio includes audio, video, computers, MIDI, timecode, synchronization, synthesizers, samplers, software, and a host of other things to know, understand, and use.

How important is all of this? It has become a vital part of every composer's working method to work in a technically sophisticated home studio. Just as you need to be technically advanced to be expressive on a musical instrument, you need to be technically advanced to get the most out of composing and recording in a home studio. The better you are on your instrument, the more you can do with it. Your studio is your instrument. The better you play it, the better you will be at making your ideas clear for those who want to hear your music. Then, and only then, can you continue to bring in other musical forces to your scores, from a few additional musicians to a full orchestra.

 Books and other materials on home studio design and use can be found on the website—www. reel-world-online.com

It is not within the scope of this book to fully explain the basics of all the technology found in the studio. There are other books on this topic. But as technology intersects with the film composer's work, there are a number of unique issues that we will examine carefully. It is not an inexpensive proposition to put together a professional level home studio. But since this is an environment in which you will be spending most of your waking hours, it's not a bad idea to make it a priority in your life.

CHAPTER FIVE

◎ Setting Up
A Studio

Staying Ahead of the Curve

How Much Gear Is Enough?

A question that seems to arise frequently is about the amount of technology that one really needs to be sufficient as a professional or even "serious amateur" (whatever that is) film composer. After all, it's not everyone's goal to be a technical whiz—some of us just want to write a cool tune, get it on the screen, and hope the check clears. Gone are the days when paper and pencil alone will allow you to get started or remain successful in this ever more competitive world. You need some gear, and you also need to know how to use it effectively. Demos are expected to sound great, and our studios frequently provide the final master for smaller films or television work. So let's take a look at what technical knowledge is enough for us to do our work.

Computers

Essential Operating System Savvy

Perhaps the most complex part of your bleeding edge existence is your computer. Personal computers, like one-day-old infants, are in near constant need of great care and forgiveness. And like children, you get out of them what you put into them. With that analogy now nearly exhausted, what do you need to know about your computer in order to maintain a well-oiled studio (beyond the fact that you should never oil a computer)?

It's very important to get to know your computer's operating system (OS). For the vast majority of composers, that's either Apple's Mac OS or Microsoft's Windows. The more you know about these somewhat complex systems the better off you may be in the long run. While I would never expect anyone to get totally nerded out with IRQs or hierarchical file structures, you should learn how to stay well organized with your computer. You should at least know how to create a folder, put a specific file into a specific folder, move a file or folder, rename a file or folder, search for and find any file or folder, and do anything else to remain calm and organized. Most of an OS's interface is designed specifically to allow you to be organized.

You should also be able to back up up all of your files in a way that is efficient, safe, and one you won't mind doing frequently. I've lost important files, as have most of my friends at one time or another. It's a painful education. I back up current projects every day (more or less), and my whole system gets backed up every week using a software utility designed for backing up precious computer data. The software nearly automates the whole process. I back up up my computer's internal drive, which contains my OS, all my applications, and sequencer files. I have several additional hard drives for my digital audio files, which are also backed up frequently.

✪ Look on the web site for hardware and software for computer backups

You should know enough about your OS to allocate sufficient memory to the various applications you may be running. A sequencer may require a certain amount of RAM, but with more complex projects it will run much more efficiently and reliably if you allocate significantly more memory. The same is true of other applications; tailor all your software to run the best way possible.

While we're at it, you should know how to install or uninstall software, and update software or hardware products such as MIDI interfaces, audio devices, a printer, internet connection, and any other desired peripherals. Many companies now offer frequent free upgrades via their websites, and it is fantastic to be able to take advantage of that, which means knowing how to set up a modem or other internet access, an internet account, and perform software downloads and decompression if needed. I've also found some handy shareware and freeware on the net—it's an essential resource for electronic musicians.

Obviously, all the above items will be rather different depending on whether you use Mac or Windows (no, they are not that similar at all, regardless of what some people say—they are very, very different systems), so you need to bone up on your system and software. I really recommend subscribing to at least one magazine dedicated to your computer platform of choice, as well as checking out a book or two on your computer's OS and general use. The manuals that come with the software we use are of frequently good use for this kind of information, if you have the patience to wade through and find it

⊗ Find computer resources on the website—www. reelworld-online.com

Sequencers
The Most Important Item in Your Studio

I often see composers who know only a small fraction of the sequencer software they own. The chant of "I didn't know it could do that!" rings loudly through the studios of too many musicians, and you shouldn't be one of them. You have better things to do with your time, like writing music, than to struggle with your essential software and not take advantage of what it offers. You should know your sequencing software like the back and front of your hand. It is perhaps the most important single item in your studio. Learn every shortcut the sequencer offers and every available key command. Try to use your mouse and on-screen menus as little as possible. The time you save really does add up, as well as lessen distractions from the task at hand.

You should also know the tempo functions of your sequencer very well, since these are of essential use to film scores. Know how to get any beat of your cue to hit on the exact frame of the picture you want, and learn how to make fluid tempo changes that support the music and still make accurate hits. If your sequencer supports digital audio, use it for recording live players and audio loops as much as is practical. Learn how to perform time stretching to allow loops and other audio to match any further tempo changes you make. If your sequencer supports digital video, using it instead of a traditional VCR will save you hours of tape shuttling every day. More on this later.

Sequencers all have the ability to perform time correction—called quantization—on your performances. This started out as a relatively simple function in earlier sequencers. You select a rhythmic value, for example sixteenth notes, and all the notes in your selected track or phrase get bumped to the nearest sixteenth. This creates a very precise, though metronomic feeling performance. When it's desirable it sounds great. As sequencers became more sophisticated they added more musically interesting forms of quantization called *grooves*. Grooves are rhythmic templates that move your notes to the nearest part of the beat with a human feel. The result is accurate but still very musical, ultimately more satisfying than its mathematically perfect predecessor. When you are composing music set against audio drum loops it can become essential to gain familiarity and experience working with groove quantization.

Samplers
An Orchestra (and More) at Your Fingertips

Samplers are one of the most essential tools you'll use in your studio in creating lifelike demos, as well as interesting scores. With sufficient sampling capacity you can simulate an entire orchestra or have any instrument on the planet at your fingertips. While many synthesizers come chock full of sampled instruments, none to date have the vividness and quality of a dedicated sampler. We should all know how to load our samplers with sounds from CD-ROM or other formats. You might want to become more fluent in your sampler's capabilities. Samplers require data storage for the sounds you use. That will necessitate adding some kinds of disk drive to your setup. You need to understand SCSI (the system that connects storage devices such as disk drives to the equipment that needs to save and load the data from those drives) well enough to know how to add disk drives to your samplers, or your computer for that matter. SCSI is actually a somewhat outmoded system, but has remained a strong standard for storage systems for many computer and musical devices. SCSI devices come in a number of variations: SCSI, SCSI 2, fast and wide, ultra, etc. There is some compatibility between SCSI varieties, but care must be given or the safety of your data and the efficiency of your system can be compromised. There are unique plug and cable types for each type as well.

✖ There is additional information on SCSI and other disk drive technologies on the reelworld-online website

You can set your system up so that a sampler can use one or more drives, or a single drive may be accessed by multiple samplers. There are SCSI devices that help enable more complex studio setups using multiple samplers, your computer, CD writer, and all types of hard disk storage. These are available from computer stores and catalogs, and some better music stores.

You should know the basics of how to rework a sampled sound to better suit a particular use. I frequently change the programming on sounds to tailor them to the way I play, and I rework my personal samples from project to project. You should be able to grab individual sounds from different programs and combine them into a new program and save that to disk. That skill alone will come to your rescue some day. You should also be able to alter the filters and envelopes on a sampler's program to make any sound work better for your style of playing and writing. For example, if you are writing a fast string line, you may want to modify the envelopes of an existing string sample to respond a little faster. (On the more drastic side is all the software available for doing sound design and sample manipulation, which while very exciting, is not a requirement for getting your best work done.) Newer software-based samplers are available that run on standard Mac and Windows computers. These are an excellent option with a great deal of flexibility and capacity.

Synthesizers
An Arsenal of Electronic Sounds

Everything about using samplers applies to your synthesizers as well. Most synths today are chock full of perfectly usable sounds without having to do anything beyond sending them a patch change from your sequencer. Still, it is in your best interest to become familiar enough with a synth so you can tweak a few parameters and make a sound better suited to a particular musical use. You should then know how to resave the sound either in place of or in addition to the original version. If you are interesting in creating a more electronic score, then it helps to be more familiar with the inner workings of your instruments in order to come up with more interesting and personal sounds.

There are lots of interesting synthesizers available. As technology improves, there are usually some interesting new varieties to choose from. And there are wonderful electronic instruments that exist only as computer software. They can run on the same computer as your sequencer, but there comes a point where your computer can only handle so much and will balk at adding another sound or sample. It probably is more cost effective to own an additional computer (or computers!) to run software-based synthesizers, samplers, drum loop programs and whatever else can be done to make noise.

Timecode
The Heart of Synchronization

Film and video are made up of frames that are numbered in order to keep track of what goes where within the body of the project. The standard method used in America and elsewhere is called SMPTE timecode. (SMPTE stands for Society of Motion Picture and Television Engineers, the technical group that develops standards for film and television post production.) Other parts of the world use similar, but different methods of timecode, though the principles remain the same. There is more on timecode later in section 2.

Any visual or multimedia-oriented composer should know enough about timecode to know when a problem might occur. That means understanding frame rates, drop and nondrop timecode formats, and the different ways that video tapes are prepared for use by a composer in post production. A composer should also know what is expected of him or her when delivering music back to the production company. That also involves knowing about tape formats and tape formatting, timecode, and other synchronization options. Believe it or not, these are not complex topics to master, and you aren't expected to be an audio engineer either. But we all need to take a modest amount of responsibility to insure that nothing will go wrong on our end. Music production is often the most distant element of the post production process, the rest usually done nearby and under more strict supervision by the editors and post production personnel.

Mixing
The Art of Balance

Perhaps all the audio engineering you will ever need to do is mix a demo and then use a professional engineer for the final mixes, which is great. On lower budget projects you may want to mix your own final masters yourself right in your studio. You should know a few things about sound mixing and using effects to their best advantage. A mix should be clean, sound great when put up to picture, have no flaws and be in a format that the production can use, which can mean mixing to anywhere from 2 tracks to 32 tracks. You should be able to set levels for each instrument you have on your mixer's inputs to get the maximum signal to noise ratio (which is the relationship between the music and the underlying noise inherent in virtually all recording situations). Your mixes should have impact, and sound realistic and musical. It takes some knowledge and practice; spending time with a good engineer can be very educational. Working with a good engineer is even better. Film sound has particulars that are unique and take practice to master. Hearing how your music sounds when mixed with dialogue and effects can either be a wonderful or frustrating experience, and the mix plays a big part in that. More on mixing later.

So how much do you know about all the above topics? Know it all? Half, perhaps? Perhaps a bit less than half? The more you know about these skills, the better able your studio will be to serve you in its true purpose—to help you make the best music possible under the most stressful and demanding conditions. You have access to all this information. It's in the manuals that came with your software, computer, and instruments. Much of it is also available on the internet, at websites from the companies you deal with, as well as other users sites set up to help others like you. There is a wealth of practical information in *Keyboard Magazine* and other music and audio magazines that are worth rereading. There are also some decent books available to fill in the gaps (humbly including my books *Synchronization from Reel to Reel* and *The MIDI Companion*, which are available at www.reelworld-online.com).

Think of it as a part of your musical education, only without any grades and a lot more fun when you're done. Every good composer is also a good music producer.

⊗ For a list of studio technical resources go to www. reelworld-online.com

Plugging It All In

Once you've decided to invest in your musical career by getting the equipment that you feel you need, how do all those pieces fit together? It's simpler than most people think, really. While no one really enjoys it, reading the manuals that come with the musical hardware and software you choose will make a big difference in how frustrated you'll be when hooking it all up and even more so when using it.

A personal studio consists of a number of sound making modules, one or more keyboards, a mixer, signal processing, audio recording gear, video equipment, one or more computers and some computer peripherals. If you have a desire to be recording acoustic sounds in your studio as opposed to merely sequencing, then you'll need to invest in microphones, preamps, headphones, and some kind of acoustical space. The following diagram shows one basic way a typical film composer's personal studio could be hooked up:

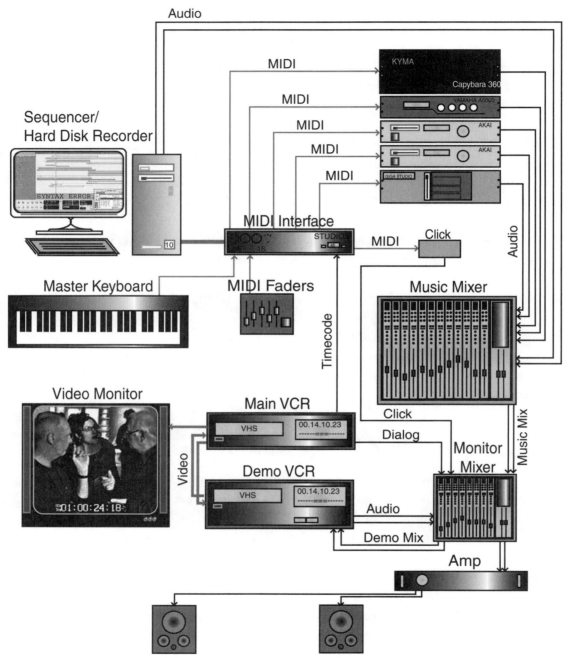

Audio

MIDI

KYMA

Capybara 360

MIDI

YAMAHA A5000

MIDI

AKAI

MIDI

AKAI

MIDI

GIGA STUDIO

Sequencer/
Hard Disk Recorder

SYNTAX ERROR

10

MIDI Interface

STUDIO5

16

MIDI

Click

Audio

Master Keyboard

MIDI Faders

Music Mixer

Timecode

Video Monitor

Main VCR

VHS

00.14.10.23

Click

:01:00:24:18:

Dialog

Monitor
Mixer

Music Mix

Video

Demo VCR

VHS

00.14.10.23

Audio

Demo Mix

Amp

Figure 2.1 Personal
music studio diagram.

The computer is the hub of the operation. A MIDI interface takes MIDI from the master keyboard and optional MIDI fader box and sends it to the computer. The interface also sends MIDI from the computer back to the main keyboard and all other synthesizers and samplers as well.

The audio from all of your MIDI gear is sent by cables to the main mixer. If you have a lot of wires, you can use bundled cables (called *snakes*) to keep things neater. Your mixer needs enough inputs to handle all the audio sent to it from all the gear in your studio. The mixer is connected to one or more signal processors that provide effects like reverb, delays, chorus, etc. Modern digital mixers also have effects built into them, though you may still wish to use other devices for quality or variety. The outputs of those effects are sent back to other inputs on the mixer. If the mixer has MIDI capabilities for automation or memory recall, then you must include a MIDI cable to go from the computer's MIDI interface to the mixer, and possibly one going back to the computer as well.

Your computer may also be used for digital audio as well as MIDI. In this case there will be an audio interface to record audio into the computer and play it back for listening, editing, and mixing. If you choose not to use the computer for audio, you will want some stand-alone form of audio recorder, such as a digital tape machine, or dedicated hard disk recorder. I find that the creative capabilities of having a sequencer with direct-to-disk recorder are creatively profound and worthwhile. Adding live players to your demos or final scores right in your writing studio and being able to edit and rework them later is a great time and money saver over going to another studio just for recording audio. It adds tremendously to the quality and sound of your work. You'll need sufficient inputs on your mixer to accommodate the outputs of your digital audio, which can be as many as you want.

While on the subject of computer-based digital audio, if you are interested in new and unusual sounds, consider looking into the world of audio plug-ins. There is a wonderful world of cool and interesting effects you can achieve using software on your computer in conjunction with your digital audio hardware and sequencer. There are a number of competing, incompatible formats, so you need to know what plug-ins your sequencer and audio hardware will support. Then have some fun experimenting with your audio recordings to come up with some fresh sounds. And software plug-ins don't only process your recorded audio; powerful software is available that performs the same functions as hardware-based samplers and synthesizers in your computer in conjunction with your MIDI sequencer. As more of these have become available, it

A list of current software based effects, samplers, and synthesizers can be found at the site—www. reelworld-online.com

is worth considering buying an additional computer (or computers) instead of standard dedicated electronic instruments.

You will be synchronized to video while scoring. You will also need to be able to hear the dialogue on the video while working. You could simply connect your VCR's audio to your TV monitor, but this won't let you mix music and dialogue together to preview how well they may blend together in context. A much better approach is what is shown in the diagram above (2.1). Unless you have a mixer with sophisticated film monitoring (typically only found in top-end mixing consoles), you can use a second small mixer to blend music, dialogue, and your metronome click source. The output of the small mixer goes to the 2-track monitor input of your main mixer. A second output from the small mixer goes to a second VCR used for creating video demos for your clients. You can do your own mixes of music and dialogue to show how cues will sound with picture and dialogue. This is very useful for those times when a client cannot make it to your studio to hear cues in person (less common in film, but more typical in television and advertising). Digital video as a replacement for the VCR is discussed later in this section.

The output of your main mixer is used to record your scores, or at least the scratch mixes and clicks you will need for recording live players or an orchestra in another studio. You can record your final mixes to a multitrack recorder, or back into your computer if it has audio capabilities. The digital audio files created by your sequencer can be exported or simply copied to another computer for use on the dub stage during the final mix.

It is feasible to make most or all of your studio components digital and have all digital connections. This makes many problems go away, but adds a few at the same time. An all-digital audio chain must be set up carefully but has many advantages over nondigital audio setups. A mostly or all digital studio makes it easier to store and recall mix and effects settings, even a "total recall" of every parameter of every mix you do. Digital connections of equipment also mean less noise and distortion and less concern about level mismatches.

Is It Enough?
Spending on Your Studio

I once heard of a first-time composer who was hired to score a film. Instead of arriving to the final dub with a tape or disk file of the completed and mixed music, he came with his sequencer and a single, cheap General MIDI synth meant for game music or karaoke. His reasoning was that this would be an acceptable way to "play the music into the film." What was he thinking? I know this gave a few of my friends a good laugh. It would appear that this neophyte composer didn't know anything about how a film score is put together and delivered to provide acceptable quality sound in a format that the engineers at the mix could work with, and was woefully under-equipped (musically) as well. But, without being cynical, this got me thinking (something I do in my spare time when no one else is around). In addition to the musical and technical know-how needed to produce a high-quality film score, just how much electronic gear does it really take to be considered "serious" in this competitive field? More importantly, what is the minimum investment in studio gear that can support a thriving career in the film muzik biz?

Some successful film composers will spend lavishly on huge personal music studios for themselves. These are both beautiful to look at and amazing in their sonic capabilities. They possess the ability to create astonishing palettes of sound: full symphonic orchestras, slamming rhythm sections, screaming guitars, massive choirs, and every ethnic drummer on earth can emanate from these state-of-the-art studios. We see their photos in the music and audio magazines, and they are the envy of many a composer. While I have invested heavily in my own studio, there are many composers with far more. Not that this is some sort of techno-macho competition. The goal is to get work as a composer, be able to do the job well and without too many technical headaches or sense of limitations. That does take some gear.

You can never be too thin, too rich, or have too much MIDI and audio gear (which will take care of the too rich part, anyway). So what does it take to get going? The ambiguous answer is "it depends."

Pop, R&B, rap, hip-hop, and techno writers and producers usually get by with a pretty spare sequencing and recording setup. This might include: drums and loops; bass and guitar samples; a couple of keyboard sounds; perhaps one decent vocal mic; a small multitrack tape machine or hard disk recorder to lay down singers and some live guitar; and a mixer and a bit of audio processing gear. It's amazing how many successful commercial recordings are done with extremely modest personal studios; a decent sequencer, a synth or two, a sampler, a modest recorder, a small mixer, and two or three select pieces of outboard signal processing gear. (Oh yes, and you need some really great song ideas to record. No problem, those are free!). Those artists are set to create demos of their music that they can send to any A&R person in the country and be taken seriously. More gear is icing on the cake. What more does one need? How about 16 or 32 or 64 tracks of audio for recording more background vocals and lots of other musicians? Absolutely. But now we'll need a bigger and better mixer, and some more outboard gear. No problem! Maybe some new CD-ROMS for the sampler? Of course! Bigger, faster computer, large screen monitors, louder amp and speakers, subwoofer, more software. You've just joined your local music store's "preferred customer" list. Welcome to the potentially bottomless shopping list of the personal studio.

What about a personal studio geared specifically toward scoring films and television? It does get a bit more complex. Most film and television producers and directors are very aware of what a good quality MIDI-based studio is capable of doing. They are on to us, they know just how cool all this MIDI and digital stuff is, and they expect to hear "the music," not just a basic demo of the score with a few samples and a drum loop. They expect to hear a complete score that sounds well produced, even before musicians have come to play.

It used to be, not too many years ago, that a composer could get into film scoring by talent, savvy, and hard work, without having an advanced degree in audio engineering and studio technology. But that really is no longer the case. Even well established orchestral film composers with no interest in electronics or synthesizers are being forced to integrate a sequencer into their writing studio just to work with those directors that insist on hearing detailed demos prior to the recording of the score. There are a small handful of exceptions. The top players in the industry, the John Williams, Jerry Goldsmiths, Ennio Morricones, etc., are typically left to do what they do best. But they built their careers in the pre sequencer era. If Jerry Goldsmith or John Williams was a young composer just getting started today, with all the talent they possess, would they be able to find work in film without a significant MIDI system? Unfortunately, the answer is probably not. And there are plenty of talented and experienced composers finding it harder and harder to get work simply because they have not invested sufficiently in a high-quality personal studio and learned to use it.

So how much does it take, technically, to have a competitive shot? Fortunately, there are many high-quality, multitimbral synthesizers to choose from that can handle many of the parts from a complex score pretty well. There are hardware and software samplers with more memory and polyphony also capable of holding a fantastic number of sounds. A drawback to these all-in-one multitimbral boxes is that mixing can be more limited or difficult if you wish to apply different

EQ or effects on the various parts. It's a trade-off between flexibility and power. It may be better to invest in a few more separate synthesizers and samplers (with loads of memory and a good sound library), as well as a couple of digital effects and a good mixer with sufficient inputs for all the instruments you have and room for future expansion. Digital mixers with automation are of great use to the composer who wants to be able to store different mixes for different cues and recall them in an instant while playing cues back for the director. In the world of good-sounding scores, more is usually more. At least gear-wise. There are computer-based hardware and software systems that can provide these capabilities: synthesis, sampling, effects, mixing, and recording. These combined with some choice dedicated musical hardware can make a fantastic personal studio.

There's something else I would like to recommend for the gear list, though you can't buy it at any music store. Whenever possible, always try to use some actual, live, human-based musicians, including on any demos you do. Even just a single soloist can bring an otherwise synth-y score to life. Hire a friend, offer a local college student some beer money (but not 'til after they play), or ask around for someone to play. People are very used to hearing the sound of live musicians, and that can't be replaced with a synth. Especially those exposed solo parts that are up front in your mix. It makes a big difference. I've found that regardless of the gear in my studio, it all sounds better when I have an experienced sound engineer help mix whatever I am doing. Not only does it help to bring some expertise in, but someone who doesn't know the music as well as you might hear it more clearly and offer suggestions to get the best mix.

Finally, keep your studio growing. The point isn't to keep up with the neighbours ("Hey honey, the Joneses across the street just got a new…!"), but to invest in your business. If you make money with your music this stuff can be tax deductible. It will also help you achieve better quality results and go for a bigger sound in future projects. As you spend more and more time writing, it will become easier to get what you want from your larger studio, which can make the whole process yet more enjoyable, which is the whole point. Isn't it?

Getting a Studio Tan
The Importance of a Comfortable Workspace

The studio is the place that a composer will spend the majority of his or her waking hours. So it is important for that place to be set up as well as possible.

One thing I've noticed over the years is that a personal music studio is not a place to scrimp. It is so much better to have a small amount of high-quality gear than a lot of cheaper, less useful stuff. There are always trade-offs with less expensive gear. Take digital effects such as reverb for example. The problem with much of the lower end audio gear out there is that they are noisier than the expensive stuff, and less realistic if you are going for a true, natural sound. I like cheap effects for odd sounds, I run synths through an inexpensive distortion unit to grunge them up, and some old Lexicons for strange effects. I have quite a bit of older gear in my studio that I use for a variety of effects and colours. On the computer side of things, there are cheap and even free plug-ins to help jazz up your sounds and your mix. You can have a lot of flexibility without going broke.

If you take your music seriously, and it doesn't even matter if it is how you make your living, you owe it to yourself to get at least a few pieces of high end, professional gear. Wait and save up if you have to. It's not for the snob factor. Good quality gear comes at a price. Many of the more successful musicians and composers I know got professional gear for themselves from the beginning of their careers, or before. Perhaps there's even some psychological effects of working with top notch gear that helps the creative juices flow. Who wants to be outshined by their equipment?

⊗ Pictures of the author's personal studio can be seen at www. reelworld-online.com

Since I spend so much time every day sitting in a chair, chained to my Macintosh, I invested some money in a really comfortable chair with a lot of lumbar support. The difference was amazing. I would sometimes get an aching back after a number of marathon days, but now that's gone. I've also reorganized my music workstation, with my MIDI and Mac keyboards, computer and video monitors, video transport and MIDI faders positioned so that I move my hands as little as possible. Going from playing to typing has become much more ergonomic. I recommend taking a close look at where you make your music and see that it is as comfortable, efficient, and inspiring as possible. I once met a composer who told me he could only write music in a small villa in Italy. That's a bit much, but it made me wonder if my music would improve if my environment was different. I'll never know, but at least I have this really comfortable chair.

To some extent, I treat my writing room/studio as though it were a sanctuary. While I do things other than just write music (like writing the occasional book), I try to keep it a special place. I don't use it as a place to work out all the problems in my life; I don't want to associate this room with things that are not about inspiration and focus. If I get a phone call that upsets me—like finding out I have to rewrite a cue I've spent days on—I usually step outside to collect myself, think things through, and then go back to work. This may seem a bit silly, but I like to keep the "vibe" in the room clear of nonmusical distractions. I find that it helps.

It is exceedingly hard not to answer the phone when it rings while I'm writing, though 98% of the time it's usually something that could have waited. But since any call could be time critical, I usually do answer it, even when I'm in the middle of composing or recording. A few times I've gotten fed up and just shut off the ringer. I don't think that's ever caused a problem. Hmm, something to ponder.

We've looked at many of the technical and practical aspects of being a composer today. If you find much of this information out of your grasp, then do what you can to fill in some technical blanks. Knowing the capabilities of your studio and all that is in it will make your life better. The technology won't get you anywhere on its own, but it can make the ride a lot more fun.

CHAPTER SIX

>Writing the Score

The Paper Tiger
Generating a Printed Score

I spend most of my waking moments in front of my computer, creating music of one sort or another, and I use all that modern technology has to offer. But regardless of the computer-based origins of my writing, much of my music is destined to be performed by actual, living, breathing, carbon-based musicians. Anywhere from a small handful of players to an entire orchestra. That means that I must transform my sequenced tracks into legible notation on paper (ugh, dead trees!) for them to read. Virtually all professional MIDI sequencers provide some degree of automatic transcription of your performances into standard music notation. Some are quite sophisticated. In addition, there are several stand-alone notation software programs with even more smarts to accurately transcribe, edit, and print your scores and parts from Standard MIDI Files that any sequencer can export.

Because of the tight schedules I work under on both film and television projects, I rarely do my own music transcriptions, although I find it a worthwhile task since I often find things in my scores I missed or could improve. Usually I work with an orchestrator on larger projects or a music prep person/copyist for the smaller ones. For the moment I'd like to focus on the smaller projects that have only a small number of players.

When I create a musical sequence, I make clear which tracks are only electronic (synths and samples to be used in the final mix) and which are to be transcribed and played by live musicians. If I have a string line that I want doubled between live and electronic strings, I will often create two tracks, one to be recorded with the samples and the other only to be transcribed for the players. I title the tracks clearly so I remember which is which. If your sequencer allows comments with the tracks, you can use that as well.

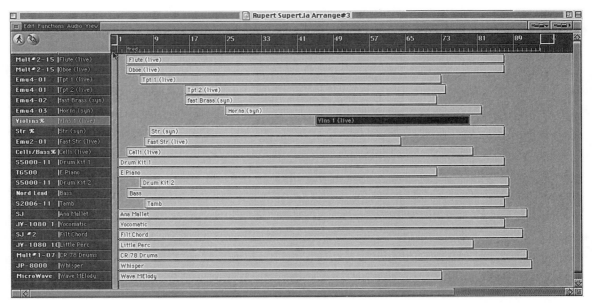

Figure 2.2 Sequencer tracks labeled for transcription

Everything I write and sequence will be auditioned for the director or producers, so the cues must sound great, even though they will be replaced by live players. If I want an instrumental phrase to sound emotional and "well played," I will often not quantize it. I want to leave it sounding human, and humans don't play in perfect rhythm (well, a few do). The wind and brass parts take "breaths" where a real player might. Strings are a little ahead or behind the beat. These parts sound good, but will not transcribe well with the computer, which is why I make a copy of the part, quantize it, mute it, and save it for the orchestrator to use for transcription only. I am always careful not to write anything that can't be played by the musicians. Recording sessions need to go smoothly and quickly.

Stay away from the extremes in range for the players unless you know who will be playing. Be careful of awkward leaps in range as well. Check that the trills or doublestops you call for are playable and not too hard. Don't make huge demands on brass to play high and loud for long stretches. These are the types of things you can learn from orchestration books. A chart of orchestral instrument ranges can be found in the Appendix.

See website for books on orchestration, notation, and instrumentation

Whenever you create orchestral parts with harmonies, such as string or brass chords, you can sequence them either as chords in a single track, or you can record each note of the chord on individual tracks. Obviously if all you want to do is play a three note chord you should be able to just go to a track, press record, and play the chord. But when the end result will need to be divided up for several players, possibly on different brass or wind instruments, each playing one note of the chord, you might want to start thinking and playing more linearly. Without going into a full treatise on the art of orchestration, each line within an ensemble should sound as musical and melodic by itself as possible. Playing parts one at a time and building harmonies will give you a better, more musical result and will be more playable by the musicians.

As my cues are sequenced and approved, I call in my orchestrator or music prep person to help me put it all on paper for the conductor's score and the players' parts. I have worked with a number of very talented people who have handled orchestration or music prep for me. They fall into two categories—computer-based and pencil-based. The computer users get a disk with the Standard MIDI Files and a tape of the music with a click track. The pencil and paper users get a tape and either a rough, unedited printout on paper of the score or a disk with the SMF that they will read from their computer screen as they transcribe by hand. The tape has recordings of each cue, with click, which serves as a guide to the articulations and dynamics of the music which may not be obvious from the files themselves.

A list of music transcription software can be found at www. reelworld-online.com

In my experience, working with pen and paper is still sometimes faster and more accurate than orchestrating with a computer. I think the reason for this is that people who work by hand have the tendency to create and think each phrase through more carefully. The unedited transcription of most sequencing programs will frequently leave in too much rhythmic complexity. It must be edited carefully, and time is invariably running out. Things get left in that an experienced copyist or orchestrator would not allow. So these two types of people come at the same task from opposite directions. Good, legible music tends to be simple and easy to read.

Computer notation programs, no matter how advanced and sophisticated, still require careful manual editing by a careful and trained eye to create the final

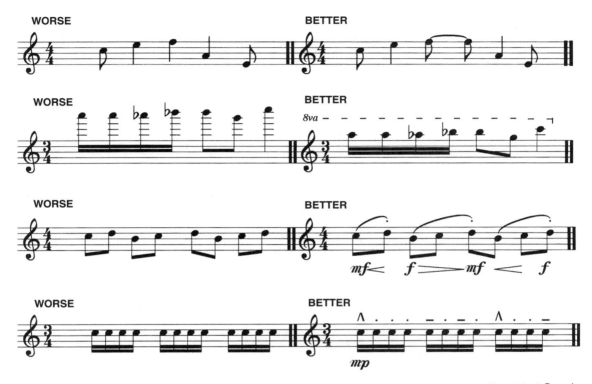

Figure 2.3a-d Examples of worse and better music notation

score and parts. I find there are a few aspects of notation that get overlooked by some of the computer-based transcribers. I would like to point out some of the more important elements of good part writing for recording sessions.

- Put the name of each cue at the top of the first page, number the pages, and tape them together before your recording.

- Never end a long note with only a whole note or a half note. It is best to end a long note tied to an eighth note for better clarity of where the note will end.

Figure 2.3e Clearer notation of note length

- Number the measures only at the start of each line.

- In general, have the same number of bars on each line.

- If the musicians will be playing to a click don't print BPMs on the score. Instead, use descriptive adjectives (i.e. bouncy, briskly, mysteriously).

- Most scores will be played once and only once—at the recording session for the project. Don't go overboard and make them look like they will be published as part of the symphonic literature. Excessive use of Italian musicological terms should be punishable.

- If a musician will be overdubbing parts (playing more than one part on multiple tracks of audio), or if two players are sharing a part, don't print multiple notes on one staff. Give each player or part its own staff on the same page.

Figure 2.4 Examples of multiple chair notation

- Use dynamics and phrase markings such as accents, staccatos, legatos, crescendos, and slurs liberally—it helps sessions go much faster when the players know how to phrase the music. The option is for you to explain every cue and wait while they scribble on their parts. Unedited parts from musical notation software can do little in this area.

- Use multi bar rests whenever needed for rests that are more than two bars long.

Figure 2.5 Multi bar rests

- Notate rhythms as clearly as possible. Avoid complex rests when they are not needed. Allow soloists to embellish phrases as desired, and give them the clearest rhythmic notation possible.

- Put the key signature at the beginning of every line, but only put time signatures at the beginning of each cue or where there are changes. If a key or time signature changes at the beginning of a line, also put it at the end of the previous line so the players don't get surprised.

- Be familiar with the keys and ranges of all the instruments you are writing for. Don't sequence out of their playable range, and be sure you transpose parts for all the non-C instruments. These can be found in the Appendix.

- Make sure that someone PROOFREADS EVERYTHING. People make mistakes, but parts for players need to be perfect. Never rely on computers or copyists to not make occasional errors. I've said this to the people who use notation programs for my projects who always assume the computer is right all the time. Mistakes can and do crop up from time to time, even though it is due to some kind of pilot error. Don't make that assumption. Check everything.

The unquantized tracks from your sequence will usually not transcribe too well. So use a copy of the track just for transcription. Tracks for transcription should be quantized carefully. Go through the track and adjust note durations for better transcription. Stretch notes right to the next beat or barline so they transcribe more clearly. Check for any short, extra notes that you might have accidentally hit. In short, with as much time as you have, polish the tracks to make them as clear as possible for the orchestrator.

The end results of your efforts, whether you collaborate with an orchestrator, copyist, or other music prep person, or just work on your own, should be well transcribed parts for all your players, and a clear, detailed score for the conductor. This will lead to a more productive and smoother recording session. Musicians also tend to play better and have better dispositions when the music in front of them looks good, is easy to read, and is accurate. There are a number of good books on orchestration, music notation, and musical instrument ranges on the website. Have them around when you do transcription or other notation, especially when writing for instruments with which you are less familiar. It will save time when it counts.

Conduct Yourself Accordingly
How to Control an Orchestra

There are few things more exhilarating than standing up in front of a live orchestra, flapping your arms about and hearing all those living, breathing people play music that you have written. I doubt that even the most jaded of composers remain jaded when it comes to this. I've conducted a number of my own scores, as well as scores for other composers. It is both a challenge and a pleasure. There are also sessions when I remain a listener in the control room, making sure that everything coming through the monitors sounds as I intended (or better).

There are those who make a life-long study of orchestral conducting. It is an art in and of itself that requires knowledge, musicality, and practice. But conducting for the film orchestra differs greatly from the conducting of symphonic repertory. Part of conducting classical music is the study and comprehension of the scores themselves. Mahler is not around to answer questions. There are expectations put upon the performance of known music, and you are compared with the others who have performed the same piece. With a film score, since no one has heard it before, there is no comparison. Your performance will be the definitive recording! And probably the only recording.

There are other differences in conducting for film. First, you will probably be working with a click track that all the members of the orchestra hear in their headphones. So you're not really keeping the time. With that rather rudimentary burden removed, what remains for a film conductor to accomplish? Plenty.

The physical act of conducting, like any martial arts, cannot be fully taught in writing. But we can describe a number of rudiments. The conductor moves the baton in a pattern that helps the players to know which beat of the bar they are currently at. While this may seem unnecessary for any decent player, it isn't the case. Film scores are recorded with little or no rehearsal, so everyone is basically sight-reading. As such there is a lot on the players' minds. The conductor showing musicians where they are in each measure becomes one less thing the players need to think about.

The basic pattern is simple:

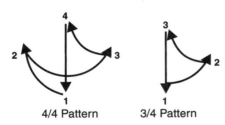

4/4 Pattern   **3/4 Pattern**

Figure 2.6 Basic conducting patterns

With these patterns in mind (there are others for other meters, as well as variations for tripletted music or fast tempos in small meters such as 3/8) you can give the musicians a clear idea of where in the bar you are. Regardless of how you show the beats, the most important information you will give the players is the location of the downbeat of each bar. This will ensure that no one deviates from the right beat. I will usually give more emphasis to the downbeat even in gentle fluid sections, though I'll really nail it for those bars with a hard accent on the first beat.

The baton is held in front of your chest, not out to either side, not too high or too low. As you swing the baton to each point in the bar, it accelerates somewhat, like hitting a nail with a small hammer. The baton swings to a beat and then stops briefly before accelerating to the next point in the pattern. Left handers, such as myself, mirror the pattern.

Now that you have the basic pattern down, next comes the nuance of it. Exaggerating the movements is a sign for the players to play louder, and smaller movements indicate playing softer. Not only should the pattern get smaller, but smoothing out the motions to be less accelerated indicates an added amount of smoothness to the playing. By snapping the baton from beat to beat in the pattern, you are asking for more emphasis on separate notes.

When a cue is about to be recorded, I raise my baton up, in preparation for the first downbeat (perhaps from the above patterns you can see why the first beat of a bar is called the downbeat). I hold the baton steady waiting for the countoff clicks to come into my headphones. Holding the baton up and motionless like this tells the orchestra to stop chatting and get ready to play. It often works. I can't predict the first click, so as soon as I hear it I move toward beat 2 of the count in bar and continue the pattern from there. I will often call out beats 2 and 3 aloud to make clear to everyone what's going on. When I bring the baton down for the beginning of the next bar, the music will begin.

Now the job shifts a bit. As I continue to lead with the baton, showing the beats and overall dynamics, I use my other hand to prepare any instruments or section for when they are to begin playing after rests. It is reassuring for players to have the conductor point to them in the bar or beat prior to an important entrance: they will play it better. I will also raise my other hand up and down to emphasize changes in dynamics. Raising my hand with my palm up means "let's all get louder" and lowering my hand, palm down means "hey, quit playing so loud, let's play it softer now."

The conductor must always anticipate the beats to which he or she wants to add emphasis. If there is a big accent or hit on beat 3 of the bar, it is too late to indicate it when you get to beat 3, so you need to indicate it on beat 2. You should always be a step ahead of accents and dynamics with the baton. To show an accent on beat 3, give a big flip of the baton on beats 2 and 3. Beat 2 prepares them and beat 3 confirms it for them. Hammer those nails! Another analogy is to think of flinging darts onto a target across the room. If you want the dart to hit right on beat 3, you need to throw it a bit beforehand. It is intuitive to most people as to when to start the throw in order to hit the target when you want to. Drummers don't start moving their sticks on the beat, they anticipate in order to have the stick strike the drum right on the beat. Even keyboard players must start moving their fingers downward early enough to get the note to strike at just the right moment. It's a subconscious act, and the same applies in conducting: you help the ensemble make the right choices by anticipating them.

Prior to recording a complex or difficult cue, I will rehearse it through once or twice, time permitting, to allow everyone to get familiar with it, and to check for any errors in the parts. I'll do this without the click track, indicating the tempo myself. The conductor's job is to keep the group of players together. When there is a soloist playing, you don't need to show them much after they have entered successfully. Instead, conduct the rest of the ensemble—the accompaniment. I will use my free hand to indicate to various players or section to play louder or softer in order to better balance the orchestra. I will not usually conduct time to a group smaller than a quartet, unless they ask for it.

Every note that starts must eventually stop; and this is another important function of the conductor. While music notation is very clear about when notes start, it is less clear about when a note ends. I very carefully indicate to the ensemble when to stop a long note by making a small circular flip with the baton or touching my fingers together with my thumb on the hand not holding the baton. Many cues will end with a held note without tempo which the conductor must cue while watching the picture on a screen or monitor.

There is no room for error in conducting. A mistake in a meter change, in the baton pattern or a miscued entrance can often stop a recording cold. It may also diminish how carefully the players watch you, assuming they are better off on their own. Be prepared and diligent. It is also the conductor's job to flag any bloopers by any of the players and stop the recording to avoid wasting time on a bad take of a cue. The conductor is the first pair of ears at the session, determining whether a take has gone right or wrong. The conductor is also there to answer any questions from the orchestra in the event that a player cannot read a part, or if an error has crept into the written parts. That means being able to read the score in any of the keys to which orchestral instruments are tuned. There are also different clefs for viola and some other instruments to be read. It feels like mental gymnastics at times, but with practice gets easier.

At the end of the session, the conductor gets to be a real hero, assuming all went well. Conducting can be physically taxing and mentally draining, but exhilarating. Short of taking lessons in conducting, or stepping in front of an orchestra cold for the first time, nothing is better than watching a good conductor take an orchestra through its paces. I've learned as much from that as I ever have from my studies. It's something every composer should do at least once before going back to hide in the darkness of the control room.

Sounds Just Like the Real Thing
(Until You Listen to the Real Thing)
The Synthetic Approach to Orchestration

Simulating an orchestra with samples and synths is a tough business. It's hard to do well, and easy to do poorly. Samples are an amazing tool for letting a director know what their orchestral score will (more or less) sound like; helping avoid major problems later on, like the director wanting changes when you are recording your score. When there is no money for a large group of players, but the project calls for an orchestral approach, then working with samples is simply the only choice. It's important to make sure a client knows there is a difference between real players and samples, and the difference can be profound, depending on the style of music and the composer's technical resources.

While samples can accurately depict what the notes you write will sound like once orchestrated, they don't truly express all that can be done with a real orchestra. Sequencing a convincing orchestral simulation that sounds better than just a demo can be time consuming. As a composer, you may not always want to spend the time it takes to make a demo sound flawlessly like a real orchestra, even if you have a sufficient amount of electronic gear to pull it off. It takes a lot of samples and polyphony to do it right. The orchestral samples found in smaller all-in-one sample-playback instruments are nowhere as good as what is available in the form of very large sample CD-ROM libraries, which have a much larger requirement for a sampler's memory and polyphony. Each instrument and section of an orchestra is capable of such a wide variety of sounds that it would be nearly impossible to make a definitive sample library of every possible sound an orchestra is capable of. It could take up a potentially massive amount of memory or storage space. But better sample libraries are available. In the meantime there are compromises—smaller samples that don't sound as rich and full, fewer bowing or blowing techniques, fewer possible dynamics, etc. You can also limit your compositional palette to what you have available.

When I was a music student, I studied orchestration and conducting, which has proven very important to me when creating sampled orchestral demos. Surprisingly, studying conducting has been just as helpful as the study of orchestration, since conducting deals with the expression and interpretation of melodic material. One time I was asked to help a friend and fellow composer

Look at the website for some of the currently available orchestral sample libraries. Go to www. reelworld-online.com synthesize a large-scale orchestral score. He faxed the score pages to me from his orchestrator to my studio, and I performed all the parts into my sequencer. The very first page I received had the marking "al talone." That was a new one to me. I looked up "al talone" in my *Harvard Dictionary of Music*, but it wasn't listed. A phone call to the orchestrator taught me that "al talone" (actually spelled "al tallone" in Italian scores, and "au talon" in French) refers to playing the violin with the near end of the bow, called the "frog," to produce a crisp aggressive sound. The literal translation of the word (for you etymology fans) means "at the heel," another term for the part of the string bow closest to the player's hand. Of course! Right in the first measure of the score was a good example of how an orchestra is capable of great subtlety and nuance not available in any current electronic emulations.

I compose my music with my sequencer, using a large set of orchestral samples, which lets me hear what each part will sound like, more or less, as I write. It's great to be able to hear just what the instruments will sound like in a particular range. Other times, if I still haven't fleshed out the composition, I sketch the music with a piano sound and then develop and sequence the orchestration later. Either way works, depending on your composing process. Here are a few ideas I use to help make orchestral demos sound as good as possible.

A list of good books on orchestration can be found online at www.reel-world-online.com

General Notes on the Character of Orchestral Sound

The orchestra is a highly expressive instrument. Woodwind, brass, percussion and string instruments sound quite different between playing softly and loudly. In other words, the changes in dynamics are both volume and timbre. Having samples of both louder and softer notes of as many instruments as possible will add to the realism of the sequence. This is less important if you are simply making demos for the director. It helps to have a way to control a little bit of your sampler's filters with a MIDI controller or keyboard velocity so sounds get slightly brighter as they get louder as is typical of most acoustic instruments. Look for samples with at least a loud and soft performance of each section.

Most orchestral musicians rarely sustain a long note without changes in loudness. They are almost always either getting louder or softer. Imitating this by the use of MIDI Volume (MIDI Continuous Controller #7) will bring a greater amount of realism to the phrasing of the music. A number of MIDI keyboard controllers have a slider for sending MIDI Volume to your sequencer. If not, you should get a small MIDI fader unit with a few sliders to sit by your keyboard to perform a variety of nuances, such as volume, filter, or a crossfade between louder and softer samples, though you will need to learn how to set this up on your sampler. Some sequencers have on-screen faders for adding dynamics to tracks. Once you have access to MIDI Volume, use it! It will make all the difference in the world for adding life to your music. Dynamic markings in scores are easily overlooked, but they provide the music with its nuance and expression. Soft notes can swell into louder ones, and vice versa. Notes marked "sfz crescendo" (called sfortsando crescendo) hit hard and loud, come down to quiet right away, and then slowly grow back to loud.

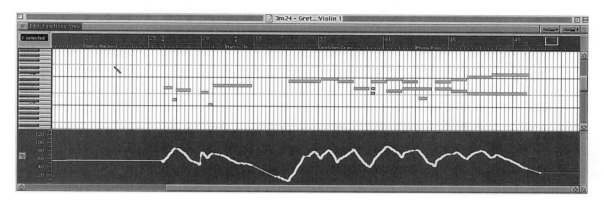

Figure 2.7 A graphic depiction of MIDI Volume as it relates to a phrase of orchestral music.

Quantizing is not very orchestral; the slight (hopefully) rhythmic messiness of a large group of real players is actually part of what gives the orchestra its sense of size and lushness. But if the music is very rhythmic, well, why not make it as rhythmically accurate as possible? It requires some judgement. If your sequencer can do a partial quantize, it may sound better than a full, 100% quantization. I sometimes prefer to play the more difficult parts in to the sequencer very slowly instead of quantizing. Depending on the nature of the sample, I may shift a track that I've quantized slightly earlier in time to compensate for a slow attack in the sample. This prevents the quantized parts from feeling behind the beat.

Winds & Brass

The key here is careful phrasing. Since these instruments are blown, in the real world they can only play for several seconds before some short pause is needed for the musician to inhale. You don't need to think about this when the part is moving from note to note, but you can't write a sustained note for two minutes without making for a problem when it is recorded. Very important is the idea of *legato* phrasing. Legato means that groups of notes are connected together and not reattacked by the musician. While most synthesizers and samplers have a legato mode (sometimes called "mono"), samples will normally re-attack the note. I play the notes overly long, just slightly, to imitate legato phrasing with greater realism. The notes overlap to blur them together. It's not really the same as a true legato (or slurred) playing, but it works.

Strings

Probably the toughest nut to crack in orchestral simulations. Slow passages aren't so difficult if you have some good sounds, but fast lines and runs can sound pretty fake coming from samples. This has to do with the fact that fast string lines are played with a single movement of the bow, and not re-attacking each note, which a sample will do. Much of it will depend on the quality and nature of the samples themselves. There are string sample libraries with programs optimized for fast vs. slow lines. There are also libraries with actual string phrases that you can just use with the touch of a finger.

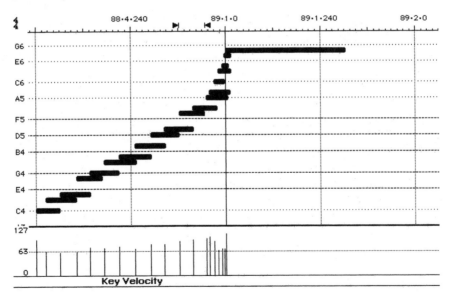

Figure 2.8 After performing a string part you may wish to lengthen the notes so they overlap slightly

Some sample libraries offer several of the more common string techniques in order to cover most of the bases (or is that basses?) of orchestral string writing. Because there can be different lines moving in different ways, first and second violins for example, I will have two MIDI channels of the same samples on the same sampler. This takes no more memory as having just one, since both programs will use the same samples. But having a first and second violin part on different tracks of my sequencer and different channels of my sampler means that I can have separate MIDI volumes for each, and thus create a greater sense of dynamics and blend.

If you are trying to achieve a very realistic string sound in your compositions and demos, it's usually far better to perform the violins, viola, cello, and bass parts one at a time. This maintains the linear feel of the way actual string players perform and well-crafted orchestral music is written. It's easy to notice when string parts are played as a chord on a keyboard. It's a different sound than the more linear method of doing it a part at a time. It can feel somewhat more modern, because it flaunts its nonorchestral style.

Percussion

There is a fairly traditional palette of percussion instruments used by the orchestra. Perhaps the most important among these is the timpani. In addition to having a wide dynamic range, they will become significantly brighter as they get louder. They are played with either wood or wool mallets depending on whether they are to be more or less aggressive. Timpani are sometimes played "rolled," which sounds best if the sample is of rolled timpani, versus attempting to simulate the roll in your sequence. The better percussion samples include two or more sampled dynamics of each instrument.

A typical percussion palette comprises: timpani, straight and rolled snare drums (which are different from the snare drums used in pop and jazz kits), bass drum, tom toms, piatti (large cymbals struck together, not hit with a stick, a distinctly different sound), suspended cymbal (basically the same as a crash cymbal, often rolled with wool mallets), triangle, orchestral bells (also called glockenspiel), chimes, tubular bells, and large and small gongs (sometimes called tam-tams). Fortunately, not long ago I got together with a fine orchestral percussionist who allowed me to sample him playing most of his instruments in a studio. In particular I had him play a number of snare and cymbal rolls, straight, with a slow crescendo and with fast crescendo. This gave me most everything I need for just such occasions. Percussion instruments are available from various orchestral CD-ROM libraries.

Harp

The harp, one of my favorite orchestral instruments, is played either by plucking the strings or strumming them (also called glissing), in which the harpist runs his or her fingers along all the strings of the harp, which are tuned to the key of the music with special pedals on the harp. John Williams uses the harp extensively in many of his scores. In particular, Williams is fond of using the lydian scale (with a raised fourth degree) in the harp while the rest of the orchestra plays a straight major or minor scale. Writing for real harp requires a thorough knowledge of the instrument as it is not a fully chromatic instrument. It's easy to write parts that are too hard, or even unplayable for the harpist.

Some harp samples include both plucks and glisses. But there are so many possible combinations of scales, keys, and patterns that it becomes somewhat cumbersome to try and manage them all. Most libraries have only the more predominant ones. Glisses are also done in time to the music in order to hit a top or bottom note at just the right beat, so again it becomes difficult to find just the right sampled gliss. In order to sequence harp glisses in a fairly realistic manner, you can perform the glisses by running a finger along the white keys of the keyboard, ignoring the tonality for the moment, then transpose the notes as needed to fit the desired scale and key. Many sequencers have transpose functions that will do this for you fairly automatically.

Putting It Together

Making good sounding orchestral demos, or simulations for a score requires practice, good quality samples, and a serious investment in sampling gear. Fortunately, there are better and better samplers available to handle more and more of these chores at a more reasonable cost. Another method that helps in creating synth orchestral recordings is to bring in key live players to add to the sampled mix. Bringing in a couple of French horn players can be a significant improvement in the expressiveness and "majesty" of certain sections of the music. French horns, for example, are capable of far more timbres and colour changes than found in any current sample library. It's quite worthwhile to spend the time and money to hire just a few musicians to flesh out the faux orchestra. This is especially true of any exposed solo passages. More than anything, samples lack phrasing, an inherent weakness of the technology. Any orchestral musician who would play like a sampler would be fired pretty quickly for lack of musicianship.

In the final mix of the music, finding a natural blend and ambience that mimics a real orchestra performing in a real hall or studio will make a difference too. A bad mix of even a very well sequenced orchestra will ruin it. Using effects improperly can also spoil what you have set out to create. This means knowing what a real orchestra sounds like. I've heard orchestral simulations, my own included sometimes, that give away the secret. Remember that about half the members of an orchestra are string players, and they sit in front. They are often the basis of what an orchestra is timbrally. Flutes that blare above a loud string passage will ruin the organic blend of a sampled orchestra. It also helps to give a good stereo image by panning instruments as they sit in the orchestra, virtual or otherwise. To put orchestral simulations in perspective, they sound just like the real thing…until you listen to the real thing!

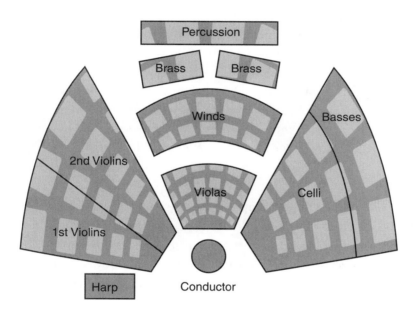

Figure 2.9 Typical seating chart of an orchestra

Loop the Loop
The Rhythms of Electronic Scoring

On the flip side of making highly orchestral film music are scores done in a more highly contemporary style and approach. Heavier use of synthesizers, electric guitars, sound design, fast sequenced rhythms, voices, world music inspired sounds and themes, unusual sonic effects, and aggressive use of percussion can be used to make a score feel modern. You can of course look for interesting ways to blend the worlds of orchestral and nonorchestral.

Ever since hip-hop and rap became popular in the 1980s, loops (sampled recordings of musical phrases or fragments, as opposed to the more typical sampling of individual notes or instruments) have become a major element of pop music, and film scores as well. There is a seemingly unlimited number of sampled loop libraries on CD-ROMs of everything from standard drumsets to exotic world rhythms, from retro style old sounds to abstract bits of noise made from who-knows-what. They can be very inspiring and sound great, since they retain the original feel and "groove" of the music or musicians that recorded or created them. As opposed to bringing in a loop last, after the bulk of a theme or cue is written, it can be far more inspiring and interesting to start with a sampled loop or other kinds of sampled sounds or phrases and compose on top of them. You can always edit the loop out of the sections where it is no longer needed. It can also be very interesting to layer two or more loops to play simultaneously and create unique new rhythms.

The tricky part about using loops in film music is the frequent need to make subtle, or not so subtle changes to the tempo in order to make the music work closely with the picture. When a rhythmic loop is created, it takes on the tempo of the original recording. The loops don't care what the tempo of the sequencer is, they play back at exactly the tempo at which they were recorded and created.

If the loops were different tempos to begin with, then you need to be able to "tune" the tempo of each loop in order to get it to stay in time with the other loops as well as the music. You can work with loops in a few ways. They can reside in a sampler, to be triggered with a MIDI note from your sequencer, and sped up or slowed with MIDI pitch bend or transposing on a keyboard.

Loops can also be created as digital audio segments on your hard drive and be loaded into a track of a sequencer or other digital audio system to be played at the appropriate moment. Most MIDI/audio sequencers have the ability to process sounds to speed them up or slow them down to match the tempo of the music. This is a great way to work, though it takes a bit more time than simply triggering them in a sampler. There are also other software programs designed specifically to work with loops. Some can time stretch loops on the fly, and some will chop a loop up beat by beat in order to allow them to be molded to the tempo of your music or to produce unique sounds. With the right program you can quickly organize and fine tune rhythmic loops to create a fascinating rhythmic framework for any music.

For information on current applications for loops, go to the website at www. reelworld-online.com

Organization
The Unique Language of the Cue Sheet

When a film is edited, it does not exist as a single object from beginning to end. Because movie film is so bulky, it is broken down into smaller, more easily handled chunks called *reels* (hence the title of this book). Typically, a film reel is around ten minutes in length, though some editors work in larger production reels that average around twenty minutes in length. With projects done exclusively on or for video, no such breakdown is done.

Each cue written for a film is typically named and given a cue number. The number reflects the cue's position and order within the film, and the number of the reel it plays in. Cue numbers are also given to the production company and the composer's performing rights society along with titles for the cue ("Lefty's Revenge" or "Harold Hangs Himself").

For example, let's say that a film has nine reels in it, each about ten minutes in length. The film will be a total of about 90 minutes long. The first cue in the film is traditionally labelled "1m1." The "m" stands for music, and it helps distinguish the music from sound effects or dialogue events on any written logs. The first digit represents the reel number, in this case reel 1. The digit after the 'm' is a number for the cue itself. The next piece of music that occurs, assuming it is also in reel 1 will be 1m2, followed by 1m3, etc.

Composers and music editors sometimes differ on how cues are numbered on subsequent reels. Some composers will number the first cue on the second reel of a film as 2m1. Other composers prefer to number all the cues of a film sequentially, and not start again with 1 on every reel. For them, the first cue on reel 2, assuming there were 3 cues in reel 1, would be called 2m4. That means it's the fourth cue of music and is on reel 2. Either method is fine. The cues will be organized by the music editor, if one is working on the film, otherwise it will be up to the composer. These numbers are primarily for the composer to stay organized and avoid losing or forgetting to write cues. The mixers will need these "m" numbers when working.

The cue sheet shows the cue number, a title (required for future royalty payments), a start time, and a duration. There is usually some description of the scene and any notes of things discussed at the spotting session of importance to the composer. It may come up on occasion that a new cue will be added after the film has been spotted and all the cues given sequential numbers. In cases like that, the new cue is given a letter after the second number. For example, a new cue put between 6m12 and 6m13 would be called 6m12A. Also, in cases where a composer writes more than one cue for a scene as a possible alternative, they may do the same thing, so there could be a 6m12A, 6m12B, etc., for various versions to play for the director. I prefer to title them with "ALT," such as 6m12ALT, or 6m12ALT2.

Figure 2.10 Cue sheet showing the end of reel 2 and the beginning of reel 3

2M16*	10.34	""Easy Smack It Up""
c2:15:10:20		MUSIC IN: At cut to int. Pressman Hotel
c2:15:21:00		MUSIC OUT:At cut to silver dinner cart
Source		(Headphone Source - Hive)
2M16B*	32.83	""Splendid""
c2:15:10:20		MUSIC IN: At cut to int. restauraunt
c2:15:43:14		MUSIC OUT:At cut to ext. bar
Source		(Restaurant Source)
2M17	1:16.18	"Fight At Bar"
c2:16:44:25		MUSIC IN: As Tyler punches Jack
c2:18:00:28		-thru drinking
Background Instrumental		MUSIC OUT:At cut to shower
2M18	2:06.69	"Medulla Oblongata"
c2:18:46:24		MUSIC IN: At ext. Lou's Tavern
c2:20:53:11		-thru bathroom
Background Instrumental		-thru 2nd fight
		-thru Tyler on bike
		MUSIC OUT:Tail out at Jack in office
REEL 3 (11 Starts)		
3M19	1:31.96	"Ozzie & Harriet"
c3:01:06:07		MUSIC IN: PreLap cut to Tyler and Jack in kitchen
c3:02:38:03		-thru fight
Background Instrumental		- thru Jack walking
		- thru talk with Irvin
		MUSIC OUT: Tail out at Walter says "I showed this already to my man here."
3M20*	1:16.01	"Goin' Out West"
c3:02:09:00		MUSIC IN:PreLap cut to Lou's Bar
c3:03:24:28		MUSIC OUT:Tail out at bottom of stairs
Source		Tom Waitts

The cue numbers should also be used when labelling master tapes, mixes, scores, and parts for any players. These numbers will keep you organized and also let you know if a particular cue comes before or after any other cue, which makes finding it easier.

Figure 2.11a-c Tape label, a score, and a part all carefully labelled

Using this numbering system keeps things organized in a way which virtually all post production people are familiar. The titles for cues are only used by the performing rights societies, so you need to come up with something. You are not obligated to use the titles for soundtrack albums or any other use unless you wish to.

Sync Up
When Your Music is Married to Film

The technology of moving images has changed very slowly over the last 100 or so years. The same celluloid strip of film with little sprocket holes has remained the medium of choice for an entire century. With the advent of television came the creation of analog video tape, a less expensive and much easier to handle medium. Analogue video tape is used throughout the production and post production of a significant number of film and television projects. Digital tape and direct-to-disk forms of video also have a place in the process of creating and producing motion pictures. Virtually all films and television programming are edited digitally on non-linear hard disk systems such as Avid, but tape is still used for distribution to other post production people such as sound and music editors and you the composer. Hopefully this will change, which will simplify things.

SMPTE Timecode

With video tape comes the need to lock together audio (tape or hard disk), video (analogue or digital), and your sequencer. This is in order to synchronize the picture and sound with the music you are composing. The standard system for machine synchronization is called SMPTE timecode and was created in the early 1960s in the US for the then-fledgling TV industry. SMPTE timecode gives each frame of a video a unique, sequential number in the format HH:MM:SS:FF (Hours, Minutes, Seconds, Frames). Developed by the Society of Motion Picture and Television Engineers, a technical group, SMPTE timecode is a machine generated audio track that can be "read" by compatible devices to indicate the position and speed of a tape. The receiving machine then regulates its tape (or disk playback) to run at the same speed and location as the timecode sender. Thus you have two or more devices running in perfect synchronization, making them function as though they were a single device. In most synchronizing setups, one device functions as a "master," sending out timecode to all the other devices in the system by cables, which read that code and function as "slaves" to it. It's a relatively simple method to work with that has been in use for some time. It will, however, phase out slowly as digital media technology becomes more common in all facets of music and motion picture production.

When you are asked to put music to picture, you will most likely be given a videotape of the final (or nearly final) edited version with a SMPTE timecode track on one of the audio channels. You'll need a decent stereo VCR to play the tape back. Professional 3/4" tape machines have the advantage of including a special third audio channel exclusively for timecode, allowing you to have stereo audio for listening to dialogue and effects. The channel with the timecode is patched to whatever device you use to synchronize your sequencer. Most every computer-MIDI interface comes with SMPTE timecode reading capabilities. You cannot put your own timecode onto a videotape as part of any film or video production. Your timecode numbers will not match the numbers everyone else is using, and you will get yourself into trouble.

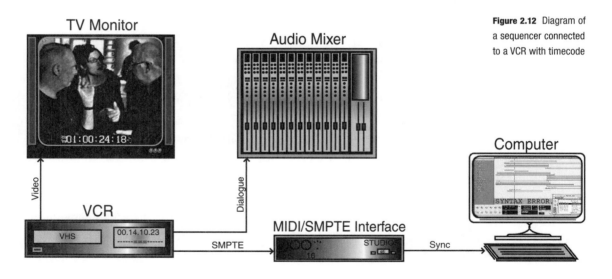

Figure 2.12 Diagram of a sequencer connected to a VCR with timecode

SMPTE timecode comes in a few different formats. Some projects use a format called *drop frame* (sometimes labeled as "df") while others are done in a *nondrop frame* (labeled as "ndf" or "nd"). You should check with the production company or transfer company that created the tape you are working with to be certain. MIDI sequencers and digital audio workstations need you to specify the format of SMPTE timecode to which you will be synchronizing. Set it wrong and your music may not sync up with everything else by the end of the post production process. If you live in America (North or South), Asia, or a few other assorted continents, the timecode found on a videotape is running at 29.97 frames per second. There are no exceptions. Even if the tape is labeled "30 fps" it really is still 29.97. Europe typically works at 25 frames per second. The video and timecode there is not SMPTE-based. It is another, noncompatible standard called *PAL*.

Film runs at 24 frames per second, but when transferred to videotape for postproduction the frame rate is changed, though the speed and duration of the film are left unchanged. Feature films are, with virtually no exception, transferred to video with 29.97 nondrop frame SMPTE timecode, while projects headed to television are virtually always post produced using drop frame timecode. Again, it's very important for you to check with the people making your videotapes, and confirm what timecode format is being used.

Once you've set up your system and you have a video with timecode to work with, you're ready to start composing your score with your sequencer slaved to your VCR. Each cue you write will have a Start Time, sometimes called an *Offset*, which will tell the sequencer exactly where in the film the cue will begin. With your loyal sequencer flawlessly slaved to the tape you can do all your scoring while watching picture, which was not easily done before MIDI and SMPTE devices became available. This means that you can write music that flows carefully to the picture, which is one of the goals in film scoring. However, it's a good idea to give the video a rest from time to time and just write some good music. This helps keep an organic feel to the music, so it doesn't simply become a slave to the picture. After you've gotten some musical ideas into your computer, set your sequencer to lock to the tape again and see how it fits the scene. Make your fixes and try it again. This is a simple and elegant way of working, made possible by some readily available technology. Digital video does it all better, and it will be discussed in greater length later in this section.

Delivering Your Final Mixes

When you deliver your music mixes back to the project's production company or your music editor, there are some variables that you need to take into account. Before you prepare to record your music, you should always talk with the people to whom you will be giving your music in order to ensure it is mixed in a format they're able to deal with. Digital multitrack recorders such as the DA-88 and digital audio workstations such as ProTools have become very popular ways to deliver music for film and TV. When mixing your music, you need to deliver mixes with 2 or more tracks along with the SMPTE timecode needed to synchronize to the picture in their facilities. When working with tape, the timecode is normally prestriped onto the tape, and then used to synchronize the sequencer to the tape's timecode. For an hour long television show, timecode for the entire hour is striped onto a single multitrack tape. With the sequencer slaved to the tape machine, music is mixed onto the points of the tape where the cues belong. The time between the cues is left blank. All the current tape and disk-based systems make this process relatively simple and pain free.

Mixing for feature films is no different, except that there will typically be more music for a longer movie format. As mentioned above, feature films are broken down into some number of reels. There is a convention used in films in regard to the hour number of the timecode in which the hour of the timecode is the same as the reel number, which makes it easier to navigate through the many tapes you may be working with. For example, a cue that starts a minute and a half into the third reel of the film would have a start time of 03:01:30:00. TV shows normally use a SMPTE hour of 01 for the whole project.

The Etiquette of Reel Changes

Speaking of film reels, it is usually required that the music never crosses between the reels due to the problems associated with shipping films to theatres in separate reels. The music should stop a second or so before the end of the reel, and not start for several frames after the first frame of the next reel. This avoids the possibility of an audible glitch where one reel ends and the next begins. This isn't a problem with some digital formats, but as long as films are still made in non-digital formats and shipped in reels, there is still a need to be careful about not scoring across reel changes. If you are uncertain about a piece of music that might need to cross over a reel change, check with the production people first. In some cases, if it is critical to the music, a scene at the very beginning or end of a reel can be moved to the adjacent reel so a cue can go uninterrupted. This is called *rebalancing the reel.*

If a film is broken down into the smaller ten-minute reels, then there is an added consideration. The reels will eventually be joined up in pairs. Reel one and two will be linked, three with four, etc. And therefor you may write a cue across a reel change provided it is from an odd numbered to an even numbered reel, and never the other way around. Make sense? As long as the cue extends across reels that will eventually be connected, such as reel 1 (odd number) to reel 2 (even number), you are OK. The music will not get chopped. You must avoid going from any even to odd reels, instead leaving sufficient silence at the very beginning and end of those reels. In the appendix you will find the calculations you need in order to write across an acceptable reel change.

I've had projects come in with the timecode misapplied, and I've also been the recipient of wrong information by the editors. Transfer houses, which are the companies that convert film to video or duplicate video tape and are responsible for printing timecode, are known for getting things wrong more often than they should. It's really important to check and double check the information if you're the least bit unsure.

Keep this in mind and you may well be on your way to delivering a perfect master tape each and every time. Ignore it and there could be a price to pay. There is less to worry about with digital audio workstations, since they don't need timecode printed on a track. They are 'virtual' systems that synchronize easily and can adapt to any type of timecode automatically.

✪ You can find *Synchronization from Reel To Reel* in music stores, technical book shops, and specialty book stores, or via www. reelworld-online.com.

If you want to learn more fascinating facts about timecode (and how to avoid getting fired over it), let me recommend at least one good book: *Synchronization from Reel to Reel*. I wrote this book to explain in much greater depth all the details that you need to know for working in your own home studio. It goes into far greater detail about all aspects of synchronization for video, film, and audio.

CHAPTER SEVEN

> Recording the Score

Working with Actual (Not Virtual) Musicians

O nce a score is written and approved, it is time to get some musicians to actually play it for you. This can be the most enjoyable, fun part of the process if you are prepared and have a good group to play for you (more about that in Section Three). I've recorded scores with anywhere from one to eighty players. Most of the small ensembles are recorded in my personal studio and the larger ones at various local studios in Los Angeles, where I work, and where most film scores are recorded. I've also recorded in other cities on occasion.

I use a *music contractor*, which is someone who specializes in putting together ensembles for recording scores. I also have certain engineers I work with who help me get the best possible sound from the group and the studio. While I am recording musicians, I am the producer, and although I am more than capable of handling many engineering chores, it is much better if I focus all my concentration on the music and the players, and not on the technology. I can enjoy working the controls with one or two players, but after that, there's just too much too think about. So on smaller projects or overdubs of soloists I just bring the players to my personal studio and record them myself. I like the intimacy of recording this way. There's no clock ticking, and I can work the way I like working best. Before starting to record your score, a number of decisions need to be made: who to have play, where to get the best sound, what gear will be involved, recording to tape or disk, in what order to record the players and cues, etc. With some practice you can learn to work efficiently and to make a reasonable estimate as to how long it takes to record each part of your score.

The *White Squall* Recording Sessions

On the score I wrote for the film *White Squall* I was, for various reasons, asked to record all the musicians in London. You would think that having the London Symphony record your music would be an absolute dream, and it is. But in reality there were also some logistical drawbacks. Recording in London cut nearly a week out of my already compressed—and panic inducing—three-week composing schedule. Preparing for the trip, sending all my synth gear (which takes several days even by the fastest means) and thus having nothing to write with, and losing a couple days with my own travel, was time I could really have used for writing and revising. However, working nearly around the clock, I finished the last cue one day early. I made preparations to send all the tapes and gear to the studio in London. One advantage to recording your scores locally is that you can spread the sessions out over several days, with composing and fixing days in between. This is a common thing to do on larger scores.

Keeping the Musicians in Time

When recording a live ensemble at another studio, you will need to record a scratch mix of your demo score along with the metronome clicks (on a separate track) from your sequencer as a reference for the musicians. At the recording session, you will need to send the metronome click into the musicians' headphones for them to play along with. The clicks are created by your MIDI sequencer and recorded onto the tape or hard disk system that is played for the orchestra. The same recording also holds synth parts and any synth orchestra that you may want them to hear for demo purposes. Some composers have two clicks tracks at the recording session. One with the normal quarter note click, and a second track with double speed click. On slower cues, if the orchestra feels out of time with the standard click, then the eighth note click may solve the problem.

The clicks should be recorded with as short and dry a sound as possible. Hi hats, snare drums, and rim shots are not the best choice. For many years the standard sound used at all orchestral recordings was from a special film scoring metronome from the Urei company. It is easily heard, and it cuts well through just about any mix. A sample of that type of click can be found online. You can use it in most any sampler.

Find a metronome click sample on line at www.reelworld-online.com

Prior to the start of each cue, there needs to be some number of count-off clicks, called *warning clicks*. There should be two bars of warning clicks at the tempo and meter of the first bar of the cue. For example, a cue in 4/4 will normally have eight warning clicks. If the tempo is fairly slow, one bar of clicks should be sufficient. The number of warning clicks should be printed at the top of the score and musicians parts, and the conductor should remind the players of the clicks just prior to the start of each cue.

While the cue is being recorded, it can sometimes be helpful for the engineer to manually raise and lower the level of the click for the musician's headphone so that it can be heard clearly in loud sections, but not bleed into the microphones in the quieter parts. Also, if any musicians do not play on a cue and be given a break, always remind them to unplug their headphones to prevent leakage into the microphones. Some engineers EQ the click to have less treble, which makes the click less likely to leak from headphones into the microphones.

Making the Transition from Home Studio to Pro Studio

If you will also be mixing your score away from your studio, you'll need to record all the synth parts onto multitrack tape or hard disk. When recording orchestra to tape, I put scratch mixes of each cue onto another multitrack tape along with the SMPTE timecode and clicks. This tape, called the *slave reel* is for recording the orchestra and soloists, while giving the players a reference to listen to. Although they don't use SMPTE timecode in the UK or Europe, opting instead for 25-frame EBU code, all the gear there accepts American SMPTE timecode just fine. It is best to not try to convert it. You don't want to change anything from the way you have it in your writing room, in case you need to make musical changes and need to sync your sequencer to the tapes. You can use the same NTSC-based video-tapes anywhere you go. I find it interesting that almost every video machine and monitor in the UK is "multistandard," that is they can play back NTSC, PAL, and SECAM tapes. No such thing readily exists in the US because nobody here feels the need to be able to easily accept tapes from abroad (not that we're geo/ethno-centric here or anything). When I've recorded in the UK, the video and audio tapes have all come through customs fine and everything has worked perfectly. Although one time my music editor, who accompanied me on the flight from LA, was detained at emigration for over an hour while they searched through all the tapes, and I feared they weren't going to admit him (he's a bit shady looking). Finally, they decided he was probably harmless and let him through.

On my *White Squall* recording trip, after one day to readjust by biological clock, we did our first recording. It was a long day devoted to a number of soloist's overdubs. I decided to record them one by one, which is very tedious work indeed, but the only way to give the mix engineer full control over the blend. It saves time in the long run to not have to rerecord a take with a full orchestra just because you are not completely happy with a soloist. I also like to be able to get a few takes of any given solo and then cut together the best parts of each in ProTools or my sequencer's digital audio tracks, something that you can't do if there is any bleedover between the soloist and the orchestra.

One real joy of going to London was that the studio was perhaps the best I've ever seen, let alone used. Air Studios Lyndhurst (**www.airstudios.com**) is a former Victorian church in the northern part of London that was converted into an absolutely beautiful sounding studio. Actually, it's two full studios and a number of smaller mixing and post production rooms, all owned by George Martin, the fellow who produced Paul McCartney's "old band." We recorded the soloists in the smaller room and then the orchestra in what they call "the hall," the massive main room of the church. I recommend always checking out the studios you plan to use before you book time in them. I've come across studios that were too small, or not as well equipped as I had been originally told. Especially when you are bringing a number of players, you can't afford to waste a moment of time. Such was certainly not the case here at Air, but has been the case in other places.

On this project I couldn't bring my engineer from LA, so I hired London-ite Haydn Bendell, a local engineer who came highly recommended and was familiar with the studio. Kate Bush fans know his work well. He was a pleasure to work with and had a great ear for what I was trying to do. He was no stranger to experimentation and gave me ample room to try ideas or forget them.

Recording the Orchestra

As I mentioned before, the first sessions were to record the soloists: harp, percussion, oboe, clarinet, sax, trumpet (who I later found out played the trumpet solo on the Beatles' "Penny Lane"!), and Uillean pipes (an Irish, not Scottish bagpipe). I had already recorded myself playing all the flutes and pennywhistles back in the US. A few of my ideas didn't work, and I either changed them or simply tossed them out. A couple of the bagpipe parts had some notes that he couldn't play, which was my fault. I fixed them as best I could but knew that I'd probably have to go back and keep some of the samples on a couple of cues. By the end of the day, we were several hours behind. Sometimes I had two musicians out in the hall waiting to play. I hate keeping people waiting, and if we went into overtime it would cost money not in the budget. About twelve hours later we finally finished, about 2 hours overtime. Not a tragedy. The musicians were brilliant and the tracks were all great. I was happy.

Recording musicians, either one at a time or in groups, takes planning. You want the session to go smoothly. Good players are patient, but play better if they don't have to wait around for technical or logistical problems to be fixed. Make sure that the mics are set up properly and there is a good headphone mix before your players arrive. Be prepared to give them a click track that is adjustable separately from the rest of the music they will be hearing. Some players, especially drummers and percussionists, often ask for unbelievable levels of click, so be prepared. With soloists, it's good to have several tracks available for them to record different takes. I like to get a few takes and pick my favorites later, when there is the time to listen more carefully. This is one great reason for using a hard disk system instead of tape—you have nearly unlimited tracks for the players. But if you need to use tape, just be ready to spare a few extra tracks. You can always erase the bad takes if you need more tracks for other things.

The next day was the big one—the London Symphony Orchestra string section, 45 players in all. If you have one musician go overtime it's not such a big deal, but if you run out of time with a full orchestra (a full orchestra can be over 80 players), you have a serious problem. They had booked the absolute minimum time we could have with the players, so there was little opportunity to make changes on the stand or for any copying errors. Ridley Scott, the film's director, and his producer came to attend. If either of them wanted changes, it was my obligation to stop and deal with them, which could have been time consuming. Although I enjoy conducting my scores, I decided to stay in the control room with the director and allowed someone else to conduct the orchestra. I think this is important. That was the time for me to listen carefully and be certain everything was sounding as I desired. I also could explain what was happening to the director and get his feedback. The conductor I hired came to the previous day's recording, had heard all my synth demos, and had received copies of all the scores in time to study. By the time of the session, he probably knew them better than I did. The musicians already knew the conductor well and respected him, which probably meant they would play better.

Making Repairs

Sitting and listening to one's music played by a top-rate orchestra is an epiphany and a real blast. This was the payoff of all the blood and sweat. As far as I was concerned, at that moment, we didn't need to press the Record button: Just let me listen. Fortunately, they did record it. Along the way, many things didn't work for me musically. I made a few changes as needed, though not complicated ones. Sometimes I would shift a line up an octave to bring it out, take a line out that was getting in the way of dialogue or a main melody, modify dynamics or articulations with the players and the like. It's so important to be flexible at a score recording. If something doesn't work, you have to either fix it or get rid of it. There is no shame in making any needed changes at the recording session, as long as they don't push you into costly overtime. In fact you should try to budget your time so that you only expect to record between five and ten minutes of score per hour. This seems to work well in most cases. A simpler score might be about to churn out ten to fifteen minutes an hour, but it is best to leave time for changes, fixes, technical problems, rehearsals, and flubs. If you are working on a package deal—meaning you are responsible for costs—then a small mistake with an orchestral session can cost you dearly. However, if a director asks for changes that take large amounts of time and put you into overtime, that is the director's choice, and the production company will be expected to pay for the extra time. Generally, orchestral recordings are not paid from the composer's package, but a reasonable budget is agreed to.

At one point in my recording, the director asked for one cue to start about twenty seconds earlier. That's a bit more of a major change. I wasn't sure if there was another cue in the same key that could be edited onto the top of the cue easily. So I found a section of the cue that could be reused as an introduction, and it was just the right length. My orchestrator was at the session and he quickly reworked it for the new cue. A copyist was also present in the next room (he was still copying the cues that would be recorded later in the afternoon) and he quickly did the parts. Within five minutes we had a new cue that could be edited onto the beginning of the original cue later on by the music editor.

Tracking Completed

With many of the more difficult cues completed to everyone's satisfaction, the orchestra broke for lunch. I had been warned that in London you should always record the most difficult music in the morning, because most of the players will go to the local pub for lunch and enjoy many of the finer pleasures life offers (in pint glasses). When they return to the afternoon session they play with great emotion, but with slightly diminished technical capacity. In general, it seems wise to record the more complicated cues first when everyone is fresh and alert. My afternoon session sounded great, though fast runs were not executed with the same ease as the morning, but they got the idea across. We worked hard to get through the rest of the score. We barely had scheduled enough time, and we were indeed running out. A few cues were a bit less well performed as I had hoped, but I knew that I could make some fixes in the mix by blending back in some of my samples. We still had several cues to go. Thankfully, a couple of easy cues were knocked out in single takes, and the performances were excellent. I had a couple of "if there's time" cues I had written, but I abandoned them. They would be synth and samples only, but they were very small cues. We got to the last cue of the day with only minutes to go. The first take was bad, and I stopped the recording before the end. We did it again two more times and finally got a good take. I looked up at the clock. We finished with exactly 90 seconds to spare! We got what we wanted! Producer and director, both very pleased with the music and the lack of overtime, shook my hand and were gone. I collapsed, nearly exhausted. That night we went out and had one hell of a celebratory dinner. It was the first time since arriving that I had a chance to see the city outside of the studio and my hotel room. Nice place, London.

Other scores I've worked on since then have not had the kind of tight schedule and budget of that one, but I think it's a good learning experience to work under those nerve-wracking kinds of limits. With bigger scores, you should be given adequate studio time. But most smaller sessions will be on a package, and that means you are responsible for any and all cost overruns, unless they are caused by the producers or director. You need to learn how to make everything at your recording sessions move smoothly and efficiently. It takes practice and careful planning. Another way to save costs is to record the cues first which use the entire ensemble you've orchestrated for, and save for later those pieces that have a smaller group. That way you can dismiss those players no longer needed and you only need pay for the players remaining. For example, if you have several cues that don't call for brass or winds, record all the brass and wind cues first and let those people go home. Your orchestrator and contractor can help you to organize these details, usually by making a sort of spreadsheet that lists what instruments play on each cue. Here is an example on the right.

Editing and Mixing *White Squall*

The day after the *White Squall* recording sessions were done, we began what was to become five days of music mixing. We mixed upstairs at Air Studios. They have a couple of special mix rooms which have no acoustic space but lots of great audio gear. A typical day went from 10AM until about 12AM, with the last day going to 3AM. Before starting to mix each cue, I'd play my original synth demo for the engineer. This gave him a very close idea of how I originally heard the music. Then I would stay out of the room for a while and let him do his thing without any of my annoying interruptions. When he felt he was close, he would bring me in to listen and suggest any changes. This worked well, and gave me a chance to learn about British television in the adjacent studio lounge. Haydn often would come up with some cool mix ideas that I'd never think of, many of which stayed in the soundtrack collaboration.

Film scores are mixed onto more than just a stereo track. This is not just because of the available surround sound formats used in movie theatres. Film music is mixed onto several sets of tracks that will allow some fine-tuning of the music mix during the final dub (see Fig. 2.16). As you are mixing your music, you don't really know how it will sound when played along with the final dialogue and effects at the dub stage. So music is mixed into several small groups, called *stems* (more on this later). But it is important to know that in order to mix film music, you will need some kind of multitrack recorder with timecode capabilities for synchronization. While composing and tracking your score, there is no real need for extensive surround monitoring. Good nearfield monitors are sufficient. Mixing is another story. You should be mixing in an environment that lets you hear the full range of larger theatrical speakers, and so a subwoofer is often used. For television mixing, a smaller monitoring setup is still adequate, though with home theatre and digital broadcast, the differences are getting smaller.

On *White Squall* we mixed to seven tracks of a digital 8-track tape machine. Tracks 1, 2, and 3 were the Left, Centre (note the appropriate Brit spelling) and Right (also called an *LCR mix*) of the orchestra and synths, with most of the bass in the Centre channel. Tracks 4 and 5 were stereo percussion, and 6 and 7 were for the soloists, also in stereo. Each stem had it's own effects, which meant we

Figure 2.13 Chart showing which players perform on each cue

CUE	ORCH	TIME	TITLE	Vln	Vla	Vc	Bs	Fl 1	Fl 2	Fl 3	Ob 1	Ob 2	Cl 1	Cl 2	Bn 1	Bn 2	Bn 3	Bn 4	Flg Hn	Euph	Hns	Tpt	Tbn	Tba	Harp	Dello	Perc	Orch
1m0	B	02:50	Opening	24	12	10	6	Fl	Fl	Pic	Ob	Ob	Cl	Cl	CB	CB	CB	CB							2			YSM
1m0 v2				32	16	24	8	Fl	Pic	Pic	Ob	Ob	Cl	Cl	CB	CB	CB	CB										BF
1m0 11/12				32	16	24	8	Fl	Pic	Pic	Ob	Ob	Cl	Cl	CB	CB	CB	CB							2			BF
1m2	A	03:05	Children Swimming	24	16	24	8	Pic	Pic	AF										Euph		2	4	2	2			LM
1m2	B	03:05	Children Swimming	24	12	10		F/AF	F/AF/BF	F/BF			Cl												2			LM
1m5	A	01:30	Witt w/Melanesians	24					Fl	BF/F															2			LM
1m6	B	01:36	Witt w/Melanesians	24	12	10	6	Fl	Fl	AF	Ob	O/EH	Cl		Bn	Bn	Bn	Bn		Euph	6	1	4	2	1			BF
1m6 v3				32	16	24		Fl	Fl	Fl		Ob	Cl	Cl	Bn	Bn	Bn	Bn		Euph	6		4	2	2			BF
1m6HZ	B			24	16	24	6					Ob	Cl	Cl	Bn	Bn					6				2			WF
2m8	B	03:27	Witt In ????	24	12	10	6				BH	BH	Cl	Cl	Bn	Bn									2			WF
2m8 v2				32	16	24	8	F/AF	F/BF	P/BF	Ob	BH	C/BC	C/EbCBC	Bn	CB	CB	CB		Euph	6		4	2	2			BF/YSM
2m9	A	05:07	Tall & Quinlund 1	24	12	10	6	F/AF		Fl	Ob		Cl	Cl	Bn	Bn	Bn	Bn		Euph	6		4	2	2			YSM
3m11	B	01:57	Staros Below Deck	24	16	24	8	Fl	Fl	Pic	Ob	O/EH	Cl	Cl	Bn	CB	CB	CB							2			BF
4m14	A	08:25	March Island	24	16	24	8	Fl	Fl	Fl	Ob		Cl	Cl	Bn	Bn	Bn	Bn		Euph			4	2	2			BF
4m14	B	08:39	March Island	24	12	10	8	Fl	Fl	Pic	Ob	Ob/EH	Cl	Cl	Bn	CB	CB	CB							2			BF
4m14R				32	16	24	8	AF	AF	BF	Ob		Cl	EbCBC	Bn	Bn	Bn	Bn		Euph			4	2	2			LM
5m16	A	02:28	Tall/Staros Orientation	24	16	24	8	Fl	Fl	AF			Cl	Cl	Bn	Bn	Bn	Bn			6	1	4	2	2			BF
6m19	B	00:47	The Grass	24	12	10	6	Fl																				YSM
6m22	A	02:35	Tall Calls Staros 1		16	24	6		Pic		Ob	Ob	BC	BC	Bn	Bn	CB	CB			6							YSM
7m23	B			24	16	24	8	Fl	Fl	Fl	Ob	BH	Cl	Cl	Bn	Bn	Bn	Bn								1	1	LM
8m25	A	Perc only																								1	1	LM
8m25				24	16	24	8	Fl	Fl	Fl	Ob		Cl	Cl	Bn	Bn	Bn	Bn							2			LM
8m26	A	08:11	B??? Dies	24	16	24	8	AF/F	F/FI	Fl	Ob	BH	C/BC	BC	Bn	Bn	Bn	Bn		Euph	4		4	2	2			BF/YSM
8m26R				32	16	24	8	FI/AF	P/FI	Pic	Ob	BH	Cl/BC	BC	Bn	Bn	Bn	Bn		Euph	4		4	2	2			BF/YSM
8m26R2				32	16	24	8	AF	P/FI	Pic		BH	C/BC	BC	Bn	Bn	Bn	Bn		Euph	4		4	2	2			
8m26R2 New Insert																												
9m29	B			24+Solo	16	24+Solo	8	Fl	Fl	BF	Ob	Ob	Cl	BC	Bn	Bn	B/CB	B/CB	2 Fg	Euph	6		2						WF
9m29A	B				16	24	8									Bn												BF
9m30	A	03:43	Tall & Staros	24	16	24	8	Fl	BF/AF	BF/F	Ob	BH	Cl	Cl	Bn	Bn	CB	CB		Euph	6		4	2	2			YSM
9m34 Bird	B		Bird	24	16	24	8	Fl	Fl	AF/BF															2			LM
9m34 Bird	A		Bird	24+Solo	16	24	8	Fl	Fl	Fl	Ob		Cl		Bn	Bn					4			1	2			LM
9m34 BRD v2	B			24	16	24	8			AF										Euph	6			2	2			BF
9m34 God	A		God	24+Solo	16	24	8	Fl	Fl	Fl	Ob	BH	Eb/Cl	Cl	Bn													LM
9m34 God	B		God	24	16	24	8	Fl	Fl	Fl	Ob				Bn										2			LM
9m34 God 11/12				32+Solo	16	24	8	Fl	Fl	Fl															2			LM
9m34v2	B			24	16																							
10m31	B			24		24		Fl	Fl	Pic	Ob		Cl		Bn	Bn	Bn	CB							2		√	BF
11m33	B			24	16	24	8	Pic	Fl	AF	Ob		Cl		Bn	Bn	Bn	Bn							2			BF
11m33 v2				24	16	24		Fl	Fl	Pic	Ob	BH	Cl	BC	Bn	Bn	Bn	Bn	Fg	Euph		2			1			BF
13m39	A	07:55	Attack On ?????	24	16	24	8	Fl	Fl	F/P	Ob	BH	Cl	Cl	Bn	Bn	Bn	CB		Euph	6	2	4	2				BF
13m39	B	07:55	Attack On ?????	24	16	24	8	Fl	Fl	F/P	Ob	BH	Cl	Cl	Bn	Bn	Bn	Bn	Flug	Euph	6	2	4	2	2			EF/BF
13m39 R1				32	16	24	8	Fl	Fl	Pic	Ob	BH	Cl	Cl	Bn	Bn	Bn		Flug	Euph	6	2	4	2	1			BF
13m39 R2				32			8	Fl	Fl	Pic	Ob	BH	Cl	Cl	Bn	Bn	Bn		Flug	Euph	6		4	2				EF
13m39 R3				32	16	24	8	Fl	Fl	Pic	Ob	BH	Cl	Cl	Bn	Bn	Bn		Flug	Euph	6		4	2				BF
13m41	B/A			24	16	24	8	Fl	Fl	Pic	Ob	BH	Cl	Cl	Bn	Bn	Bn											BF

needed three of everything we used while mixing the score. This multitrack mix gave the dubbing engineers (the people who mix the dialogue, music, and effects for the actual film soundtrack) control over the elements we provided. Because the film was being mixed in Dolby Digital format (DDS), they wanted us to provide them with separate tracks for the stereo surround speakers as well as the sub woofer channel. We discussed doing this, but opted to leave it simple and let them move the music into the surrounds as they saw fit. This was a relatively simple mix. Other mixes I've done have been far more complex and extensive, with more stems, and more LCR mixes.

The number of tracks to mix onto, and how to split out different parts is a decision that changes on each project. Some dubbing mixers want as many *splits* (another term for stems) as they can get. Some mixes I've done have taken up as many as 32 tracks. Some have been as little as just 2, but most have been between 8 and 16. Any part that might need special handling or might be viewed as controversial is best kept separate from other stems.

For many of my mixes I set up my computer, sequencer, MIDI interface, and a sampler in the studio control room in the event I want to do any touchups as I mix. I have SMPTE timecode sent from the master tape or audio workstation to my computer so I can run the original MIDI sequences along with the recording of the orchestra. One thing I love is having rhythmic delays on percussion and other parts of my music. I then can send MIDI Clock from my sequencer to an effects unit to set the exact tempo of a stereo DDL (Digital Delay) in the studio. This way I can set it once and forget it. In London we occasionally found synth tracks that were in need of some last minute tweaking. I was able to sequence in new parts or edit the existing ones and make fixes on the spot. I requantized and slipped several parts in order to better fit them with the timing of the orchestra and other players. You can't expect live players to sound like a sequencer, in fact you don't want them to. When you get a good, expressive performance of a line that has to match a synth part, go back and adjust the synth part if needed. A few cues had spots that I thought needed a bit more polish. I recorded a couple of new parts with the synths I brought to the studio. Having sequences available during a mix can be a life saver, and worth the hassle of getting and setting up some gear in the studio. It's also very simple to record any fixed tracks in your studio to digital audio and bring only those new tracks back to the studio for inclusion on the mix.

On numerous scores, I've brought in wonderful players to do some improvisations on some of my cues. By getting a few different takes for a particular solo

I can try the piece several different ways. I will fine tune and tweak those solos until I am happy. With written solos, I will get a few good takes and then pick my favorite phrases from each. During the *White Squall* mixes, while my engineer was working on another cue, I took all the takes with soloists, a scratch mix of the music and a click and put them into a ProTools system we had upstairs at the studio. There I assembled the final versions of the solos from my favorite parts of each take. I love working this way. It allows both the player and myself to be experimental and creative, and not be concerned with one "perfect take." I was very pleased with the results. I took the final edited solos back onto the master multitrack back downstairs. Hard disk recording, both within my MIDI/audio sequencer, and then in ProTools when mixing, are fantastic in that they provide the tools to carefully improve the sonic and musical quality of everything I do. I have come to rely on it for virtually everything I did.

On to the Dub Stage

When a music mix is completed (and a bottle of champagne dispensed) the music is delivered to the dub stage. The dialogue and sound effects editors will have compiled all their work onto dozens of other tracks. You need to prearrange with the sound supervisor exactly how the music is to be delivered—analogue tape, digital tape (which format), or hard disk-based workstation. In the case of the latter, all kinds of last minute tweaks can be made, which can often times save a cue if the director is having any second thoughts. I've made a great many changes right there on the dub stage that would have been impossible any other way. Cues can get longer or shorter and melodic entrances can be delayed or brought forward in a relatively musical fashion. Having multiple music stems comes in very handy for editing. You can stagger edits to make them much less apparent. Delivering music to the dub via hard disk has become common, and for good reason. Your music editor will be able to make last second changes on the stage. In fact, you as a composer have less need to be at a dub session as the music editor (if there is one on the film) until later in the mix. And as hard as it can be, it is best to keep an open mind when the mixers experiment with your music in ways you may disagree. Dub sessions can be very political, tenuous events. I've found that it's OK to speak your mind to the person in charge, usually the director, and let them make the final choice. If there is time for experimentation, then ask to try out an edit or a change in levels, otherwise just let the process flow as best as possible.

I've learned a lot about film music during dub mixes. Things can sound and feel so different than in your own studio. I've learned about keeping music simple in order to have maximum musical and sonic impact. Too much "stuff" in an arrangement or orchestration is lost by the time it is blended with sound effects and dialogue and lowered to its final (and often very low) level. Cues with too many small parts, rhythms or counter lines will seem to vanish or turn to mush. It's better to have as few elements as needed to get your musical point across, and make sure that each of those ideas really counts and has full impact. Many ideas that work well within the context of my room don't cut through a dense film mix. In the real work of a film soundtrack, usually all you hear at the end are the main elements, your primary colours. Think of this as musical conservation of sorts.

As for *White Squall*, the first major studio film of my career, the film opened to mixed reviews from the press and came out at the same time as some real blockbusters. It was not a box office success in the US and only did well in a handful of countries. My only satisfaction came from the work itself, what I learned, having a great opportunity to write some interesting music, hear it played by brilliant musicians in a great studio, work with Ridley Scott, one of my personal favorite film directors, and know that he was happy with my work. It was an honor, an adventure, a lesson, a thrill, a grind, and a stepping stone for the future. Had the film been a success, the phone would probably have started ringing right away. But it has been a great addition to my resume, and the music has been licensed and reused numerous times for television logos and was featured in the Olympics. That made me quite happy.

Samples Run Through It

Creating Samples & Loops for Mark Isham

Mark Isham's music, from his first score to *Never Cry Wolf* to his music for director Alan Rudolph's films and his Oscar-nominated score for *A River Runs Through It,* has defined a genre of liquid, minimalist film music. At once both ambient and jazzy, Isham has the ability to communicate a great deal within the confines of very few notes. He has also proven himself quite innovative in both the worlds of electronics and the traditional film orchestra. He is unique. When I was working as a synthesizer programmer and sample jockey I was very excited when he called me to work with him.

The first project was called *Fire In The Sky*, based on a (supposedly) true story about a Midwestern man who is briefly abducted by a UFO and how the experience impacts his life from then on (hint: no longer fun at parties). The majority of the score was for a fairly standard film orchestra. But an 18 minute sequence of a flashback of the encounter with some aliens and the nasty medical experiments they perform on him (not for people squeamish about their eyes) called for a unique and heavily electronic palette. I did almost all of my work for the film right at home and gave the results to Mark early enough so that he could experiment and compose with them at his home. No studio work here.

I put together a group of odd percussion instruments for Isham's samplers made from banging together bits of metal and glass in a reverberant hall and then radically retuning the results. I also took some truly odd sounding bowed piano sounds from a sampling CD and put together programs that would have them pitch bend in a couple of interesting ways. One was to double the program so each sound plays twice, one version with no pitch bend sensitivity and the other with some. Thus, as he played the sound and moved the pitch wheel of his synth, the sound would detune with itself in various amounts. I've used this trick with other sounds such as voices and strings as well. Another approach to warping the sound is to once again double the sample so it triggers two copies of the sample when you press a key, and then set a pitch envelope to one of the copies so it automatically bends down (or up) whenever played. The result, like the MIDI pitch bend version, produces some very odd effects with both pitched and unpitched sounds. Making the pitch envelope's speed and depth MIDI velocity sensitive will produce unlimited variations to the sound.

I finished all the samples and also created a bank of custom synthesizer textures for Mark's Korg Wavestation which resembled the bowed piano. We then met at his home studio to go through everything. We threw out the sounds he didn't like and made numerous variations on the ones he found more inspiring. He was now ready to sit down and make some music. Mission number one accomplished.

Mark thought of me once again on his next project. "Hey, make me funky!" was the call to arms, not the first thing I'd expect from Isham, but the beginning of a fun project and a chance to use some of the cool drum loops and other hip-hop nasties that I love and collect. The film was a comedy with Whoopi Goldberg and Will Smith.

What made this project the most fun for me was the amount of creative freedom I was given. On two particular cues, Mark wrote a pretty complete frame-

You can visit Mark at his website at www. markisham.com.

work and then told me to add anything I wanted to them. He gave me his scratch mixes, which I loaded into an audio track of my sequencer, which I could use to synchronize my sequences and samples to his music. From there I put together drum loops, a new, very hip synth bass line (in my humble opinion), sampled voices, kalimba, some other African drums and some whacked out, funky noises from my noise collection. I put together a lot of tracks of material—more than was needed—so he could choose the parts he liked. I think it's important to go into a session overly prepared whenever possible. It helps to beat the odds. I made mix demos on which I overlaid my parts with Isham's originals; then, I made a recording of just my new bits. I returned to his studio and played them for him, and he was very happy with everything.

He was recording the final music in the studios at Capitol Records in Hollywood. I recorded all my parts to a small digital recorder and brought it to the studio where they were recording a live rhythm section. I then took the live tracks back home to do final tweaks in order to match his band's grooves with my own. I had to slightly change the tempo of my sequence and retune the drum loops to exactly match the new click. This done, I recorded six tracks of my parts, separating out the drums, bass, percussion, etc., to make it easy for the engineer.

I took the recording back over to Capitol early the next morning. Locking the two machines together, we transferred my parts onto some empty tracks of the master. During the transfer, I heard a couple of things from my tape that did not feel exactly in the groove on the master. Using the offset feature of the synchronizer we could slide them in time until they felt right and then retransfer just those problem tracks. Finally, it all sounded right. You need to be very meticulous with grooves to be extremely precise. I wish all sessions would go this easily (unfortunately, they don't).

In earlier times, session players would cart around racks of gear to every session in order to accommodate any possible situation that might arise. That is rarely the case any more. Programmers and synthesists work from their own studios and can bring the results of their efforts to the session as sound files or digital recordings to be merged with the total project. It's a great way for artists of all kinds to collaborate. With MIDI files and better audio file compression technology available, collaborations via internet have become more common. I have used MP3 file compression on several occasions to send and receive music all over the country and the world. The possibilities are limitless.

Walk like an Egyptian

Working with Exotic Musicians

The Dreamworks animated feature *The Prince Of Egypt* has a score by Hans Zimmer and songs by Stephen Schwartz. The score draws from Middle Eastern musical influences, but is by no means an "ethnic" score. It features a full, standard orchestra, and some very cinematic-style themes, rhythms, and harmonies. I produced all the Middle Eastern recording sessions, which included winds, plucked and bowed strings, and lots of percussion. The charts were very complex, with frequent tempo, key and meter changes, as is often found in music for animation. There was also nearly 90 minutes of music to record.

I first turned to some of the acknowledged experts of Arabic music that I could find in Los Angeles. I learned about the various instruments used in the region both today and from antiquity. I went out and got some Arabic, Persian, and other Eastern and North African folk and classical CDs. As a woodwind player myself, I have a fairly extensive collection of eastern instruments that I play in varying degrees. All of these instruments are limited in their scales and ranges, possibly adding to their charm as well as their authenticity for playing those styles of music. Bringing them into a full blown film score would be a challenge for even a top-notch Middle Eastern musician.

Middle Eastern folk and classical music is almost entirely based around improvisation. There are traditional themes and melodies, but they are meant to be interpreted by the musicians, not played verbatim. Asking a traditional musician to play a new, nonindigenous melody, and to play it exactly as written (assuming they read western notated music at all), is asking a lot. Or so I quickly learned once I brought some authentic master players to the studio.

My initial plan was to load the synth demos of all the film's cues into a ProTools digital audio workstation, allow each player to listen to a theme, commit it to memory, and then perform it in small sections. I would then edit these all together into final performances. Painstaking and slow perhaps, but at least it would have the qualities of an authentic performance while still being accurate to the score. My first sessions were very frustrating. While the quality of musicianship was very high, what I required simply went beyond the scope of what a traditional folk or Eastern classical artist does. I did not want to hire studio players simply to play western instruments.

The final solution was a combination of things. I created some woodwind samples that Zimmer could use with his sequencer. While this made for a number of great sounding passages, it didn't do it for the real critical solos. Samples can't get that great phrasing you hear in a great solo player. For woodwinds, we needed a gifted wind player with a great collection and knowledge of eastern instruments as well as a fantastic sight reader. I ended up performing the majority of solo and ensemble winds. We used flutes and reeds from every part of the world, selecting them for timbre and scale. Because these instruments were unable to perform in many of the keys required by the score, I used a great plug-in called Auto-Tune from AnTares Systems to retune any unplayable notes. In performing the score, I would play all the lines as closely as possible, but if there was a flat or sharp I couldn't hit, I would just play the note closest to it (a painful process to listen to at the sessions) and then go back later to repitch it in the computer. Add to this the fact that most Eastern instruments are not in tune with Western scales, so they sound blatantly out of tune (and they would say the same about us!). By the time the score was done, hundreds of notes had to either be corrected or tuned to the live orchestra, a process that took many days. I was grateful for my tireless assistant engineer who took shifts with me to get all of the tuning and editing done.

The strings and percussion were much easier. Everything was still done straight into ProTools for easy editing. Because there were sampled and quantized percussion in the score to match, I wanted control to tighten the timing of the live drummers within reason, since I didn't want to lose their great sense of timing. I was able to put together a drum ensemble that not only could play fantastic Middle Eastern instruments such as dumbek, daf, tumbek, and others, but they could read music as well! They improvised rhythms based on the demos, and the charts indicated mostly just when to start and stop. The trickiest thing was for them to play on the first bar of a new tempo. It made being rhythmically tight very hard. The solution was to copy two bars of the click, which we had in ProTools, of the new tempo and paste it into the space just prior to the tempo change, something you can only accomplish easily with a hard disk system. This gave the players a two bar count-in to the new tempo, even though it didn't match the music in that spot. The result was flawless tempo changes by the drummers.

The strings consisted mostly of Armenian virtuoso oud player John Belazekian, who also played some mandolins, a tar, and even some violin. The oud is a Middle Eastern version of the lute. Belezekian is both a popular player in a number of Middle Eastern ensembles here in Los Angeles as well as a top call studio player with impeccable sight reading skills. He still requested and took several days to practice some fiendishly difficult parts, which he executed brilliantly.

While there are some beautiful Eastern bowed instruments, such as the komanche, Zimmer specifically asked for a Chinese string instrument called the *erhu*. It is a two string violin-like instrument whose sound is haunting and exquisite. By asking around I found a wonderful chinese player who came in to play on a few cues. It was geographically incorrect to feature the instrument, but it has such a unique, voice-like quality. It provided something wonderful to the score.

Recording folk musicians from other parts of the world involves both knowledge and patience. First you must know what each instrument can and cannot do, and also have a clear sense of the type of music usually played on it. You should also learn about the individual players you plan to have play for you, and what they bring to the session. I will often get together with them and have them teach me how to write for their instruments. In my own scores, I have used a number of brilliant folk and "ethnic" players. I try to create an environment both musically and technically that allows them to do what they do best. Few want written charts, preferring to learn the music by listening to a demo a few times. While they can play themes that I create, I don't expect them to be able to do them the same way each time. It's part of the beauty of the collaboration between different types of music and musicians. I find that by spontaneous recording and careful editing, I can get the best possible performances without making difficult or unreasonable demands on these players. There are also great musicians that I work with who have studied music from other cultures and can perform in these styles without being from that part of the word. I include myself in this category. I have gotten some beautiful performances from these players as well, though there is something unique about working with a musician who grew up in the culture you are exploring musically.

In the final analysis, the main thing is to get your music recorded the best way possible, so it sounds great and reflects the intent of the music. If that requires musicians from other lands, great. If it means working with studio musicians with some knowledge of other types of music, then that is fine as well. The people who went to see *Prince Of Egypt* didn't know that every sound meant to be "Egyptian" was actually a blend of instruments and musicians from a great many countries. They got a listening experience that fit with the mood and style of the story. Film scoring isn't about musicology, but working with knowledgeable and virtuosic players from different parts of the world is a great experience both musically and culturally and can give a score the flavour of far away places.

In the Mix

Beyond Stereo to Surround

As movie theatres made the transition from analogue sound (Dolby Surround and its imitators) to digital sound, the possibilities and requirements of film sound have increased. 5.1, 7.1, DTS, SDDS, Dolby Digital, and other competing surround sound formats have added a greater sense of immersion for the audience and have radically improved the quality and consistency of film soundtracks. They also add to the technical requirements of the soundtrack mix. Theatrical and home surround sound presents soundtrack engineers with the capabilities of placing or moving sound around in space, separating any special low-frequency material (big booms or drones), and placing sounds in different parts of the theatre, in front, to the side, and behind the audience.

As a composer, your main concern is not so much how to mix for a specific surround format, though there are some issues regarding the analogue surround format still used in some television, video tape, and low-budget feature films. More important is that your mixes have sufficient separation of elements to allow for the greatest amount of flexibility on the dub stage. Dub stage engineers highly desire the music spread out over several stems, so they cannot only rebalance, but create an ambience by panning elements into the various available surrounds as they wish.

When mixing to multiple stems—each of which can be stereo (L R), three channel (L C R), or more (L C R and either split or mono surrounds)—you might choose to have stems for orchestra, percussion, choirs and other vocals, soloists, synthesizers, and any other sounds that have the potential to get in the way or be buried by other effects or dialogue. Larger studios that are set up for film score mixing have a larger number of busses on their mixing consoles to send various stems to tape simultaneously. That also means that each stem needs to have its own set of effects devices, such as reverb or delays.

Smaller studios and even personal home studios can still do film mixing, but it will be a little less elegant. Your stems are mixed one at a time, so that the same outboard effects can be used for each without bleedover from stem to stem. These multiple passes are kept in sync by the use of timecode sent from the master multitrack recorder to the sequencer playing the music. In some cases you can even use your sequencer's audio recording capabilities to record your mix stems back into the sequencer itself as it is playing. These tracks can then be copied into a hard disk editor for any final tweaking or to move to the dub stage.

As needed, tracks from the sequencer are muted for each recording pass. For example, only the percussion tracks are played when the percussion stem is recorded, and so on, until the entire cue has been recorded to tape or disk.

Theatre in the Surround

Dolby Surround has been the international standard for analogue 35mm movie theatres. While it has been replaced by the various digital audio formats, it still has a place in movies and television, as mentioned earlier. There are some drawbacks in working with analogue surround sound that the composer and mixer should be aware of. Let's look at how it works and how to best avoid its pitfalls while taking advantage of the effect of theatrical surround sound.

A Dolby stereo movie theatre is equipped with three sets of speakers behind the screen and a set of speakers which "surround" the audience (see fig 2.14a-b). Each set is capable of a discrete track of audio. The three front speakers handle the majority of sound. The need for the third center speaker helps to compensate for very wide screen formats so as not to leave a "hole" in the sound. This need comes from the pre-shoe box-sized "Megaplex" theatre days when most movie theatres were large and equipped with big, wide screens.

Though standard Dolby Stereo systems contain four tracks of audio information, the sound is actually encoded and placed onto two physical tracks on the 35mm motion picture film, or on the videotapes you rent. This keeps Dolby stereo films compatible with ordinary stereo film with no center or surround channels. By what magic do the Dolbians get four channels onto two tracks? The basic answer is "by encoding unique phase relationships between the channels of the original audio tracks and then looking for those unique phases upon playback." In other words, they muck around with the sound. But some of the spatial data can get lost in the Dolby matrix encoding process. Let's take a closer look at how the matrix does its thing:

- Sound on the film's left channel comes out the left speaker.
- Sound on the film's right channel comes out the right speaker.
- Sound on both channels comes out the center speaker and is removed from both the left and right speaker.

- Sound on both channels but 180° out of phase with each other are placed only into the surround speakers.

A Dolby encoding box is used when the movie sound is mixed and mastered to produce the special phase shifts, and the decoding box used at the movie theatre (or in your Dolby Pro Logic receiver at home) looks for those relationships and sends the sound to the appropriate channel.

There is also a limitation in a Dolby stereo soundtrack recording for both the dynamic range and the frequency bandwidth. Both are somewhat limited relative to a standard digital or even analogue studio recording. Much of the limitation is due not to the Dolby process, but to the fact that the final mix goes onto an analogue optical track on the film—a technology that dates back to the 1930s and has changed very little since.

If done without some care, the left and right channels of each stem of your mix can collapse into mono. If that isn't bad enough, when a sound is played in the center of the Dolby Surround matrix, it is removed from both the left and right speakers and sent only to the centre speaker. So not only will there be no sense of width in your music, but you'll only be driving a single speaker. The people who mix sound for films don't like to hear too much music or sound effects coming from the centre speaker since that is where the majority of dialogue emanates from, so you want to keep it as clear as possible. That isn't to say that you cannot pan sounds into the center of a Dolby Surround mix—you can and should. But you must take care in not overdoing it so that too much comes from the centre alone.

The key is to keep the left and right channels of your music mix as different as possible without being lopsided or overly panned. A good Dolby compatible mix should still sound decent on a normal home stereo system, with music spread from left to right. But by exaggerating the stereo field somewhat, you will be able to maintain stereo width in the theatre.

Here are some of the ways I've found to keep as much stereo image as possible in the Dolby Stereo Matrix :

- If you are recording music with stereo samples, detune the left and right sides by one or two cents. If your sampler has a function to modulate the sample's start times by key velocity, apply this to one side of the sample only. On audio tracks, you can experiment with a pitch shifter to change one side slightly.

- Don't be subtle in your panning of sounds that you want left or right. If you want something to come from the left, pan it way left. You can still have

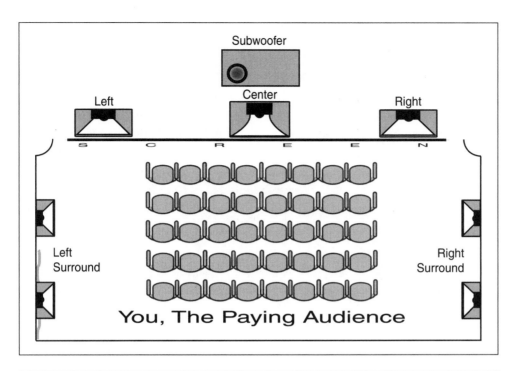

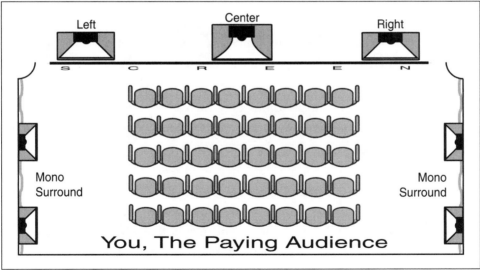

Figure 2.14a-b
Speaker placement in
surround format

sounds that are in degrees of pan from centre, but don't bother panning something just a little to the side.

- If you have enough synthesizers to do it (or use a multitrack recorder to over-dub), use two similar sounds instead of a single patch, and pan them hard left and right. For example, to have a lush stereo synth pad that will stay stereo in the soundtrack, choose two similar pads which compliment each other from two synths. Pan one hard left and one hard right. Even if they are from stereo synths, pan both sides of each synth to one side. The stereo will still be far better. Many stereo synths rely too heavily on their on-boards effects to achieve their "stereoness." Many of those sounds are almost guaranteed to collapse into the centre in the Dolby Matrix.

- EQ each side of a stereo sound differently. This is best done on your mixer. By altering the EQ of each side, you can change to sound enough for the Matrix to take it out of the centre.

- Experiment with the on-board effects of your synth. Some of the effects that will often spread the sound are stereo pitch shift, stereo delay (delay one side more than another), chorus, flange, and rotary speaker simulation. Some settings will put the sound well into the side speakers, while others will put the sound back into the surrounds. Be careful of putting too much into the surrounds though, they are of very limited frequency or dynamic range, and some loud sounds will distort. Also, some film mixers who prefer only to have sound effects in the surrounds will hate you and pull down the level of your music.

- One of the best ways to get a good stereo image is by applying a small amount of delay to one side of a stereo pair. This will instantly widen the sound for both digital and analogue surround sound systems, as well as on any stereo systems.

- A stereo reverb, can "suck" to the centre channel although you have its outputs panned hard left and right. This can be corrected by inserting a short delay (15mS- 60mS) on one side of the reverb, which tells the Dolby system that the reverb is in fact stereo and to keep it left and right.

Analogue Dolby Surround has a limited life. It is all but gone from movie theatres and will no longer be used on digital broadcast television. But since analogue television and VHS tape format will stay around for a while, as will smaller films without "digital surround budgets," it makes sense to be aware of how to work with Dolby Surround.

Smells like Team Spirit

The Music Editor

There are a number of people who inhabit the film composer's world. Certainly there is the director for whom we work. There will be producers as well, and executives from the studio or production company involved in making the film. Then there are the people on the composer's "team," depending on the project: orchestrator, engineer, musicians, music contractor (who hires the musicians), possible musical collaborators, and then the person who often keeps the whole bloody mess from falling apart. I speak of the music editor.

I've worked with a number of wonderful music editors on television and film projects. So instead of going on and on about the topic, I've decided to let award-winning music editor Adam Smalley speak for himself.

Q: When does a music editor get involved in a project?

A: Hollywood puts a lot of stock in recruited audience screenings, for which they need a "temp" score. So, very often, the music editor is involved before the composer is even hired. The temp score is music taken from other film scores to give a sense of where music might be needed. If the director screened the film with no music at all, it would be disastrous for an off-the-street audience.

Q: Do you help pick the type of music that might help influence the actual score?

A: Often the director has an idea of the composer he might want to hire, and indeed, if there is a composer attached to the film I will use as much of his or her previous scores as possible.

Q: So what is the first item of business you do with the composer when they start working on the project?

A: The first day on the job is what is called a "spotting session." It's where the director, composer, and music editor sit down with the rough cut of the film and decide where the emotional moments are. We often will spend two days breaking down the film and deciding where music goes. Later on I will fine-tune it down to the frame.

From the spotting session, "spotting notes" are created. They describe action, length of scene, and placement in the movie. For instance, "1m1" is the first piece of music in reel 1 of the film (a film is broken down into 10 or more reels during post production). The composer will use the notes as a sort of "bible" for all of the music in the film. They will refer back to the spotting notes to remember where the music should start and stop, and also to remember any specific emotions the director conveyed at the spotting. Being a film composer is inherently an isolated job. It's nice to rely on a music editor at 2 a.m. just to have someone to bounce around ideas with. It's a balance between editor, friend, therapist, and producer.

Q: What does a music editor do during the weeks that the composer is actually writing music?

A: Very often there are a number of temp screenings with different versions of the film. The composer has to be updated with the latest version, and the temp music conformed (re-edited to match the new edits in the picture) for those said screenings. In many cases I'll spend more time with the director than the composer will, and I'll relay the director's sentiments to the composer. Depending on the film there may be a number of songs that need placing and editing.

Q: How often will the cut of a film change while the composer is at work writing?

A: With animation, not very much, because it's so expensive to reshoot. With action films there can be enormous numbers of changes. I think it's due to digital film editing. When the director can ask for variation after variation at the click of a mouse, there tends to be a lot more trial and error. On the last film I worked on I got five versions of the same reel in the same day.

Q: Are there things you do to prepare for the recording of the music once it's written?

A: Depending on the composer, there are various needs. The metronome click for the musicians must be in sync with the picture that will be projected at the recording session. This also gives the director something to watch while the music is going down to tape. I take the click output of the composer's sequencer and record those to the master tape for the session. In some cases we'll bring the sequencer to the session for recording and rehearsing. The conductor will often like a visual "streamer" (an animated line that moves across the screen to warn of an upcoming transition) when difficult tempo changes are pending or a cut in the film needs to be hit musically.

I keep track of videos to be sure that we always have the right version of everything, and that nothing is ever missing from the session.

Q: Are you as involved in all or mostly all-electronic scores?

A: There's a lot less pressure, because I don't have 100 musicians waiting for me

Figure 2.15 Spotting
Notes

"DOUBLE JEOPARDY"
MUSIC SPOTTING NOTES
FEBRUARY 25TH

1M1	**1:12**	**"DOUBLE JEOPARDY-MAIN TITLE"**

01:00:10:05	**MUSIC STARTS** ON FADE UP PARAMOUNT LOGO.
01:01:12:07	FADE UP **"DOUBLE JEOPARDY"**
01:01:13:07	TITLE IN FULL
01:01:17:07	BEGIN FADE OUT TITLE
01:01:18:07	TITLE FULL OUT
01:01:18:19	BEGIN DISSOLVE TO FISHING SCENE
01:01:22:15	**MUSIC TAILS** AS CAM PANS DOWN TO SHORE LINE AS LIBBY: **"OKAY, HELP ME WIND."**
UNDERSCORE	**NOTE: IT WAS DISCUSSED THAT CUE WOULD BE "IDYLLIC, WITH SOMETHING OMINOUS, THOUGH NOT TOO MUCH, ON TITLE." IN THIS VERSION, THE BEDROOM SCENE HAS BEEN LIFTED.**
	NOTE: EXTENDED 26 SECONDS. 2/24

1M2	**1:21**	**"PARTY SOURCE"**

01:02:04:25	**MUSIC STARTS** ON CUT PARTY AT PARSON'S HOUSE.
01:03:34:22	**MUSIC IS OUT** IN PROGRESS ON CUT NICK AS HE JUMPS UP TO MAKE A SPEECH.
NON-VIS SOURCE	**NOTE: SOURCE MUSIC TO BE PURCHASED. IN TEMP, WE USED THE BILL EVANS TRIO DOING COLE PORTER'S "YOU, THE NIGHT, AND THE MUSIC."**

to find the next scene to record, but the process is the same. Sync is essential. Keeping track of every change or fix is still part of the job.

Q: What happens after the score is on tape?

A: Mixing. The last several films I've done were mixed directly to Protools and track assignments had to be decided upon. Choices have to be made as to what instruments need isolation on their own tracks to keep as much flexibility as possible at the final mix as well as the creative balance within the music.

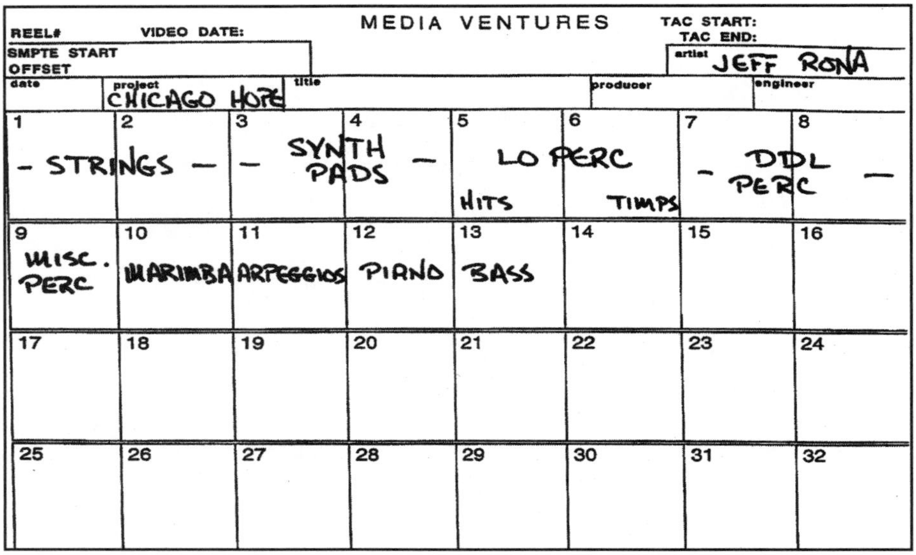

Figure 2.16 Typical film mix track sheets

REEL# VIDEO DATE:	MEDIA VENTURES	TAC START: TAC END:

The chart reads:

MEDIA VENTURES

REEL#   VIDEO DATE: TAC START: TAC END:
SMPTE START
OFFSET   artist JEFF RONA
date   project CHICAGO HOPE   title   producer   engineer

1	2	3	4	5	6	7	8
— STRINGS —		—	SYNTH PADS	LO PERC		— DDL	—
				HITS	TIMPS	PERC	
9	10	11	12	13	14	15	16
MISC. PERC	MARIMBA	ARPEGGIOS	PIANO	BASS			
17	18	19	20	21	22	23	24
25	26	27	28	29	30	31	32

I will also prepare dubbing log sheets that will be a road map of tracks and placement of music for the dubbing music mixer.

Q: How do you work with the dubbing mixer?

A: One of the important elements is simply having a consistent set of ears. Someone who had heard the music with the composer and can recreate the sound in a different room. I've heard horror stories of dubs that didn't have a music editor and the dubbing mixer left out the piano melody simply because a fader was down and had never heard the music before. The dubbing stage is the final mixing process in the life of a film. It is a big theatre where the dialogue, sound effects, and music editor bring their various elements in and mix them all together. Each of us has our own mixing engineers. The director will orchestrate a final mix with all of us.

It is an ongoing process of changing various music cues on the spot to further fine tune all of the elements. Very often this is the first time everyone will see the film with all the sound elements, and they sometimes conflict. To serve the film, it is our responsibility to make all the elements work, and that sometimes requires some drastic editing. For example, on a recent film the director felt that one cue ended too soon. Keeping the integrity of what the composer intended, I copied a phrase from a different cue and worked it into

Figure 2.17 Dubbing log sheet shows which tracks are playing at any given moment

Out 1 Mono/Unassigned Page:01 Final
- S 1 5m24A Cello-02 L 111.11 – 167.10
- AV 1 5m24B Orch-02 L 184.03 – 296.03
- VC 1 5m26 Orch L New-01 421.08 – 527.14
- VV 1 5m28 Orch-01 L 715.15 – 822.10
- WW 1 5m29 Orch-01 L 927.15 – 1293.09
- XX 1 5m30 Orch-01 L 1296.01 – 1391.08
- AA 1 5m32B Drums-01 L 1552.14 – 1911.05

Out 2 Mono/Unassigned Page:01 Final
- S 2 5m24A Cello C-02 111.11 – 167.10
- AV 2 5m24B Orch C-02 184.03 – 296.03
- VC 2 5m26 Orch New-01 421.08 – 527.14
- VV 2 5m28 Orch C-01 715.15 – 822.10
- WW 2 5m29 Orch C-01 927.15 – 1293.09
- XX 2 5m30 Orch C-01 1296.01 – 1391.08
- AA 2 5m32B Drums C-01 1552.14 – 1911.05

Out 3 Mono/Unassigned Page:01 Final
- S 3 5m24A Cello-02 R 111.11 – 167.10
- AV 3 5m24B Orch-02 R 184.03 – 296.03
- VC 3 5m26 Orch-02 R New-01 421.08 – 527.14
- VV 3 5m28 Orch-01 R 715.15 – 822.10
- WW 3 5m29 Orch-01 R 927.15 – 1293.09
- XX 3 5m30 Orch-01 R 1296.01 – 1391.08
- AA 3 5m32B Drums-01 R 1552.14 – 1911.05

Out 4 Mono/Unassigned Page:01 Final
- AV 4 5m24B Drums-02 L 184.03 – 296.03
- VC 4 5m26 Perc L New-01 421.08 – 527.14
- WW 4 5m29 Perc-01 L 927.15 – 1293.09
- XX 4 5m30 Perc-01 L 1296.01 – 1391.08
- AA 4 5m32B Perc-01 L 1552.14 – 1911.05

Out 5 Mono/Unassigned Page:01 Final
- AV 5 5m24B Drums-02 R 184.03 – 296.03
- VC 5 5m26 Perc R New-01 421.08 – 527.14
- WW 5 5m29 Perc-01 R 927.15 – 1293.09
- XX 5 5m30 Perc-01 R 1296.01 – 1391.08
- AA 5 5m32B Perc-01 R 1552.14 – 1911.05

Out 6 Mono/Unassigned Page:01 Final
- S 6 5m24A Rhodes-01 L 111.11 – 167.10
- VC 6 5m26 Gtr L New-01 421.08 – 527.14
- VV 6 5m28 Gtr-01 L 715.15 – 822.10
- WW 6 5m29 Gtr-01 L 927.15 – 1293.09
- AA 6 5m32B Gtr-01 L 1552.14 – 1911.05

Out 7 Mono/Unassigned Page:01 Final
- WW 7 5m29 Gtr C-01 927.15 – 1293.09
- AA 7 5m32B Bass C-01 1552.14 – 1911.05

Out 8 Mono/Unassigned Page:01 Final
- S 8 5m24A Rhodes-01 R 111.11 – 167.10
- VC 8 5m26 Gtr R New-01 421.08 – 527.14
- VV 8 5m28 Gtr-01 R 715.15 – 822.10
- WW 8 5m29 Gtr-01 R 927.15 – 1293.09
- AA 8 5m32B Gtr-01 R 1552.14 – 1911.05

Out 9 Mono/Unassigned Page:01 Final
- AV 10 5m24B Sax/Rev F/X-02 R 184.03 – 296.03
- VC 10 5m26 Dobro L New-01 421.08 – 527.14
- WW 10 5m29 Wurli-01 L 927.15 – 1293.09
- XX 10 5m30 Pno/Cymb-01 L 1296.01 – 1391.08
- AA 10 5m32B Synth Drms-01 L 1552.14 – 1911.05

Out 10 Mono/Unassigned Page:01 Final
- AV 11 5m24B Sax/Rev F/X-02 R 184.03 – 296.03
- VC 11 5m26 Dobro R New-01 421.08 – 527.14
- WW 11 5m29 Wurli-01 R 927.15 – 1293.09
- XX 11 5m30 Pno/Cymb-01 R 1296.01 – 1391.08
- AA 11 5m32B Synth Dr-01 R 1552.14 – 1911.05

Figure 2.18 Cue sheet

"We Were So Close" Performance Rights

Date:	June 14, 2000
Title:	We Were So Close…
Description:	Feature Film
First Airdate:	10/12/00
Music Editor:	George Washington

CUE: **1M1**   Title: Opening
Composer: John Smith (ASCAP)
Publisher: 50% Smithmusic / 50% Something Else Music
Affil: ASCAP
Length: 1:30   Usage: Main Title

CUE: **2M2**   Title: A Shrink
Composer: Boom Boom Band
Publisher: 100% Modern Sound
Affil: SACEM
Length: 1:00   Usage: Source

CUE: **3M3**   Title: Jarvis and Computer
Composer: John Smith (ASCAP)
Publisher: 50% Smithmusic / 50% Something Else Music
Affil: ASCAP
Length: 2:00   Usage: Background Instrumental

CUE: **4M4**   Title: End Titles
Composer: John Smith (ASCAP)
Publisher: 50% Smithmusic / 50% Something Else Music
Affil: ASCAP
Length: 3:30   Usage: Background Instrumental

Total Music:	Background Instrumental	7:00
	Source	1:00
	TOTAL	8:00

the end of the cue that needed extending. With some careful editing on the ProTools system, the change is undetectable to anyone except the composer.

Q: Is the composer ever there with you during the dub?

A: The composers I have recently been working with are usually on to their next film by then. But occasionally the composer will make an appearance, though won't stay too long. It's a difficult adjustment for the composer to hear the music behind all the dialogue and sound effects.

Q: Is there anything left after the dub is finished?

A: There's a certain amount of administrative work. The production companies require that I deliver licensing sheets (sometimes called "cue sheets") which are a log of every piece of music that ends up in the final mix of the film. They include the length of each cue as well as the names of the composers and publishers. Master tapes have to be logged and delivered. And all digital equipment has to be backed up in the event that we might need to come back and make any adjustments or fixes at a later date.

Q: Do you work on lower budget projects? Is a music editor really needed every time?

A: On lower budgeted films there's less time and money to make changes so the need for a music editor is less. It's broken down into spotting, composing, and dubbing. Not much room for temp scores, but the basics remain the same.

Q: How did you learn to do music editing?

A: I apprenticed for a short time with the grande-dame of music editing, Else Blangsted. I made relationships with a few composers and built up a clientele of loyal customers. I've now taught a few newcomers how to edit film music. Music editing has changed in the last few years with the increase in temp screenings. There's much more work for the music editor to do on a film.

Q: So, any regrets?

A: None. Well, there was that girl in 12th grade…

Sounds Good to Me

The Film Score Mixer

So you've written a great score, and now it's time to record and mix it. Alan Meyerson is a well-rounded sound engineer who has been successful in both the record and film worlds. His album credits include Brian Ferry's *Bete Noir*, New Order's *Technique*, Cameo's very cool *Word Up*, and OMD's hit *Sugar Tax*. As a film mixer he's done the scores to *Gladiator*, *Thin Red Line*, *The Prince of Egypt*,

As Good As It Gets, Face/Off, The Rock, Crimson Tide, Speed, Mission Impossible 2 and many, many others. Here's a few questions with Alan Meyerson:

Q: How do film mixes differ from album/song mixes?

A: The first obvious difference is that we mix in "surround sound" using LCRS (Left, Centre, Right, Stereo Surround) and subwoofer channels. This gives a lot of flexibility for positioning your sounds and greater sonic freedom for the final film mix. You get to move the sounds around in space more than you might with a straight stereo mix. It's my job to accentuate what's happening on screen musically. When you mix a song, it's all about the lead vocal. Everything is shaped around them to make the vocals shine. In score mixing you shape the mix around the dialogue or the picture itself. For example, in *Speed*, when the elevator falls down the shaft there was a sample of a string screech that was doubled with a live orchestra. In mixing that cue we made sure that the abrasiveness of the music cut through the blazing sound effects.

Q: When you mix a score, how do you deliver the music?

A: I typically deliver on ProTools. I try to get the best possible fidelity, and I've been using the Apogee AD8000 converters as a front end to either system. I deliver "stems" which are separations of different instrumental groups. For example, a typical cue may have orchestral LCR, stereo percussion, stereo synths, stereo surrounds, and mono subwoofer tracks. That's a ten track mix.

Q: If you need to keep it simpler, say 8 tracks or less, how would you mix a score?

A: I would do an LCR mix, stereo surround, and a stereo "solo track" which would have anything that might need to have extra control in the final dub, in case it conflicts with a piece of dialogue or effects. When I'm doing an action score like *The Rock* , I put more of the music into the surrounds to punch up the movement on the screen. On a nonaction film, I'm less concerned with the surrounds, so I might do a mix with LCR music, stereo percussion, and stereo solos—a seven track mix.

Q: What outboard gear do you find the most important for good film music mixing?

A: A very high quality reverb, like the Lexicon 480L, a few good EQs (I use the Manley Massive Passive and Avelon AD2055 EQ a lot) and compressors (such as the Neve 33609). I also need to have a few good mono DDLs available because in the world of Dolby SR (nondigital) film mixes certain sounds will tend to "fold in" top mono unless I delay one side. I'll use delay times of 13 to 50 milliseconds on one side of a stereo sound. This keeps them in stereo in either digital or analogue surround sound. I have 2 busses on my mixing board dedicated to delays, one for the left side and one for the right. I bus any stereo sound I want to "spread out," some left and some right so the mix doesn't get lopsided.

Q: Do you need to mix music on a board that is designed for film music, or will any good board do?

A: Any good mixing board will do. I've mixed scores on Euphonix, which are specifically configured for film mixing, but I've also used standard Neves, SSLs, APIs, and other good mixers for film projects. I once mixed a small, low-budget film on a 1972 vintage API. It's one of the best sounding scores I've ever done.

Q: What about smaller, home studio mixers?

A: I've used them all for film and television mixes. They have far less flexibility—fewer aux sends, fewer busses, lower quality EQs, etc. The Yamaha 02R has come a long way for doing film mixes. It has a built-in surround sound matrix similar to bigger boards designed especially for film sound.

Q: What about monitoring your mixes? What speakers do you like to use?

A: My speaker of choice these days (at least this week) is the Quested 2108 series, which are available either powered or unpowered. With powered monitors I can go to any studio, big or small, and set up a monitoring system that I am familiar with, and know what I am getting. For a full surround mix I use three speakers for the LCR, and some smaller Questeds for the surrounds. A subwoofer is nice to have, especially for big action film style music, but I can create a subwoofer track and monitor it in my regular left and right speakers.

Q: Can you do a decent film mix with just left and right speakers?

A: Sure! I will pan my LCR mix to simple stereo with the centre channel panned to the centre. If I am doing a surround track I would need at least one surround speaker behind me.

Q: How do you record an orchestra for a film score?

A: I use a great room and some fantastic mics. I like Neumann M50s for recording a large group, such as an orchestra. I place three of them in a LCR pattern 10 feet above the conductor on a boom stand called a "tree." I put up "spot

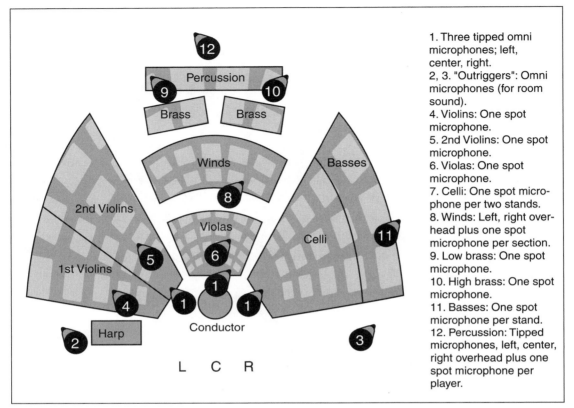

1. Three tipped omni microphones; left, center, right.
2, 3. "Outriggers": Omni microphones (for room sound).
4. Violins: One spot microphone.
5. 2nd Violins: One spot microphone.
6. Violas: One spot microphone.
7. Celli: One spot microphone per two stands.
8. Winds: Left, right overhead plus one spot microphone per section.
9. Low brass: One spot microphone.
10. High brass: One spot microphone.
11. Basses: One spot microphone per stand.
12. Percussion: Tipped microphones, left, center, right overhead plus one spot microphone per player.

Figure 2.19 Orchestra layout with microphone placement by engineer Alan Meyerson

mics" for certain sections of the orchestra. For example, I like Schoeps CMC5 for high strings, Senheiser MKH40s for low strings, and Royer ribbon mics for winds and brass. I like different microphones for different percussion instruments, though a favorite is the Neumann KM84.

I will record the orchestra on 15 or more tape tracks. Later I'll mix that with synths and any other elements of the score for the final mix. My favorite storage medium for orchestra is still 24-track analogue, 15 ips, Dolby SR. However, 24 bit digital sounds almost as good!

Q: Is mixing an all synth score any different that recording one with live musicians?

A: It's different because many of the composers I work with deliver their tracks directly from their keyboards in stereo pairs, so I'll forgo a centre channel. On *Replacement Killers*, we had no centre channel in the music, but we did create a stereo surround track using delays and reverb. I work with composers while they are still writing to help make each synth sound its best by using delays, eq, compression, chorusing, or whatever. That way they are composing with sounds that are very close to how I would eventually mix them. It makes for a much smoother and faster mix.

Q: Do you ever attend the final "dub" mix of a film, when the music dialogue and effects are all put together?

A: All the time. I've developed good relationships with the dubbing mixers I work with. They know what to expect from my mixes and they like my work. Occasionally I get to do the dub myself. I've lived with the score for quite a while, so instead of handing over to another engineer, I can help tweak the mix to fit into the film as perfectly as possible.

Q: How do you get drums and percussion to cut through a mix without overwhelming the music?

A: I use some compression. I use an Aphex Dominator on the stereo percussion bus, which eliminates overmodulation by putting a "brick ceiling" at whatever level I want. It's a very, very good tool. I use a bit of general compression on the percussion, like the Imperial Lab "Distressors" to let it "pump" a little.

Q: Any final thoughts about making a film score sound great?

A: Don't let the mix get in the way of the music. It's so easy to get caught up in individual sounds and forget about the big picture, sonically. It's important to remember that it's the music that counts. I'd rather hear someone say "great score" than "great mix."

Q: Why is your dog named Squirt?

A: I thought it would be funny to have a huge dog named "Squirt," sort of like a WWF wrestler named "Tiny." When he was 5 weeks old he had huge paws, I thought he'd be 80 pounds or more. He only made it to about 25 pounds now. Oh well. He comes to every mix I do. He's my secret weapon.

Perspectives

Hans Zimmer

Films include: *Mission: Impossible 2, Peacemaker, Gladiator, The Lion King, Backdraft*

JR: Your career and your musical style as a composer have been closely linked with technology from the start. How would you describe the way technology has influenced your compositional approach?

Hans Zimmer: It absolutely made it possible. There's a big difference between me and someone who plays well and can write [music] on paper. The technology is about finally having a musical instrument that I can play and write with. Most of my writing happens in my head, and now I have a way of getting it across. It has made communication possible.

JR: Do you see a relationship between the way technology has evolved and the way your writing approach has evolved?

HZ: When I only had 16 monophonic tracks in the old Fairlight CMI (an early sampler), I really got my counterpoint chops together. I still do most of my string parts in a 'monophonic' way. I probably would have learned bad habits had the technology been better back then.

JR: Tell me about your musical experience prior to your film scoring career.

HZ: I was doing commercials. Before that I was in a band and busy being a session programmer. I was the synth whiz kid in London. I had a Prophet 5, a Yamaha TX 816 rack, a Roland System 700 modular and the Roland MC-8.

JR: What was your first opportunity to score a dramatic picture?

HZ: Being an assistant for Stanley Myers (composer for the *Deer Hunter*). I knew technology and he knew about the orchestra. The first thing we did was a Nicolas Roeg film called *Eureka*. I got to do a couple of little scenes in it.

JR: What did you learn about film music from him?

HZ: I learned about musical language. In *Eureka* there was a scene with Gene Hackman finding gold in Alaska. It was rather a spectacular shot. I asked Nick (or "Mr. Roeg," because I was so terrified of him) what he wanted and he replied "The sound of the earth being raped, dear boy!!" From that whole experience I learned that you need to talk to film people in a different language. You can't be technical with them. You use emotional language. Over the years, the more I learned about musical language, the I more I learned that it is not that helpful with musicians either. Years later, when I was doing *Gladiator*, I started to talk to my musicians only about the feel and emotion of the scene. I tried to describe the colors I was after, and never used "pianissimo," or "mezzo forte." "Really loud," or "really soft" are equally accurate words to describe musical dynamics.

JR: I know you did a number of films under Stanley Myers. Let's jump to the first film score you did on your own. How was the experience? What went well? What went didn't go well?

HZ: The only thing that didn't go well was me, which is to say my head. I was so terrified all the time. It was a film called *A World Apart*, an autobiographical story of a good friend of mine. So here I was looking at an actress on the screen acting the life story of someone I knew very well. Somehow, whenever I would get really stuck, this wonderful kind of "telepathic help line" came in. I'd be struggling along when the phone would ring. And it would be my friend Shawn on the phone saying "just thought I'd give you a ring." I'd say "Well, thank God for that, because I have no idea what to do here. How did you feel at that

moment in your life?" That was a big help. Everybody loved what I was doing. I was just afraid that the other shoe would eventually drop and it would all go terribly, terribly wrong.

That little film got me *Rain Man*. But that fear of being "found out" has never really ceased. Just recently in *Mission: Impossible 2*, I was being reckless and saying "Biggest movie of the year, let's not use an orchestra like everyone else, lets use a rock and roll band instead!" Seemed like a great idea. When we went to the preview screening, I had to use all my acting skills not to let anybody see how incredibly terrified I was. Would the audience just start throwing popcorn and whatnot at the screen because the music ruined the film? When we saw the audience polls, and the music scored really highly, I relaxed and said "O.K., I am going down the right way, so let's really go all the way here."

JR: In film writing, do you look at what you do as self-expression or as strictly doing what other people expect you to do?

HZ: Totally self-expression. My job is to watch the film, and then come up with an idea that we can discuss. I think part of my job has to be bringing something new to the project.

JR: But there are typically expectations. Temp scores for example.

HZ: True. After *Rain Man* I worked with a director who said "Can you do that *Rain Man* thing?" and I said "No, I can't. Your movie, in my mind, doesn't lend itself do that."

On the other hand *Peacemaker* was temped entirely with my own score to *Crimson Tide*. When producer Steven Speilberg said "don't change a note" I knew he meant "don't write too far from the style, it actually works very well." As it happens I like writing in that style, and for *Peacemaker* I could try writing better at that style.

JR: You have a really good dialogue with directors that you work with, don't you?

HZ: Yes. When I start a film, I sit down with the director and ask him to tell me the story. That way I figure out what kind of film the director wants to make as opposed to what the script writer wanted, or even making my own version of the movie in my head after the script. I want to know where WE are going to go. However, a situation like this depends on how confident the team is. If the concept is solid and the initial idea is good and fits where everybody else wants to go, then there has to be give and take. It's about making the film better, ultimately.

JR: Do you feel you have always had a good first instinct, or is this something that has grown with your confidence?

HZ: On *Mission: Impossible 2* I started getting a little lost in the middle of the project, from all the pressure. After a number of frustrating meetings, producer Tom Cruise said "But Hans, all that stuff we talked about before we started shooting, that little tune you wrote, where is it? Your first instincts were so great." Some of the scenes hadn't turned out in a way that lent themselves to using that tune that Cruise liked so much. So they graciously re-cut the scenes in order for me to have the opportunity to go back to my first instinct, because that really was serving everybody, including the movie, the best.

Since then I've realized that I have always gone back to my first instinct, I just never realized it.

JR: One thing I have always admired in your relationships with directors and producers is your keen sense of when to fight for something you believe in, and when not to.

HZ: You have to come to a movie with a position of strength, and you have to come well armed. I have an imaginary "gun." It has maybe nine bullets in it in, of which three of them are "silver bullets" I use for winning arguments. The first six bullets are for minor points I want to make. The three silver bullets are for when I really want to hang on to an idea which I think is really good for the film. In these cases I will be outspoken and try and make my point. However I can only do it three times, more or less.

JR: What do you think makes great score?

HZ: It depends entirely on the movie. If I think it has great music in it (and great music can be a lot of things) that also works for the film. The music really does need to add something to the film to be great. Is *The Shawshank Redemption* a great score? Absolutely. It serves the film in a brilliant way and you can also listen to the CD on its own. I think that if everybody works at the pinnacle of their imagination and creativity, you can't help but end up with great music that not only fits the film but also stands on its own two little feet.

JR: Do you find that you work differently when you work with a first time director versus veteran directors?

HZ: You know, I haven't worked with a first time director for so long, I can't really say. There is, however, something about veteran directors that makes life a lot easier because they already had to go through that experience where they must surrender their film to the composer, because that really is what happens. They are in charge, in control, all the way from the script. They know how to change lines for a writer since they can write at least a little bit. They know how to look at a scene and place the actors and even act for them. They know if the lighting is right or not.

But when it comes to music it becomes an incredibly complicated conversation for them because they don't have the technical language of music, and so they have to surrender their movie and trust you. You have to respect what they go through, and you'd better be on their side.

JR: What is the most enjoyable part about film scoring? Is it the process of working with the film makers, is it being alone and actually having that time to write, is it when you are towards the end and your starting to bring your team together to flesh out and record? Or is it when the movie is actually finished and you can sit down and simply listen to it?

HZ: Well, because I'm a procrastinator, the most enjoyable part is spending time with the film makers in the cutting room and figuring out what the film is. The actual sitting alone by myself and writing can get pretty hard.

JR: Do you feel that you have times of inspiration and times of non-inspiration?

HZ: Sure! The one good thing I learned over the last few years is that if you're just sitting there knocking your head against the wall, go home and sleep on it. It will be there the next morning. Let the subconscious do the hard work.

JR: What is the hardest part about scoring a film?

HZ: Writing a good tune. The idea is easy. The style and the framework, that's easy. But to then actually put into that something that has some aesthetic value, that's always the tough one.

JR: Does talent equal success?

HZ: No. But it depends on what you mean by talent. I think that some amazing composers probably find it very hard to communicate with directors. I communicate well with directors, and they know that I come from a place where I want to serve the movie. The other half of my success stems from my knowing how to get the job done and write the music.

Ultimately, I do a movie because it interests me. Sometimes it's the subject matter and sometimes it's the people. With Terry Mallick (director of *Thin Red Line*), I worked for a year on the film, but I didn't write music for a year. Fifty percent of the process was talking to Terry about the movie and never ever mentioning music in those conversations.

JR: Bringing a composer into a film is much like casting an actor.

HZ: Yes, I'm cast as an actor into a role in each movie I do.

Mark Isham

Films include: *The Net, Home For the Holidays, A River Runs Through It, Trouble In Mind, Fly Away Home*

Mark Isham: To me the excitement of this job, what really moves me foremost is seeing the job which I'd set out to do completed to my utmost satisfaction, and secondarily, of course, to the satisfaction of my employers. I think it's in the nature of the way that I've come to see the job. That, and the realization that what I've accomplished is exciting.

A film composer is in control of a language that is without a doubt the most subjective language in our planetary culture. I have done actual tests on this! It's of no surprise to anyone, but just to verify it for myself I tested music that was to my mind very programmatic. You listen to this music and it told you a very particular story. You're on the Scottish Moors, the piper comes across the glade, you enter the countryside church, the choir there is singing, etc. I played this piece of music for people expecting a programmatic response. When I asked them what the story of the music was telling them, they'd say, "I'm in the bazaar at

Marrakesh and the snake merchant has just approached and he's got five new cobras to sell me." And it went on and on like this. No two people's reactions to the same piece of music were anywhere near what I expected, nor anywhere near resembling each other's.

But programmatic music has been with us historically for a long time. Beethoven could title a piece "The Pastoral Symphony," or Vivaldi could title something "The Four Seasons." That's all you need, and then you can get a sense of the music's flavor. Well, in film we have a lot more than just a descriptive title. We have picture, which, other than the story itself, is about as objective as you can get. We have the dialog, which is slightly more subjective in describing emotions and talking about things. If you're working with lyrics and songs, you have poetry, which is about as subjective as words can get. And of course we can't leave out the sound effects guys! [Laughs] So music has a very pivotal role in this combination of elements.

JR: It sounds like what you're saying, perhaps, is that music is the most internalized of any art form.

MI: In that it speaks uniquely to each individual hearing the same thing, yes. It draws upon an individual's personal experience with life. And yet, you're dealing with a language. A very specific language that has dictionaries and tools and conjugations, form, and whatever other rules as might occur in a well conceived, well-used language evolving through culture.

JR: Do you think about those rules?

MI: Those become the whole mystery of being a film composer, because if you are dramatically inclined you could categorize it all! I'm sure that it has been done. In fact, I've seen books in which academics have attempted to categorize the emotional qualities of various musical events. The sweeping upward motion to a major sixth implies great triumph of the will. The downward motion of a minor third indicates loss. You could go on and create sub-categories, ad infinitum, of this sort of stuff, and I suppose people may do that.

JR: It would be a dangerous book in the hands of some producers.

MI: Exactly! But the truth of the matter is that there is this element that feels slightly magical and mysterious in the manipulation of this. To me, still as a film composer, I can try and build what I think will be predictable things into a score, but the structure of what I'm attempting to create will undoubtedly change.

There are magical moments, such as when you take that cue you've written for the death scene and put it up against the virgin's love scene, and it plays better. The magic imparted by that un-intellectualized creation characterizes the real high points for me. When you get it to work just right you can see the emotional impact you now have with this totally personalized communication, which is then added to those other more objective ones. You then get to see how much the final result can be such a tremendously powerful experience for each individual audience member.

Basil Poledouris

Films include: *Cecil B. DeMented, The Jungle Book, The Hunt For Red October, RoboCop*

JR: Do most filmmakers understand the process of music?

Basil Poledouris: I think music is abstract enough of an idea and enough of a commodity that as composers we basically make a lot of choices that the client, the producer or director, is unaware of, nor should they be. I'm not aware of a lot of things a director has to do—his or her internal mechanisms. But you get the job done. I think they're still dealing with dramatic concepts in dramatic film, and for me it's about realizing the director's or the producer's vision.

JR: Do you think you banged your head against the wall when you were starting out?

BP: I know I did, and I think a lot of that probably has to do with insecurity. Like making sure that I found the right way to approaching something. There are a lot of approaches to the same problem. I don't think there's just one anymore. Give ten film composers the same scene, you're going to get ten different approaches, ten different kinds of scores. I always assumed there was just one way I could write, and that was either because of my limitations or insecurities or whatever, and I stuck to it. It was my style and, to a certain degree, people expected it. I was hired for it. But now it's different. It's changed a lot for me and I think there are a lot of different kinds of movies.

JR: There are so many interesting ways to make music.

BP: Yeah, I suppose there always were. It's just so much more accessible now. You can try out ideas without having so many limitations. You have the luxury of experimenting with electronic instruments, whereas before it was a gamble. It was only the gutsy that would push things.

JR: Do you know why you get hired to do a film?

BP: It's generally because of a film I've done prior to it. It speaks to the new project and someone hears something in there; the most notable example in my career was Paul Verhoeven hearing *Conan the Barbarian*. He really wanted me to do *Flesh and Blood* because of that. *Conan* had that kind of medieval thing that he was looking for. Randall Kleiser hired me to do *Blue Lagoon* because of something he heard in *Big Wednesday*. There was a kind of warmth and quality to it. I don't think any of us could define it. There's an emotional response to it. You might be able to analyze it intellectually, but in the end it is emotionally that kind of response you want people to have for your scores.

JR: You were using electronics as early as anybody.

BP: Yeah, absolutely. I always added the electronics as an orchestral color. But not until MIDI and the sophisticated sequencers came

along that we have now was it possible to do a mock-up of the whole instrumental pallet. I think that's changed my attitude about how I approach film scores a lot.

JR: I know that the bar has certainly been raised with all this gear in terms of what directors expect to hear when they walk into a composer's studio. You're exceptional in the fact that you're such a good pianist that you can dazzle a director by playing and describing a score.

BP: Used to be, thirty years ago.

JR: You know what I mean. There's lots of composers who don't really play piano very well, but are able to do their work from using their MIDI gear.

BP: Do you see any pianos in here? We need to get rid of the preconceived notion about how we approach scores now. That's the difference. Before, it was: Spot a movie, go away and write for a while, then meet with the director to play maybe a couple of main themes on piano, and no more. Six weeks later you show up on the scoring stage, and that would be the first time [the director and producer] ever had an idea of the score beyond the piano sketches. Now it's totally different.

It depends on the director. I think particularly that younger directors expect that process of working with the composer and hearing almost a full realization in the electronic mock-up form of what the score's going to be. I don't mind that, though it's more time consuming for me. I know what it's going to sound like, but it takes time to sequence and review. Then it opens the door to change. Sometimes that change is very positive, but sometimes it isn't. That's where the collaboration comes into play. You talk about the possibilities. You explore the alternatives. Sometimes you end up where you started, but sometimes it goes in a different direction that can be very exciting.

Marc Shaiman

Films include: *South Park: Bigger, Longer and Uncut, Patch Adams, In & Out, The First Wives' Club, When Harry Met Sally*

JR: Let me start by asking you what you were doing before you started scoring movies?

Marc Shaiman: I moved to New York when I was 16. I started as a vocal arranger for cabaret acts there. I was Bette Midler's vocal arranger and writing a lot of off off-off-off-Broadway shows. I was very busy just doing everything that had to do with music and show business.

JR: So you were a composer before you started in film?

MS: More like a songwriter with eyes on being a theatrical composer. Listening to film scores was something I enjoyed, but I wasn't a film score aficionado. I was into music, show business, movies and plays. So I was aware of film music, but it wasn't something I was specifically focused on.

JR: At what point did you make a transition into films, and more importantly, how did your earlier musical work influence what you did when you started?

MS: It definitely influenced me, for better or for worse. Film writing is so much like arranging. You have a melody, and then you have to figure out different ways to conform that melody or those chords to work for a scene. Sometimes that's bad, as when I will continue to try to make a theme work (and my arranging chops will allow me to keep texturing it to be playing throughout the scene) when in fact I should probably be going for texture and not trying so hard. So my arranging is sometimes a bad habit of trying to hold onto a full 30 seconds of a melody, when in fact it should just be a chord or a rhythm. But on the other hand, I often think that I see a movie like a singer, and I'm the accompanist playing for it. That's what I really am, an accompanist.

JR: That's a fantastic way to look at it. And you're aware that sometimes your music absolutely has to step up to center stage.

MS: That's completely how I approach it. It's not like I think: "That's my M.O."

JR: For better or worse, you're very well-known for the comedy scores that you've done. I don't think there's anything harder to do in film scoring than what you do (and what you do so successfully). What do you think makes a good comedic score?

MS: It is hard, and there are moments I'm as ashamed of it as I ought to be! It's that incredibly hard thing of knowing when not to write "funny" music. But I have a sense of humor that just can't help being in the musical style I'm writing. So hopefully it works with the movie, and hopefully does not overtake the movie too often. There's nothing worse, [using] the comedy trombones and all that kind of stuff. But I'm not afraid of stepping out. However, I was recently called on the carpet for *The Kid*, which I scored in two weeks. It was the only time I ever did one of these "come in at the last second" scores. The director was loving what I was doing, stepping around and dancing jigs of joy and leaving my studio so happy every time. The best score he'd ever had!

And I got so beat up in the reviews, which I kind of anticipated because of the style of music. I've done enough of them now to know. There is a bold stroke element in that score. So there was no time to think about what you were writing, or to be subtle. There was just no time to do anything except write something and then move onto the next cue. And when the director's loving it, it is nice! So you keep going.

JR: Do you think about things other than what the director feels when scoring a film? How important is your director's response.

MS: Very important. I've never been in a situation where I was so at odds with a director that I tried to stamp my feet and be immovable. But luckily, it hasn't happened so much (or else I have a selective memory). I'm usually in tune with a director, and I have them come over every few days and they hear everything and comment on everything. The people with whom I've had successful collaborations say they know that even when I roll my eyes and take in my breath, they know I'm listening. And I'll make the adjustments. I find ways to adjust things to make everyone as happy as possible. I'm lucky, in that I've never had a situation where it was obvious that the director and the producers were unhappy.

JR: Now that you've done quite a few movies, how do you think your approach has changed from when you first started?

MS: I wish I could somehow erase all of this experience and be a little freer. I feel guilty of having fallen into the same grooves or patterns, musically. That's the bad thing about getting similar kinds of movies. It's hard to sometimes find a different way, especially when you know that that's what they want, and it's coming naturally to you. It just sort of happens. That's what happens after 35 movies or whatever it's been. But I look at the posters for the first 10 movies I did, and they were all different. Maybe they're not so different in that they're all movies that I scored (and I was chosen for them). I'm looking at them right now: *When Harry Met Sally*, musically speaking, is not very close to *The Addams Family*, which is not very close to *City Slickers*, which is not very close to *A Few Good Men* or *Sleepless in Seattle*. During my first 3 years, I had more variety in the kinds of projects on which I worked.

JR: Do you think that typecasting and pigeonholing is something sort of endemic in the biz?

MS: Of course, that's the way it is in all life. Not just showbiz, but throughout life in general, people always compartmentalize you. Things could be worse. But I think I did an okay job on *Misery*, which is the first movie I ever wrote music for. I wish I could get more films like that. I watch little moments from *Misery*, and I think: "Would I write that now?" Because it's much more free-form, in its way. I didn't know anything about clicks! So what I said to you about accompanying the movie was more in evidence than ever. It was really me there just playing. The poor orchestrator had to figure out how to conduct it and write it out so it could be clicked. And yet it was much freer. That's what I meant when I said I wish I could erase. I'm still not a slave to [the click track] now; I never have been. But I'm more so now than I was in those first three years. And I also thought, "Gee, it took two hours for the orchestra to play this cue!" I'm going to have to learn the click. My expressive clicks that I create from my playing don't translate to the orchestra necessarily. Sometimes an orchestra will sound more emotional getting to play not necessarily with a click but with a steady tempo then to try to play like a pianist (breathing through the same piece of music playing a little faster, a little slower). But when you've got that big orchestra, trying to find that heartbeat can be more emotional.

JR: Do you feel that you're a more confident composer than you used to be?

MS: You happen to have caught me at a low confidence moment. The reviews from *The Kid* really knocked the wind out of my sails. Not only the reviews, just where I am in my life. I'm cocky and have a high opinion of myself, and yet I can totally beat myself up. I mean, listen to me the last ten minutes!

JR: What are some of the most valuable things you've learned on the job?

MS: It's the old cliché: less is more. It's such a cliché, but those moments where I realize that my trying to hit a cut or make a melody last two bars longer than the scene really needed to be. So I wrestle with it to make it fit the scene. Then three months later I go see the movie and wonder "Why did I have to do that? Why couldn't I have just played that moment as just texture and not have played the melody to that extent?"—that kind of stuff.

Now and then I think that I try to force a square peg in a round hole, but I have the chops to pull it off.

JR: I've always felt that there's never been a single note of music in a film score that wasn't

approved by virtually everyone before it gets dubbed. When you're working with a director for the first time or on a repeat basis, how do you communicate? How do you interact?

MS: You know everyone's personality is different, so it's different with each person. What can I say, hopefully, is that my personality is a part of it. It's weird to say out loud, but it is true. I think people enjoy coming over here and hearing music, enjoy being with me (until I fall into the well of misery). I think that's a big part, and an enjoyable part of it. I've been lucky enough to always be pleased with the directors, so I've never had an awkward relationship that's like … [whispers] "Oh my god, I'm really not pleasing this guy."

I've been lucky enough to not have to deal with producers with too much to say, (at least not until it's too late), except of course the fact that once every two years I've worked with Scott Rudin, a producer who's completely hands on. His is really the only situation like that, where the producer is more involved than the director. And again, the relationship with him is like the relationships that I have with most directors, which is very difficult because he's been in New York for the last six years. So it has involved videotapes, ISDN lines and satellite feeds. It's ridiculous!

JR: Do you have a good relationship with technology?

MS: You know, I have the basic love/hate relationship with technology. I'm not like you, but god knows I make use of it all! I do love it and I can't imagine what it would be like in the golden age with just timing notes and perhaps a Moviola. It's hard to imagine not being locked to picture at least, hearing things back and experimenting. Yet the great all-time scores were written like that, and there are hundreds of them!

I have no formal training. I had to learn by hit

and miss. I've figured out a lot of orchestral colors through the use of synthesizers. And conversely, I've learned how the synthesizer is sometimes so unable to create a sound that the orchestra can. I'm constantly learning that the orchestra will not sound—direct, crisp and exact—like my synthesizers every time. I've dealt with directors who, as glorious as the orchestra sounded, told me that it sounded so much better at my home studio, and I agree. Then a few weeks later I listen to the real orchestral version and compare to the synth version and we all ask: "What were we thinking of, favoring the synth version?" The thing about the synth is that it's all me playing, so that my sense of humor and my emotions are in every single part, whether it's an oboe part or the volume swell on a field drum roll. It's all my playing. There's not a single note that goes by that doesn't have my character. I think that's why the synth mockup has a certain flavor. It's a professional challenge to be able to achieve that with the orchestra.

JR: You're also a very accomplished piano player, so you could probably sit down at the piano and impress the hell out of a director by presenting a theme and playing it really well.

MS: Yes as far as playing a theme or a mood I can do that, except when you have a big chase scene, or something really percussive. Those are things that I don't find myself doing as much. Also because I haven't had a chance to exercise that side of me. But there's no doubt that I can sit by the piano and make it work. I was blessed with that.

JR: Has your agent been an integral part of your life?

MS: Ahh, certainly yes. The movies I get most of the time are owing to previous relationships from previous movies I've done, or another relationship I forged on my own, whether Billy Crystal or Bette Midler, who were my ins for the movie industry. I can look at 90% of the posters on my wall at least and do a six degrees of separation to either one of those people. It's a bit complicated. I don't even know how to answer that question. But my agent is an enabler in the whole overlook of the situation. Although he listens to my feeling about being burned out now and then, he will always dangle some other thing in front of me. But I've been as guilty of that myself really, of hearing about something, having to look into it, and suddenly I'm on the job and it has nothing to do with the reality of what I'm capable of dealing with. I do work here all by myself! I have no underlings laboring alongside me, whether credited or not. I write every single note by myself. I don't know how some of the guys can do it with seven or eight movies a year, I don't know how they do it….

JR: I think you probably do know how they do it.

MS: Sure I know. It took me up till a couple of years ago to trust and not feel guilty letting an orchestrator fill in the proper colors once I had established the tone of the movie. And of course with Jeff Atmajian I have such a complete trust, and would feel lost without him. I know that I can give him a really well worked out piano version of the cue, and don't have to say a word to him. And he will still deliver just what I had in my head. It doesn't mean adding notes really. I don't have to add much more. About 80 to 85% of The Kid was delivered as four-handed piano parts. And I learned the difference between orchestrators, how certain people can make that flower bloom and others just get by. Anyway, I don't want to say something bad about the people who have saved my life repeatedly. You really see what some people can bring to it. There are no added notes except for realized harp runs, although I love doing that. Playing that, adding all that in, I love doing that. But I finally have learned to let go when there's a real crunch at the end [of delivering a score].

JR: If you ever talk to younger composers, do you find yourself giving a particular piece of advice that rings true for you?

MS: You know what, I feel like I'm always depressing when people call or write me. I can only talk about what I've done, how things happened for me and the way that I write. It's not really helping anyone to follow that same path, it's so specific and individual. All those cliches where famous people tell you that if you don't want to do it every single day all the time, don't even try. Ha Ha! What can I say is not uplifting at all.

My agent once said go to a video store, find a scene from a famous movie that didn't have music in it, and write music to that. A producer or director will immediately see a star and it will just get more interested watching it and listening to it. He brought up a great example of a really long, fantastic, classic chase scene from *What's Up Doc?,* with Barbara Streisand and Ryan O'Neal. [Director] Peter Bogdanovich chose to not score at all, and it's like a twenty minute chase on the streets of San Francisco. So he said, take five minutes of that and score it if you want to show your comedy chops. At a symposium I brought up that a scene in *Sleepless in Seattle* that I scored; [director] Nora Ephron had dropped the cue, in order to give more impact to the song which preceded it and came after it. Maybe she was right. It was still a terrible phone call when I heard the news. So there's this great scene in the movie where Meg Ryan is listening to Tom Hanks over the radio in her car. It would be a great scene for someone to take and write a beautiful theme to. That's a piece of advice that I can give.

> Career

CHAPTER EIGHT

> Beginning A Career

How Do I Get Started in Film Scoring?

Zen koans are these simple, poetic questions for which there is never a single correct answer. Some Zen koans are even more tricky than this chapter title, because frankly there is no real single, simple answer to the question of how to get into the business of scoring films. Everyone who has developed a career in film music has found a unique way. We can look at some of the ways that those composers successful in the business (and it is very much a business) became that way.

Live Where You Work

Without cynicism, let's skip the topic of talent. We'll assume for now that you are ready for that first big break. The first item to look at on a career path is—and this shouldn't be much of a surprise—it really helps to be as close to the action as possible. While there are numerous successful composers who live outside of the major film production communities of Hollywood or New York, there is an inherent liability in being far away from where the majority of product is made. There are a handful of major cities in the world that can support the careers of scoring composers. Convenience is looked upon as a great commodity in the movie biz. While it is possible to be successful in scoring commercials, local promos or shows, logos or other music for radio, television, industrial videos, games or other new media from any number of locations, the bulk of movies and TV are primarily made and scored in LA and NY. That's where the work is done, and that's where the work is.

Should you find yourself transplanted to one of these metropolises, or decide to make a go of it wherever you are, then what? Go to music school? Seek professional work of some kind door to door? Wait tables while scratching out stunning music by a dim bare light bulb all night until your fingers bleed from inspiration or orchestration?

How Important Is a Music Degree?

While many of today's more successful film composers come from an academic background strongly based in music, their academic training itself did not get them any work in film. If you feel that you still need to learn more about your craft, and there are film music courses somewhere near you or somewhere you want to go, then by all means take some classes, learn and enjoy. However, be aware that when you finish, you will be in exactly the same position you were before in terms of a professional music career. Universities do not create successful film composers—talented composers find the ways to become successful. Most producers do not get excited learning of a composer's academic excellence. It's all about what you can do, how well you can do it, how quickly you can do it, and what you have done before.

⊗ A list of schools offering courses on film music can be found online at www. reelworld-online.com

Windows of Opportunity

So how do new composers get a leg up in the film industry? Usually by some unique combination of talent, hard work, luck, ass kissing, apprenticeship, dues paying, more dues paying, demo hawking, nepotism, and those famous right place/right time situations. How did Danny Elfman or Michael Kamen or any number of today's in-demand composers get where they are? Achieving a certain amount of visibility in music outside of movies, like rock 'n' roll or other pop music, helps, as is also true of composers like Randy Newman, Hans Zimmer, Mark Isham, Anne Dudley, Stewart Copeland, Craig Armstrong, Graeme Ravel, Cliff Martinez, and many others. Their non-score albums are showcases for a unique style or talent that gives film people a sense of what is possible with them. There is also some amount of celebrity attached to a composer who sells records outside of the film soundtrack genre.

Other composers have found success by slowly working up the ranks of film scoring; from student films, short films, trailers, documentaries or TV toward the top rung of the movie scoring food chain. I believe it is far harder today to become established as a composer of "serious" film music without having some form of existing recognition. The resumé you include with your demo is often more important than the music for many people, since it lists what you've done prior. You will always have a better shot when you have several good, recognizable credits to your name. The first question any prospective employer will often ask you is, "what other projects have you done?" They will want to see that you have completed real work of a similar type and scale successfully in the past, and they may want to know that at least some of your music is similar to what they are looking for. The quality of your work may sometimes be less important than the notoriety or success of your previous projects. As shallow as that may seem, it is sometimes, though not always as simple as that. And here is a brief caveat: never ever lie on a resumé. They are checked, you will get found out, and lose any chance at working with those people. Fortunately, on a smaller low-budget project, where a more experienced, and typically more expensive, composer is unavailable, you will have your best shot strictly based on the quality of your music and what the director or producer thinks of you in your initial meetings. First impressions at face to face meetings count.

If you've put together a good quality demo, what do you do with it? Who do you send them out to? Unsolicited demos are neither appreciated nor accepted by most potential employees (including directors, producers, music supervisors, music agents, production companies, film studio executives, etc.) You must first make contact with these semi-mythical creatures via some means. For some that means is the telephone. For others, it's the cocktail or dinner party (see what I mean about being close to where the action is?). Connections do get made at social events. Make contacts whenever possible.

Apprenticing with a Successful Composer

Much of the work that came to me when I was getting started was from recommendations from other composers. I was very fortunate in this way, since I worked for several years with a number of successful film composers who have been very gracious in passing my name along on projects they couldn't (or didn't want to) do. This is one reason why an apprenticeship, paid or unpaid assistance to a successful composer, can be a valuable part of one's education in film. Apprenticeship also helps teach you about the "realities" of composing for film, something not taught in music schools. Knowing how to compose music, even very appropriate music for a given film or genre, does not fully prepare you for what goes into successfully executing and completing a score. Again, I do not mean to say anything negative at all against formal education if you feel you need to hone your craft. However, music is music, while working in the movies is another thing altogether. How do you convince a director or producer that you're the right person for the job? What do you say to a producer who tells you that your music needs to sound more emotional, when you've poured your heart out onto paper (or your sequencer) for a month? How do you put together a recording session that cannot fail? What do you do when it fails? How do you deal with the unions, ASCAP and BMI (the organizations that collect performance royalties for composers), contracts, royalties, publishing or soundtrack album deals? How do you pace yourself on a project where you need to write more music per day than you ever have before? Who are the people you need to ally yourself with in order to accomplish the best results in the least amount of time? Is it considered acceptable to ghostwrite for another composer, or to have someone ghostwrite for you? What kinds of musical motives are guaranteed to be thrown out of a film? Is it OK to criticize any aspects of a film you are working on in front of the director or producer, even if it would help improve the film? Are there certain jobs, people, or things you could do that could ruin your career? How would you recognize them?

So much of this is best learned when working closely with a working composer. We'll touch on some of these topics later in this section, but nothing takes the place of learning by simply doing in a professional environment. And you really must be prepared to work very hard to get started in a very competitive field. Complaints are not welcome in most situations. Going the extra mile before being asked is always a plus.

The business of film scoring is a maze, one where you are, by turns, both the mouse and the cheese.

The Demo

Just as most actors audition in order to have a chance at a role, composers too must audition for work by submitting a demo recording of their prior work. In addition to the demos I make of my scores, I've also listened to a number of demos sent to me by other composers interested in scoring films. I get these because people are interested in feedback on the quality and style of their music as it compares to those who are already scoring pictures. I'm reluctant to act as a musical advice columnist, dispensing suggestions or criticisms about other people's compositions. After all, who am I to criticize what anyone else writes? My own musical career is still relatively young. I work hard and I've had some good (and a few not-so-good) breaks along the way. Like most, I need to prove myself almost daily.

The Makings of a Good Demo Tape

I've listened to dozens (perhaps even scores!) of demos sent to me by various composers wanting my feedback or help. I have stopped accepting or listening to demos for a variety of reasons. While there are some legal concerns, the main reason is that I am simply not comfortable passing judgement on other people's music. But some recurring trends among these many, many demos has compelled me to make a few general comments on how a composer puts his or her best musical face forward in order to get a better shot in the film and TV music world. In other words, what makes a good demo?

- ## Genre Showcase

    Film music has an ephemeral, identifiable, if hard-to-define quality. Although many styles of music work well in films—every style of music ever created has been adapted to the service of film—there are recognizable conventions in film score that continue to work again and again and are sought after by film makers. In general, film producers and directors are looking for music that functions in specific, "cinematic" ways, that sound like some film scores they have heard before and loved. If your music completely bends all established genres of film music to the point of breaking, if your music falls outside of the styles set by any known composer or successful film score, then you may have a problem. While you should strive to innovate, you must do so with at least some sense of acknowledgment to all that has come before you. You are hopefully adding a new brick to the wall of successful film scores and composers. You take what has come before you and make it into something new, but within certain stylistic bounds. Neither Stravinsky nor Bob Dylan were successful film composers, they did something different.

    I studied contemporary classical composition in music school. It was a great, though academic education that taught me a lot about writing music. It did not teach me about composing for the screen; it wasn't designed to. I started becoming aware of film scores and started buying soundtrack albums while a student. That was my first real lesson in scoring. The next was to eventually meet established film composers, first through some music classes, and later as a working musician and then as a composer myself. But I do not put any of my more "serious" contemporary music onto a film score demo. It simply doesn't belong. Neither does jazz, pure pop, or other musical styles, unless you are selling yourself as someone to write those kinds of "source music," which is music that appears in a film on a radio or in a club. But that is not film score. If you want to show yourself as a film composer, then keep your demos focused on film-style music.

- ## Melodies: Concise, Focused & Memorable

  One of the most important—and often overlooked—factors in film music is a great, memorable melody. I recognize that some great moments in film score history are from dense or atmospheric cues that would not be considered especially melodic. Virtually all successful composers have at some point in their career written a memorable theme. Don't neglect that. People bond with melodies. It is how most people hear music. It's also the most elusive part of composing for film. Melodies need to be stated clearly and concisely, at least once. Melodic repetition, within reason, is a tool for structure and development. It is a part of human nature to require some repetition in order to understand and memorize new things, including melodies.

  The other important element to film score style, as mentioned in the first section of the book, is *focus* and *economy*. In other words, don't have too many things going on at a time. Keeping things focused will also help to make your melodic ideas more clear and easily heard.

- ## Variety: The Spice of a Diverse Sequence

  A good general demo of your music should be varied and well sequenced. Put the best stuff first. Don't put more than one piece on the demo that shows the same style and musical approach. Each cue should show something unique. Don't put similar pieces next to each other, every cut on the CD should have contrast to the ones around it. Cues should be nonrepetitive within themselves and should not have any long sustained sections or long intros. Edit if you must in order to get to the heart of the cue quickly and make it a good listening experience. Demos must stand on their own musically because there is no picture to go along.

• Plagiarists Need Not Apply

Don't rip off music by another composer to make a demo. I've heard a few of these. I'm not talking about imitating elements of the style of an established film composer—there's nothing wrong with that. I mean emulating an actual piece of music from a film score (or any composition) too closely. In general, you can't fool anyone but yourself—somebody along the way will figure it out. The point here is that you may stand a better chance of finding work if your music has some elements of the sound or style of a currently successful film composer, but not if all you do is recreate some tune from some film. Where's the creativity in that?

You probably have heard the saying that "good artists borrow, and great artists steal." It's true to a point. Every artistic style develops gradually over time. Each important new artist within a field or genre builds on top of what came before and does not start from scratch. There are some exceptions, but I think this rule applies well to the movies (or television). The great composers who have succeeded in the real world have done so by adding their unique voice to an existing form, while also embracing the basics created by those who came before them.

Learn from today's most successful composers. Find scores that really move you, and figure out what it is about the music that works, both emotionally and how it supports the picture.

• Including Appropriate Material

When you do put together a demo for a specific project, be sure that there is some music on it that exactly fits what the producer/director is looking for. Most nonmusicians have very little musical imagination to understand what you are capable of beyond what you give them. If you get the chance to submit a demo for a car commercial, be sure that at least one piece on your tape sounds like a car commercial. What does a car commercial sound like? If you can, ask them before you submit the demo. There is nothing wrong with asking those kinds of questions ahead of time, and it shows that you are concerned and on the ball. Then either find something you've already recorded or write something that fits their description. Same goes for any project you have a shot at.

• Your Demo Reflects Your Abilities

Be sure to never submit a demo for which you are anything less than proud. There are no excuses, and no one will know what you are capable of beyond what they actually hear. You will always be competing against people with more experience and more gear than you, so make the best of what you have. There are no points given for complexity—only imagination, expressiveness, appropriateness, and a good sounding recording. Don't assume that the people listening to your music will be able to hear what you could do with more resources. They rightfully will assume that what you put on your demo is exactly like what you will deliver on the job. No more and no less. Avoid overly synthy sounding demos, which are usually perceived as cheap sounding. Get live players on your demos.

• Credits Where Credit Is Due

Remember, it's your work that counts. If you are looking for professional work, don't supply superfluous information about yourself. And in this category I would include your educational background. No one in the professional entertainment business will care one bit if you graduated with honors, got a prestigious academic award, slept with your teachers, starred in the school play, scored the school play, or any other facet in your life other than your "reel world" musical credits, period. You have a far better chance of breaking into the scoring biz if you are a former (or current) member of a famous rock band than if you have a degree in music; recent history bears me out. How you learned composing is of no ones' concern other than your own and that of whoever paid for your lessons. If you are asked to submit something along with a demo, it will be a list of credits, and that's it.

Why are credits so important? As mentioned before, there is a huge difference between knowing how to compose music technically and being able to deliver the right music for a project. That, along with the ability to deliver it on time, under budget, well recorded and mixed, with great sounding musicians, with all legal and payroll affairs properly handled, and with the right attitude when changes are requested (for the fifth time). Credits say to a producer or director, "I know how to do it right, and I've already succeeded at it before." It boils down to trust. Can you be trusted with their very precious project, and money? Good question. A diploma does not answer it. Acting like a professional does. Like they say, nothing succeeds like success.

• Be Yourself

This may be the most important and difficult aspect of making a demo: be yourself. You have a better shot at something if you are the only right person for that job. If you can provide a musical element that sets you aside from the rest of the pack, then you will have a much better shot. Don't be bland. Composers such as Ry Cooder, for one example, score films because they do something that no one else can. They are unique. So are you, and it is your job to prove it. Tread that fine line which distinguishes you, while maintaining the "screen sense" that is part of the genre of good film music. It's not easy, but, as Tom Hanks said in *A League of Their Own*, "Hell, if it was easy, then everybody'd do it!"

- ## Judging a Book by Its Cover

  On a somewhat more mundane note, a demo should also look as good as it sounds. Among other things, this means it should be a CD and not a tape. This is expected by producers, directors, and music executives. If you don't have a means of making your own CDs, then either get it or make friends with someone who does. Make the label and cover look good as well. Use a printer instead of handwriting them. Include your contact information on the cover and the CD label as well, in case they get separated. Don't go too crazy with fancy graphics. Your name and contact information should be clear and easy to see, as well as names for all the cuts on the back. Your name and contact information should also be on the CD itself in case it gets lost from the case.

The List
More Advice on Getting a Start in the Film World

As it stands, writing film music is hard, hard work. I assume most of you know that, but I want to be sure that you do. If you are lucky enough to have a serious scoring job, with a serious deadline, there's a pretty good chance you'll be losing a serious amount of sleep before it's done. If you're not willing to make personal sacrifices of your weekends, evenings, social events, vacations, and even some relationships, then be warned: this job may not be for you. Of course, any film composer has free time to do other things like any other semi-normal person, and some manage their time carefully enough to accommodate work and some play at the same time. But virtually all of the composers I know have become experts in sleep and social deprivation at one time or another. This isn't a glamorous profession, but it's a great life if you are ready for it. Here are some points about getting a start in the film scoring world:

- As described above, have a demo that shows what you can do, with no excuses about its technical or musical quality. Anyone who may hire you will want to hear your work, and will compare your music with every other demo they get. They don't care how you made the recording, what gear you used, or how much it cost. It has to sound like the real thing. That means music in a film score style, with themes, melodies, good performances, with a range of emotions and feels, and good quality, listenable mixes. I recommend having some music played by at least a few live players because of how much it enhances the emotional impact of the music to the listener. Most all-synthesized demos sound poor in relationship to their live recorded counterparts, unless the style of music dictates an all-electronic approach.

- Be prepared to do some demo work on "spec" (meaning for free). If you are just getting started, and don't have a resumé with any significant professional work on it, you must prove yourself to any prospective client. (You should be willing to do a demo to picture as a way to show how your work will apply directly to the project.) Make it clear up front that is what you are doing, so there are no misunderstandings about doing the whole job for free. There have certainly been occasions where composers have donated their time and efforts in order to prove their abilities in exchange for nothing more than the credit, or a good meal. It may set a bad precedent, but it can also open the door to better projects in the future.

  You may also wish to donate your service and talents for a project that seems worthwhile. Such projects might include: a promising student film; a well-made, small independent film; a public service announcement; a documentary; anything that supports a charity or other worthy organization; or doing a full-blown demo to show off what you would do for a paying film job. Some things are more important than money.

- *Work with people who are better at what they do than you are at what you do.* In other words always seek out the best possible collaborators. This would include musicians, singers, engineers, recording studios, orchestrators, music editors, programmers, and anyone else you might work with on your projects. Don't feel the need to work in a vacuum. Get help whenever needed. On your first scores there are many potential problems that could cause you to fail. By working with experienced people you will avoid most of the possible pitfalls. You will be surprised how many experienced professionals are willing to help out a new composer if they have the time and like what you do. There is never harm in asking. Take what you do seriously. *Think like a pro from the very beginning.*

- If possible, align yourself with a working composer. Be an apprentice, even if it pays little or no money and has long hours. It is the one best way of learning how the business really works. Make yourself useful, become of value. Eventually it might become a job that pays while you can continue to hone your skills and your contacts. If appropriate, you may get the chance to help out with writing some music, possibly to make the fixes that are frequently required on certain cues, polish up MIDI sequences, write source cues, or even write some cues on your own based on that composer's themes. Be warned though: it is not acceptable ever to take clients away from someone for whom you are working. It is a breach of personal and professional ethics and can be very damaging to your future career.

- Promoting yourself is one of the more important activities you can do as a composer. Get on the phone, call music supervisors, ad agencies, or other people in your area that are likely to hire a composer and introduce yourself. Offer to send a demo. Build relationships. Make connections and meet people. There are lists of names and numbers in some industry contact books that you should be able to find at a larger book store or the library. Both trade publications *Daily Variety* and *The Hollywood Reporter* do annual film music editions with excellent contact lists.

See the appendix for more information, or check online at www. reelworld-online.com

- Artists with unique musical styles can become more noticeable. There isn't really such a thing as "generic film music." In general, most successful composers have a unique style which their musical background often reflects, while, at the same time, they have the flexibility to apply what they do well to the rigors of a film project. It is to your advantage to develop a personal style of music that both expresses who you are as a composer and has the capability to fit into the genre of film, television, commercials, games, industrial films, or whatever type projects you are aiming towards being involved with.

- Be persistent in your efforts, and be patient. While stories abound of overnight successes, big breaks, and accidental discoveries, most solid careers build slowly over time. Mine certainly has been that way. It can take years to get a foothold on a musical career. And there are no guarantees after your big breaks that your foothold will remain. You will always be working on your career while working on your music. Even the most well established and successful composers continue to promote themselves in various ways to keep the flame of their career lit and growing.

- Once you have established a relationship, continue to nurture it. Stay in touch with the people you have worked with through calls, letters, holiday cards, and CDs. Personal relationships are at the heart of a career.

As mentioned previously, there are advantages to living in Hollywood (which is really a euphemism for Los Angeles) or other major cities with active post production in order to work in the film and television music industry. But don't hop on a bus quite yet. There is no advantage to being in a film mecca without some credits or at least the possibility of some real work. While lots of composers have successful careers outside of LA, NY, or a few other major places, it helps significantly to be where the action is. While some projects are done by some remote means of sending videos and demos back and forth, few directors or producers enjoy working this way. I've seen attempts at long distance relationships break down because of the lack of proximity during the intense parts of a project. Things happen fast in this business. There is not always time to send sketches or demos back and forth to other time zones. Delivering demos via the Internet, though quite possible, isn't a real substitute for sitting in a room together with your client. Still, it would be very rash to move to a new city without some way of support for yourself right from the start. Either that, or save up so you can work for free and get by. It is quite possible to get a start and then eventually grow as a working composer in any number of cities around the world. There are projects that require music in most cities—independent films, commercials, industrial films, local TV, and radio promotions are all projects you can do most anywhere you live, and start developing a resume. So much of career development depends on what you really want to do with your life. Think about your real goals, both short and long term. Then decide how to go about achieving those goals, and where that might take you.

Learning By Doing
10 Things Film Composers Taught Me

As a score begins to take shape, it becomes time to work with other musicians at recording sessions or to schedule meetings with the director. Prior to writing my own scores, I was a synthesist and sound designer for a number of Hollywood film composers, which had me working side by side with the composer. In addition to being my job, it also became my apprenticeship in the scoring world, since it required me to stay with those composers for days or weeks at a time. I worked intensively on their scores and watched how things got done in the "reel world" both by what went well or poorly on technical, logistical, and political bases. Attending recording sessions and those incredibly important composer/director meetings was very educational for me and I learned a number of important lessons for composers and those who work as part of a composer's support team.

1. Be prepared. Nobody wants to hear you explain why you could have done a better job under different circumstances. Learn the tools, be organized, and be ready before you need to do or show anything, and know what to do if something goes wrong. Be able to find everything you might possibly need for the session. Have a thorough understanding of the processes being used so you can flow with it.

2. Remember: It's not always what you can do, it's what you can do in ten minutes. During recording sessions time is money, and thus time is every producer's enemy. If a problem comes up that stops a composer or musician from working in any way, it needs to be fixed any way possible. It's not uncommon to make adjustments and even significant changes to a score during recording sessions, but you need to learn how to make things flow quickly and efficiently. If you can't do it, be sure someone there can.

3. I've seen some people use recording sessions or director/producer meetings for a bit of showing off either musically or verbally. It's not a good idea. An assistant's job is to make the film's composer look as good as possible. It's poor etiquette for any subordinate people to grandstand. Ghostwriters cannot, unless allowed, speak up about the cues they've written. Soloists shouldn't be handing out cards unrequested. And so on down the line. A composer puts a team together to accomplish something, but remains captain of the ship until he or she chooses to point out the efforts of the others. Hopefully, if all is going well, everyone is congratulated and credited in front of the director or producer. Hopefully, if things do not go so well, the composer will not use the opportunity to lay blame.

4. Learn to take criticism gracefully, no matter what. Most scoring projects have a good amount of pressure associated with them. No one is necessarily on his or her best behavior. There are lots and lots of fragile egos in the film industry,

sometimes in unexpected places. And it never hurts to give compliments when it feels appropriate, as long as you are not obviously kissing butt.

5. Anticipate needs. It always helps if you know what you are getting yourself into. There is a lot of planning that goes into a film score and the recording sessions to be sure that everything will go smoothly and efficiently. What equipment should be available? Is there anything you need to borrow, rent, or have repaired to be ready? The biggest obstacle to all this is usually communications, or lack of it more specifically. There are a number of people involved in any score project, from the director to the musicians, musical contractor, engineers, dubbing mixers, editors, etc. There isn't always a system in place to ensure that everyone who needs to communicate does. If you are working on a project, either as programmer, assistant, co-composer, or composer, be sure to get something going so that critical information is always where it needs to be. I remember playing a cue for a director who seemed very uncomfortable as I was playing it. I was sure he didn't like it. When it was done, I coaxed him to tell me what he thought. He told me that he liked the music a great deal, but that the scene had been cut from the film several days prior. So why didn't I know that? Why did I have to waste several days of my time? Lack of good communication.

6 & 7. Don't complain and don't make excuses. Nobody really wants to hear how hard your job is, who on the session you don't like, whose music sucks, or how crummy the studio is that you're using. Too often, complaints are just veiled excuses for why things aren't going as they should. There's little room for these at a recording session or a session with your clients or collaborators. In more private moments, then the chance for some belly-aching or dishing is fine, to be sure. But choose those moments carefully. People love to gossip and you might say something critical or negative that gets around. It could end up costing a friendship or an important professional relationship.

Excuses just don't cut it at sessions or meetings. What matters is results, not why you can't or didn't achieve them. That might sound like a lot of pressure, but hopefully this will not happen often for you. The goal is to work through a problem to a solution, even if the answer is a compromise (as it so often is). Hopefully fixes can be made before anyone is affected by them. Naturally, there will come a time when you just can't do what someone wants, and it's important to be honest and graceful about it. Sessions can be postponed, but union musicians require a two or three day warning or they must be paid anyway. Cancelling a meeting to play music for a director is better than wasting anyone's time.

It is alright to be demanding on the people with whom you are working. After all, your reputation and further success is based on how well everything goes. If someone is causing problems, don't just sit there and hope the problem goes away. Demand that the problem be fixed right away. For example, if you're not happy with your engineer's sound or speed, say something. If a musician is not giving it their best shot, speak up and try to inspire a better performance. Suggestions are usually more useful than complaints. Some people are tyrants, and some people are collaborators. I prefer the latter to work with, and to be when working with others. I am demanding, but I've never worked with someone who performed better through threats, coersion, bullying, or shouting. I think that those who do are not serving themselves in the long run.

8. Leave as much of your ego at home as possible. There will invariably come a time when you will be working with people not nearly as together, prepared, organized, or perhaps as talented as you are. Recording music is most always a team effort between the composer and those people hired to realize the score—musicians, orchestrator, engineer, tape or hard disk system operator, contractor, etc. The main goal is to get great music made into a great recording. Just as the composer is the boss at the recording sessions, they are also at the call of the director and producers. Last second changes are not that uncommon. Even if music has been listened to and approved, minds get changed, and that is their prerogative.

Learn to take suggestions and requests gracefully. As always, the composer's main job is to make the producers and director happy. Even if your favourite music is about to be altered beyond recognition, that is just part of the job. Some film makers are more willing to debate the merits of a cue than others. Some are more dictatorial in their collaborative style. If you firmly believe that you have written something that truly serves the film, then by all means speak up and explain what you are trying to do. It may make you unpopular for the moment, but you need to show, in as gentle a way as possible, how changing something in the music may ruin the desired emotional effect and not be in the film's best interest.

9. Never be late. This may seem like a little thing to some people, but it's a pet peeve of mine so I've got to throw it in. Some people are really lax about this,

and it never ceases to amaze me. On most professional sessions, it's not tolerated, and nobody cares what went wrong with your car or that you had to be taken to the emergency room. On film and TV projects, there's never any question about sticking to the schedule.

This would be a top 10 list, but it only has 9 things in it. Maybe number 10 should be "sometimes you need to forget the rules." Maybe it should be "anything worth doing is worth doing right" or just "remember to have fun." If you've worked on any type of project you should have your own set of rules to go by. The end result of all of this are meetings that go smoothly and professionally and recording sessions that are productive and fun.

Agents

Having a Representative on Your Side

Some composers consider the acquisition of an agent to be the Holy Grail of career success. "If I only had an agent, I wouldn't have to go looking for work, it would come and find me." Well, that's not quite wrong and not quite right. An agent is a tremendous ally to a working composer, helping to insure an optimal working situation for the composer. They handle most of the business aspects of a project and make sure those elements are covered to the composer's best advantage. They can also ensure that legal problems won't occur as a result of the work. They protect and help a composer achieve some of their goals.

Agents do find work for their composers. Almost all major film work will come through an agent. Most major producers and directors don't deal with composers who don't have an agent. They prefer not to talk business with creative artists. Other directors will just hire their friends to score their projects, hire someone whose nonfilm music they like, or find someone through a chance encounter or recommendation. Many composers get work when a film they score becomes very successful. That will attract many new prospects. Agents makes it their business to know what upcoming projects are looking for composers and make contact with the production companies directly in order to offer their composers for the project. They do tremendous research to find possible projects for their clients. Some producers or directors may already have some idea of whom they want to score their work before coming to an agent, while some welcome input from agents based on musical concepts.

If you are interested in getting an agent, the best way to do it is to approach one when you already have a firm offer of a project. Let them handle the negotiations for you and take their 10 percent. Since the job is already yours, you could certainly do it on your own and not have to pay the commission. Often, a good agent will be able to enhance the negotiation sufficiently enough to compensate for their fee. Even if that is not the case, bringing a job to an agent shows them that you are not starting from scratch and that you are willing to work toward your own success; that's what they need to see in order to select you as a good prospective client. If you are getting work, and want to bring your projects to an agent, you should probably contact several and talk with them, get a sense of what they do and what they would do for you. Look at their roster and see how their clients are doing. If possible, contact some of the agent's existing clients and ask them about their experiences. There is more about agents later in this section.

CHAPTER NINE

> Career Challenges

Orchestral Maneuvers in the Dark

My First Score for a Live Orchestra

While it is important to put together a home studio capable of producing demos of orchestral scores, there is no replacement for the real thing. I spent a great deal of time, effort, and money putting together a studio for cool electronic scores as well as decent sampled orchestral scores. After doing a great many all-synthesized scores, I got my first small opportunity to compose and record a score for a live orchestra. Ah, a room full of people with expensive instruments and pieces of paper with a bunch of black dots in front of them. My job? Those black dots!

What qualified me, at the time a mere synth-and-sample guy, to write a score for orchestra? Honestly, nothing did—well, almost nothing. I did study music, though I was not a great student in school. I played in some orchestras and classical ensembles (I was a trained flute and piccolo player), studied composition, orchestration, and conducting. Some of those skills had languished somewhat while I pursued my interests in higher technology. Now was a chance to set aside those cool synth noises and do something in a more traditional setting. I recognized a great musical opportunity. I turned my sequencer on.

Sizing Up "The Critic's" Needs

The project was relatively simple, an animated series for television called *The Critic*. It used a medium sized ensemble of about 35 or 40 players each week. The show's usual composer had to deal with a small emergency that week, and since I had arranged and produced the show's main theme music, the producers remembered me and asked if I could step in on short notice. Orchestrally speaking, I had a specific palette to work from, based mainly on the show's main theme—strings, woodwinds (featuring a somewhat jazzy clarinet), French horns and trombones, and a standard rhythm section of piano, bass, and drums. After watching a video of the episode I was to score, I added two trumpets and an accordion player to the roster, since parts of the show had some Cuban and Hispanic elements. I loaded samples or all these instruments into my samplers, along with some added Latin percussion. I decided that with the short time I'd have to record the orchestra, I would do the Latin percussion and electric bass myself (besides, those parts are really fun to do!). I now had the sonic template I'd use for the whole show all ready at the touch of a key. I also set up a track template in my sequencer so each cue was laid out the same, named by instrument, whether I used every instrument in the cue or not. This would simplify things for the orchestrator, who would have a very quick turnaround time as well.

I hired on a great orchestrator to assist me in the transition from sequencer to score paper. Most composers use an orchestrator, both for tight schedules and for their expertise. The orchestrator fulfills the vision of the composer and, if appropriate and needed, will embellish it, just as a good musician in a rhythm section might. I'd known orchestrator Bruce Fowler for many years (in his former life, he was a trombone player with iconoclast rockers Frank Zappa and Captain Beefheart), but, until then, we never had the opportunity to work together. While the sequencer I use can print out a score and parts, there is a great deal of essential detail that is needed in an orchestral score which gets left out, such as precise dynamics and articulation markings. Bruce could also give me much needed suggestions about string or wind voicings unfamiliar to me, and ensure a good sound from the group. I wanted this session to go smoothly, so working this way made it that much more certain it would. As I was sequencing (or "composing" as it used to be called), I kept in mind always that the end result would be different once the real orchestra played the parts.

Working on a Tight Schedule

I received the video of the show late on a Sunday night, and the recording session was already scheduled for that upcoming Thursday morning. In that time span I had to write all the music, get it approved, hand it over to Bruce so he'd have enough time to do the orchestrations and send them off to get copied. Then I'd record my timecode, clicks, and synth percussion parts to the multi-track (along with a scratch mix of my demos), then show up at the studio for the orchestra session by 8 AM Thursday. The show had some 30 plus cues—it was time to push some buttons. Oh, television!

A pleasant surprise came on Monday, when I spoke to the show's producer for the first time. I asked when someone would be by my studio to listen to my cues and approve them. He said, "Oh, we'll just all come to the recording session. See you Thursday!" Well, well! I'd never done a project where the music wasn't demo'd and completely approved before the actual recording. This was an unusual situation. Normally I would be thrilled, but I was apprehensive that things might go horribly wrong. After all, I was working with these producers for the first time, let alone being my first orchestral session.

Writing the music was great fun. Knowing there will be an orchestra means not having to worry so much about my sequenced performances, since all would be replaced by the live group. For thematic consistency, I integrated elements of the main theme into several of my cues. I also wrote a few themes as well for the characters. One of the recurring jokes in the show were very humorous parodies of popular films. This meant writing some cues in the style of the score being parodied. One clip was in the style of Spike Lee's *Malcom X*, one which was a weird cross between *Terminator 2* and the classic French film *The Red Balloon* (a sweet children's story), a Mel Gibson action movie, and so on. These had to be musical parodies as well, which meant to approach them very seriously, and just a little over the top. Since the orchestra I was recording wasn't as big as some of these cues would require, I subtly embellished those cues with my samples. For the remainder of the underscore, I stuck with just the live players.

On Tuesday, I had Bruce Fowler over to give him the first half of the music. We went through each cue. I played him my synth demo, told him what I was going after (tender, scary, triumphant, etc.), and we discussed some orchestral options. For the most part, my demos were exactly as I wanted them played by the orchestra, making his job easier. I gave him a tape with my demos. Each cue was slated with the cue number and title to prevent any confusion. Most importantly, I recorded the click along with the music so he could discern the exact rhythms on sections that might be loosely performed or where the tempo makes any sudden changes.

I also took advantage of my sequencer's notation capabilities and gave Bruce a printout of each cue. I also gave him a disk with MIDI files of the cues. Anyone who's used a sequencer with transcription capabilities knows that they all require some amount of tweaking to get them to look like well notated and edited music. For most of the parts I was not quantizing (a sequencer function which makes the rhythms more precise), so the transcriptions were pretty rough, but they did what was needed. Bruce got an approximation of the score, which accurately showed all the correct notes in the music.

Figure 3.1 A cue in both the computer printout and what Bruce did for the orchestra

The combination of rough score and decent demo, along with our brief chats gave Bruce everything he needed. Off he went and left me to write the rest of the music.

On Wednesday, after three very long days, I finished. Bruce came and picked up the last of the music. Now I had to prep tapes for the session the next day. I checked with an engineer at the scoring studio and got the specs on how to record my elements of the score the same way as all their previous episodes. I found out how many tracks they normally record onto, which tracks they usually reserve for prerecorded synths, where to put timecode and clicks. At the time, they were still using analog tape(!), so I rented the same type of multitrack machine used by the studio and had it delivered to my house. It was too wide to fit through my studio door, so it remained in my kitchen and I ran cables to it from my studio. I recorded SMPTE timecode for lock-up to video, the clicks for the musicians, scratch mixes of all the music for reference, the bass, drums, and percussion that would be used for the final mix, and some separate sampled strings for the bigger cues. My engineer and I finished tracking everything at about 2AM the night before the session. I had to be at the studio at 8AM. I got a little sleep, then headed over to the studio in the morning.

At the Studio

I got to the studio before the musicians and handed over the master tape to the studio engineer. He put the tape on and played some of it. "What did you use to generate this timecode? Some cheap computer MIDI interface? It's junk!" Although I knew that was a ridiculous thing to say, I was getting nervous. The last thing I needed now was technical problems or an angry engineer, especially with the so-very-important timecode, which is needed at a scoring session to lock up the audio and video tape machines so we can watch the picture while recording or playing back the music.

The engineer was quite unhappy about having to chase down the problem between my tape and their gear. Then it occurred to me that this was exactly his job. It turned out that as an older engineer, he was somewhat biased against what was new technology for the time. Eventually, the timecode was working fine, and everything was up and running. A false alarm. I could finally exhale. The musicians arrived and tuned up. Things were starting to hum along.

Soon, everyone was seated, the parts were passed out, instruments tuned, microphones positioned, and levels set on the mixing console. Time for the downbeat of the first cue. It's an amazing feeling to have a whole room full of people all playing music that you've composed. One of the reasons that producers are still willing to fork over the cash needed to record an orchestra is for the wonderful experience of being with all those people making music. When it works, it is a real high. There is no other time during the making of a film or TV show that so many people are gathered for a single coordinated effort. Making live music is a tremendous rush. And, after many, many more scores, that rush has not diminished for me.

The session itself went amazingly well. I was completely nervous the whole time, but did my best to hide it under a veneer of "composer's cool" (Film Business Rule #1—"Instill confidence. Avoid doing anything that will make your clients as nervous as you actually are"). I had Bruce conduct the session, since he knew the completed scores better than I did, and also so I could remain in the booth with the producers and director. Bruce did a great job, and I could listen carefully to the orchestral results of my sequencing labours.

Making the Producers Happy

Since the producers had not heard a note of the score prior to the recording session, the possibility existed that there would be cues they did not like. Making significant musical changes on a scoring stage with an entire orchestra waiting is far different than editing a track on a sequencer. Orchestral dates are expensive, and the clock ticks on mercilessly. Running into overtime is not looked upon kindly by the people who sign your checks; they may not hire you again. Fortunately for me they were happy with everything and asked for only minor and easy to make changes, such as lightening up an ending chord or making a comedic hit a little broader. Everyone was having a good time at the session, listening to the music, telling jokes, and making a near continuous stream of phone calls. Since then, I've done other orchestral scores that required more effort to make a cue work to everyone's satisfaction. Even with music that has been previewed and approved, people do change their minds on occasion and will ask for fixes at the last moment. It's a fact of life to be dealt with using as much patience, poise, and grace as you can muster.

At that *Critic* session I was not given the opportunity to request specific players for the orchestra, something that I now do routinely. I was asked to use all the same players as in the show's usual orchestra. As a result, there were some problems. The brass players were mainly from the jazz world, and had problems with a few of the more difficult classical solos I had written for them. It took many takes of one particular cue to get a decent take. I was never completely satisfied, but had to keep moving. I learned a lesson then to be much more demanding about knowing the key soloists in the orchestra. Think of it like casting a role in a movie. Good players are rarely generic. Some are classically oriented, some are jazz, some are rock, etc. If you can, you must match the player to the part or score style. When you work with a musical contractor (more on that later) this is what you discuss when putting your ensemble together.

Because of those cues that the brass had such a hard time with, we ended up going about a half hour into overtime, but only with a small group of musicians. No one seemed to mind, and I was told that this was par for the course. The music, while not a lot of minutes, consisted of over 30 cues, which takes time to rehearse and record. In general, you can expect to get between five and ten minutes of orchestral music recorded per hour. A little more if it's simple and you have a really good group, or less if the music is tough or the group isn't so great. Fewer but longer cues go faster than having many shorter cues, even if the overall number of minutes is the same. On this session, it took longer because of a few problems in the group and having so many shorter cues to do. On subsequent scores I've done, I've been able to get through much more per hour, and maintain good quality.

While we recorded the orchestra to the multitrack, we were also mixing the live group along with my synth parts straight to a 4-track master (left, centre, right, and mono surround for TV) with timecode. This way, if there were no mix problems there would be no mixing session—once the orchestra was done, the score was mixed! Just like in the old days. We rebalanced one cue and remixed it from the multitrack. Overall, the mixes sounded great, and I was glad that I pre-recorded my bass, drum, and percussion tracks in my studio—it saved a lot of time and sounded great with the real orchestra.

The session was now over. Hands were shaken, thanks and congratulation were conveyed all around. The producers hung up their phones and exited en masse to their cars. Now the studio was dead quiet. Ahhhhhh, mission accomplished! I went home, ate some lunch, and took a much needed nap. The show aired just three days later. Another one bites the dust. Technology and tradition worked together for the common good, and why not? I've done many orchestral recordings since, but you always remember your first.

Fired
When Bad Things Happen to Good Composers

Let me tell you about a phone call I once got. It was from a good friend, a composer just getting some breaks in his career. Let's call him Arnold. Last time I spoke with Arnold he had just gotten a job to score an independant film for next-to-no money. He had gotten the job only after doing about six demo cues for the director for free, which is really above and beyond what is to be expected from most composers. But when he called me, he was nearly speechless.

"I got fired today" he said in a barely audible voice

"What are you talking about?"

"They kicked me off the film, simple as that. I don't even really know why. After all those cues I wrote for them, and finally hiring me over a bunch of other composers, now it's over. And I've written about nine cues they haven't even heard yet! This is terrible! What do I do? Should I try to get it back? Will I ever work again?"

I asked Arnold to back up and tell me the story from the beginning. It seems that he had met the director some time back on another film. It went well, and at the end of the job the director promised him that they would work together again. But it wasn't so simple. The director needed the approval of the film's producer on all music matters, including choosing a composer. The producer had some potential composers he was also interested in, along with Arnold, the new director's choice. As a result, several possible composers were each given a scene from the film and asked to take a crack at scoring it, on spec. Sometimes this is the only way to get a shot at a film until you are a more established composer. After Arnold, along with who knows how many other composers, scored numerous cues for numerous scenes, the process of elimination came down to selecting him anyway. The deal was made, and he soon received a check for one half of the agreed-upon fee, a typical arrangement, with the other half paid upon delivery of the recorded score.

But don't pop that champagne cork yet. Not long after he began the job, the problems began. For although Arnold was selected based on music written for the actual film (and not just a general demo), the director then decided that none of the demo cues were actually ready to be used in the film. A turnaround from his support when the demos were being written. The director had done a thorough temp score for the film to see how certain kinds of music worked in specific scenes, and he wanted the final score to be reminiscent of his temp music. In fact, he wanted the final score to sound just like his temp score. Note for note. This was not good.

Time to write, and rewrite. And rewrite, and rewrite. What my beleaguered friend soon found out was that this was in fact The Director From Hell. A great guy, but a real maniac about the music. Nothing could please him. If every minute detail wasn't to his liking, he rejected the entire cue. It was either "too many notes" or "I don't like that rhythm" or something else. But most often it was "It's just not like the temp score, listen to it again." This was starting to get on Arnold's nerves. How does a composer write music that is a personal expression, when what they are asked to do is write like someone else? This can shake confidence.

Arnold felt that while he would be glad to write in the overall musical style of the temp music, he wasn't willing to just rip it off. And yet, that's exactly what he was being asked to do. It appeared that this director wasn't going to settle for anything other than a direct takeoff of the temp score, and Arnold decided to fight that idea on both ethical and creative grounds. It is important to mention here that composers are personally liable for any copyright lawsuits that emerge as a result of any musical pilfering. If you are asked to rip of a piece of music for a score, you are the one in trouble, not the ones who hired you and asked you to do the rip. This is spelled out in a legal document that every composer signs on virtually every project called a *Certificate of Authorship*, or "C of A" for short.

Time went on. More and more music was composed. The film's deadline began to loom, and still not a single note was approved. Arnold was getting discouraged and even a bit desperate. The director was oddly confident that all would turn out well somehow, but would conclude each meeting with "just listen to the temp music here." Arnold was treading deep water and didn't know what to do. The answer came soon enough.

The director called Arnold into a meeting with himself and the film's producer, and an amazing, if not somewhat surreal idea was put forth. It seemed that the film's producer was also a bit of a composer as well, and would Arnold mind collaborating with the producer in order to possibly speed up the process. Arnold was bewildered, disheartened, and just a bit offended. Still, it is a composer's job to make the director happy (and to make them look good). As it happens, the producer had brought a tape with some thematic ideas for the film. But after all the enthusiastic talk of collaboration, the director ended up not even liking the producer's music all that well (he obviously felt secure enough to just blow off his boss). Back to square one for Arnold.

Arnold continued to write with the producer for a few more days and played some more cues for the director. Even after all this, nothing was getting approved, no matter how close to the temp music he would get. He felt that the director would only accept music identical in phrase and rhythm to the temp, which would be out-and-out thievery. The director would pick apart a cue by saying "There! That third note is wrong! The melody shouldn't go up there! Listen to the temp." Through all his rewrites though, Arnold refused to simply rip off the temp score. He wanted the music to be his creative invention, though in the style of the director's wishes. They were at a creative impasse.

Finally (and perhaps not a moment too soon), Arnold got the call. The director, politely and even apologetically, explained that his services were no longer required. Perhaps they would work again on another more fitting project. After three weeks of constant, futile work, Arnold was bewildered and crushed. Such a thing had never happened to him in any of the films he'd done. In fact, he had been on a pretty good string of growing successes before this. This was hard to take.

What are the repercussions of being fired from a film? Would his peers hear about it? Would other directors or producers know about this? Would he be marked as a composer unable to take direction or fulfill a director's wishes? Was it a question of talent? Was this preventable or avoidable? How would he explain this to his friends and colleagues who knew he was scoring this film?

Now you may be thinking "what about the money!?" Though not required, he decided to voluntarily return half of the money that he had been paid for starting the project. Oh, how I wish he would have asked for advice, because returning the money was a mistake. In the professional film scoring world, no one is ever asked to return money paid as a creative fee just because a score isn't going to be used. He earned that money—several times over. It was the production's decision not to use what they had asked for, something a composer is not responsible for. Whether you complete the score or not, it is not your fault that they change their minds or that they not like the music you create. If you quit, that's a different story. You return some or all of the money. But that's it. Never return money, even if asked.

I sympathized with Arnold on the phone for some time. One thing I felt compelled to point out is that of all the successful film composers I know, I don't know anyone who hasn't lost a job at least once, including myself. Sometimes the combination of a particular composer with a particular project simply doesn't work, be it for personality, or creative reasons. It's an unfortunate and painful part of the music biz, though it doesn't necessarily spell career derailment or disaster. All the same, it doesn't feel good.

After I scored two successful seasons of the TV series *Homicide*, the makers of that show decided to go with someone else. I wasn't really given a full explanation, though part of it involved my being in LA while the show was being posted in NY. It didn't matter; I was out of a job I liked, and I felt badly about it. Being "philosophical" didn't really help at first. I certainly didn't know at the time that it was the best thing that could have happened to me since it led me to some far more interesting work that I couldn't have done had I stayed with the show. Things like this happen for good reasons, and if you can get the message behind the events, it usually leads to better things.

So what was the message for Arnold? It is very unlikely that this small project will have any impact on his career. I pity the poor composer who inherited the job. Some "jobs from hell" just don't have happy endings, and it's better to get out while you can. Just how much aggravation is alright for you in your work? The people on my friend's film didn't operate in what I considered a very professional way, so what should they expect for results? But there's lots of unreasonable, unprofessional, and difficult people in the film biz, and at some point you will end up working for one. You can't always spot them ahead of time, because they are often very nice people who are just very hard to work with.

On the other hand, what about Arnold's refusal to give the director exactly what he wanted? Should he be surprised that his attitude, which said the score must be "his own artistic expression" and not what was requested from the director, would lead to his dismissal? Forget the legal aspects of this, because you can rip off a score without running into trouble if you change a few notes. This is a tough question, and there's no one right answer. Your job as a film composer is to both give the director what he/she wants, but also to use your best musical judgment and help the film find the best possible score, even if the director or producer is not convinced at first. I've been in situations where the director enjoyed challenging me and then allowing me to defend my decisions. I've been in situations where a producer had no interest in my opinions if he didn't like a cue. I was expected to make the changes and play them for him.

If a director or producer asks you for a pizza, do you give them filet mignon? I think the answer is that, unless you have a very close relationship with the people you are working for, and can differentiate between what they think they want and what they really want, pizza is the way to go. But it has to be a gourmet pizza. After all, in the reel world, you aren't making up the menu, you just make sure everything tastes as good as possible.

Letting Go
Two Examples of How NOT to Deal with Film Producers

Two composers I know had both just completed film scores. One of them, I'll call him Neil, has scored a number of hit films in the last few years and has really learned the ups and downs of the scoring world. The other composer, I'll call him Bob, a successful recording artist with a large following, had just finished his very first feature film score. Both Neil and Bob are great composers, and the quality of their work is not in question. The difference in their experiences is in how they handled what happened to their scores once they recorded and turned them in.

Neil called me one day to complain about how his music was being treated after he finished it. The producers of his last three projects all made significant changes to the films, re-edited many of the scenes that had music. In some cases, they had even gone back to reshoot parts of scenes, thus changing the tone and pace of them greatly. A music editor was called upon to take Neil's score, put it into ProTools, and chop it up to fit the new edits. Neil worried that the music suffered as a result. It was as though his music was being treated as raw material for them to fiddle around with, with no regard whatsoever for the music's original integrity, intent, or form. Neil works very hard to make each piece of music he writes fit perfectly to the scene for which it is intended. At the dub sessions it was hard for him to see how so much of it came out so differently than he had planned. In some cases, the director had moved cues into scenes other than the one for which they were composed.

As a successful recording artist, Bob was used to having a great degree of artistic control in his music, and when he was asked to score his first film, he was thrilled to hear that he would be able to maintain a great degree of control here as well. That's a wonderful situation to be in. The film's producers wanted a score that sounded like his instrumental music anyway, so they basically left him alone to do what he does best. Everything went well, too. He finished over half the score before even playing anything for the producers. And when he did play things for them, they asked for very few changes. They were happy, he was happy. So far, so good.

The problem came in the very last scene of the film. Bob wrote a song for the scene. He collaborated with a lyricist, brought in a singer and other musicians, and recorded it. He did this entirely on his own, and didn't play it for the producers until it was mixed and finished. But they decided to go with a different piece of music. Bob nearly went mad. He argued fiercely with them. They didn't budge, because they were very pleased with what they had. The rest of Bob's score was approved, recorded, and mixed, but he hadn't handed in the master tapes yet. He decided that if they wouldn't use his song, they wouldn't get the rest of the score either. He was willing to return his entire scoring fee if they made a fuss about it. He felt that strongly about the song and its place in the overall film score.

While the desire for artistic integrity is laudable, making demands to the producers or directors of a film or holding your score hostage is not an acceptable action. As songs have taken a greater and greater role in film soundtracks, making way for them has become a routine occurrence. Usually it is decided ahead of time which scenes are for score and which will have songs. The music supervisor, if there is one, will start the process of finding the best songs for the scene. This is also a part of the spotting sessions, deciding which cues will be songs vs score, though there is always the option to change direction. This means that the composer will usually not be called upon to score a scene that will be replaced with an existing track. If it does happen your choices are to respond with some grace, or find another scene for the cue, and adapt it. To hold a score hostage in order to get personal demands met is a near sure-fire way to lose your job and career.

Fortunately for Bob, a level-headed partner of his was able to talk him down off the career ledge that he had put himself on. He turned in the master mixes, they used his song as source music in another scene earlier in the film, and asked him not to bother coming to any mixing sessions for the film, or any screenings either. In his personal attachment to his music, he had shot himself in the foot. As much as they liked the score he did, he'll never work for those people again.

Interestingly, the end result in each case was more or less the same—the directors and producers were happy with the scores, and both films went on to be critical and box office successes. Hard to argue with that. What was tough for Neil was hearing his music changed so much. Recut, remixed, moved around, and otherwise messed with, Neil felt like his music had fallen upon partially deaf ears. The music he worked on with such technical skill and artistic sensitivity was treated like set decoration. Neil was resigned to this just being the way things sometimes are in his job. Neil could be fairly philosophical about it, however: It would be better in future projects. Most scores are not chopped apart. Some scores are saved thanks to judicious editing.

In my own music career I have learned to accept the sometimes capricious nature of the film and TV worlds and the people who inhabit them. It's a difficult lesson at times, but one which gives you a greater ability to collaborate with people of all types. I've had cues that took me days to write tossed out of films because the director later decided that "maybe the scene doesn't really need music after all." I've had cues moved so that big loud hits now inappropriately hit on nothing. I've had cues mixed so low against the dialogue and effects that they might as well have just been a simple synth pad instead of the complex orchestrated pieces they were. I've had the drum tracks faded out of cues that were completely percussion-oriented. I've had cues faded up in the middle, and others faded out in the middle. This is simply the way some film makers think and work with music. It is theirs to tinker with as they see fit, no different than any other sound effects. Conversely, some film makers think very differently. I've had the pleasure of hearing my scores intact and mixed just the way I'd heard them in my mind's ear. Those experiences can give you a wonderful feeling of artistic collaboration, mutual respect, and the sense that you are working with someone who respects and likes music as much as you do.

It is natural for any composer to take care and pride in everything he or she does. You strive to make everything perfect. Each note, phrase, sequence, instrumentation, performance, and recording should be the absolute best possible. You want to put your heart and soul into your work, and I believe that it is critical that you do so. Yet, at the same time, once you have completed your assigned task (and remember, you are the one being hired by other people to help them with their projects) it is time to simply let it go. Buddhist monks and Hindu yogis spend their entire lives learning to let go of their emotional attachment to things. One time I had the pleasure of watching a group of Tibetan monks spend weeks creating an enormous, unbelievably complex and beautiful artwork made from different colours of sand. When it was done, they held a brief ceremony in which they simply swept it up with a broom and threw it away. The beauty for them was in its making, there was no reason for them to leave it around just to have it decay or take up space. They had perfected detachment from the fruits of their labour. There is a lesson here for many of us. Once something is done, it is done. Time to let it go and move on. Think of this as the "Zen" of film scoring: Be passionate and caring about every note you write as you write it. But once you are done, let it go. It no longer belongs to you. This simple thought will help you keep things in perspective.

Once, a successful R&B composer and record producer I know said something to me in passing that stuck with me. He said, "You know the difference between you and me? You think of your music as fine china, and I think of mine as paper plates." It took me a long time to really figure out what that meant, but eventually I got the core of his meaning. He wasn't saying that my music was any better or more important than his. It was strictly an attitude, and I believe that in many circumstances of a professional music career, a very healthy one. He knew how to remain casual about the making of pop music. Film music does, arguably, aim to be something higher and more artistic and lasting than a pop song. But still, don't be precious about each and every detail in every piece you compose. Do your very best all the time, but don't get caught up in every detail. Think about the big picture. Focus on the end result, and what can achieve that. Do your work and then let it go. Time to sweep up and move on. Not only might it make your music making experience more pleasurable, it may just help you be a little happier when your work is finished.

So, Are You Up to Speed?

How to Get a Lot Done in a Very Short Time

They say that to make it in most businesses, it's not what you know, its who you know. To that, I'll add the Reel World corollary: Sometimes it's not what you can do, its what you can do in ten minutes. This is the world of hellish deadlines and merciless schedules—projects turning into wild rides—and you're the bus!

A number of years ago I was working with composer Basil Poledouris (See interview on page 161) on a movie he was scoring. The deadline was tight, and we were holed up in a small recording studio, sequencing and recording keyboards. Basil has just written a lengthy action cue, and I was sequencing it into the computer. The phone rang; it was the film's producer. He was very concerned about this particular cue and wanted to hear it right then—over the phone! Though it wasn't finished (there were a number of live instruments to be added which we weren't sequencing), Basil, with a look of resignation on his face, held the phone up to the speakers and played it for him. I can only imagine how poorly it sounded on the other end of the line. No surprise, he hated it and didn't care what was missing or how lousy the phone made it sound. He wanted it changed and wanted Basil to call him back within the next two hours (he had a dinner date to attend) and play him the revised music.

I still remember Basil just sitting there, with his head in his hands. This was a complex piece that took him quite some time to write, at least a couple of days. Now he had to conceive a new approach, compose it, sequence it into the computer, and play it for the producer in the next two hours! What do you do in a situation like this? Do you tell the producer no way, and play it for him when it's good and ready? Do you put up a fight and try to get him to change his mind, or at least wait until he can hear it in person? There are times when any of those options might be valid, but in this case the answer was to just do the best possible rewrite, call the producer back, play something new for him, and hope for the best. That's exactly what Basil did. He put something together right on the spot as fast as he could. We threw it into the sequencer, and he called the producer back. Sure enough, he liked it and made his dinner date as well. We fell down exhausted (for about fifteen minutes before getting to work on the next cue).

Explaining Impossible Deadlines

So how can a piece of music written in an hour beat out one that took days, or weeks for that matter? Well, it happens more often than you might think. Orchestral film scores are often changed right at the recording session, with the entire orchestra sitting and waiting while the composer figures out what to do. Imagine the pressure of having to make changes in a score that took days to compose, with thousands of dollars being lost every minute, and with the producers, director, engineers, and up to 100 people waiting for you. Did you remember to bring your good pencil and a big eraser?

Perhaps one advantage you have when forced to rewrite a cue quickly is that now you know exactly what not to write, because you've already written it. You also have the advantage of having the director or producer's direct involvement, which nearly always means that they will like the results that much better. They feel somewhat responsible for the new cue.

The scoring schedule on most films has become incredibly tight, and continues to become tighter. In many cases, even a project being scored with a very tight schedule won't actually be released for weeks or even many months afterward. The reason for this is (as it so often is) money. It costs a film production company a lot of money to keep the editors, mixers, and support staff on the payroll while the composer writes the score. They can't be dismissed, because they will be needed again when the music is ready, and in the meantime those people might find other work and not be available at a critical moment. This is a result of the shift from the old Hollywood studio system, when everybody working on a film was an employee of the production company. They were thus always available, unlike the current way films are made—entirely by independent contractors who are hired for a specific project and then let go. As a result, stringent schedules are set and carefully adhered to. Sometimes a lucky break will occur, and a week or two may get added (usually not because the composer needs the time to do a better job, but because something else in the film is taking longer than expected).

Film and TV projects all have deadlines, which is typically the first day of the dub. A dub can last anywhere from a few days to a couple of weeks depending on the complexity of the project and the budget. When you are hired to score a project, the first thing that you may need to discuss is when the project dubs. This is your target date to have the music composed, approved, revised, recorded, mixed, and edited into the production tracks. Each day of the dub will mix a certain number of reels of the film. It is usually acceptable to deliver the music during the subsequent days of dubbing. Dubs often start with some preliminary dialogue work and then go on to add the music and effects. As long as you stay ahead of the dubbing engineers, you can deliver your score in parts all through the dub schedule. This can be tricky, so always stay in contact with everyone so as to avoid the experience of not delivering the required music on time.

One of the toughest aspects of working on tight schedules is that it is often very difficult to predict just how long it may take to write a new piece of music. Can you write five minutes of music in a day? How about in two days? There are a lot of factors which may determine that—complexity of the music, amount of inspiration, difficulty of the dramatic elements of the film, approval of the director. In a three to eight week schedule, it may take several days to come up with a main theme idea, but then things might flow quickly from there. Maybe they won't. It's difficult to predict inspiration.

Composer Mark Isham, in talking about his musical evolution from his first film scores, says that one of the biggest differences is in how fast he can write. In his earlier scores, he might take three or four tries at a cue before coming up with something that works for him. Now his first instinct usually serves him well, and he can move on. He still puts in tremendously long days toward the end of a project, getting little sleep for days at a time, but for the most part he has learned his pace.

When I started scoring my first film and television projects, I was overwhelmed by the schedules. In TV it is a new episode nearly every week for months on end, with as little as three days between spotting and dubbing. At first it took every waking moment of my life, six to seven days a week, and little time for luxuries like sleep. Over time I was able to do each score in a shorter amount of time, without resorting to recycling older cues or relying on set cliches. I would continue to try new things out every time. But I developed a "groove" and things flowed faster. With my films, I may often take a major percentage of the schedule to write the first theme or themes. Lately I will write a number of themes, sometimes as a suite, without watching any picture to try and set the tone for the score. I will take the time needed to make them sound really great. But the pace picks up over the time of the project as more cues can be based on my existing themes and motifs.

When you get called upon to do a score, be ready. There may be no time to tweak your studio or figure out why your computer crashes with new software. There are no excuses allowed for not delivering your best score on time. No last minute requests for extensions or begging will help. You simply do it. I've left my studio to find the sun rising many, many times. It is rare to have a leisurely schedule to be able to write slowly and carefully. Some of the best scores I've ever heard were done at near blinding speed. Some composers who know their own speed limitations can make demands for more time and get it if it is early enough, but that takes some clout or understanding. You do the best you can in the amount of time you're given. It's a bit like a race to the finish line—it wouldn't be as exciting if you had all the time you wanted.

As Al Green once sang, "It's all in a day's work."

The Politics of Dancing
The Diplomacy of Scoring

There is much practical and perhaps even essential knowledge about all that goes on from the time you get a scoring job to when you finish it. It should come as little surprise to learn that the entertainment business has a wide range of personalities and egos. How you deal with the people you work for can make for a huge difference in the enjoyment of your work. It's about relationships.

The music you compose for a project will always need the approval of those in charge of the project. That includes the director, the producers, and sometimes executives from the studio or production company music department. Most every project you'll do will have at least one of each. You compose, you demo, they listen. You either get a thumbs up, thumbs down, or some specific requests for you to revise some or all of your music. It seems simple enough, doesn't it? But this can be the most critical and political aspect of your work.

Most facets of the entertainment field are about relationships: Making them, building them, developing them, and nurturing them. This can and will have a major impact on your work and career. When you are hired to compose music for a project, your job is to bring all of your technique and style into their service until they are happy. While pleasing yourself should always be an important part of your musical life, your final goal in working in film or television is to also please and satisfy your clients—the people that chose you and are going to pay you. This may seem obvious, but it isn't to everyone. It is your goal to help them get the best possible score, and you must not allow your own ego (or theirs!) to impede your progress.

There are so many personality types: secure, insecure, brash, quiet, articulate, inarticulate, honest, dishonest, powerful, and low-man-on-totem-pole-with-an-attitude. With each one, I do my best to learn about them. How they like to work, what they expect of me and the music, and what I can expect from them. I do my best to be an ally, and even a friend. And, yes, I stroke their egos as well. I get to know them and share things about myself. It makes a project more personal, fun and enriching when I work with people whose company I enjoy. I hope the same is true for them. It doesn't always happen—and that's OK. Sometimes a job is just a job, and at the conclusion we simply go our separate ways. I always express my gratitude, and hopefully they will want to repeat the experience of working together, and will call again when their next project is ready.

Because music often comes so late in the game on a film project, it's not uncommon to have tensions and conflicts between some of the other people involved with the production, none of which has anything to do with you. Nonetheless, it can have an effect on your work. You may find yourself getting feedback from too many people, or not enough. One person may really like a cue, but another will ask for a rewrite. You must find out the true chain of command in order to know to whom you should ultimately listen. I believe in knowing the pecking order with the producers and director. Who do I answer to? Who does that person answer to? Will that person want to deal with me directly? Usually it's clear and simple, but because of the egos (and the high financial stakes) that often accompany a big project, you need to be aware. You may only answer to the director, but if a producer disagrees with that director and asks you to change the direction of the score, what do you do? Who do you listen to?

Other Peoples' Problems

One way to approach those occcasional internal conflicts and disagreements is to keep it from becoming your problem. Stay out of the politics that may go on within a project's production team. It may not always be possible. But with considerable tact, humor and diplomacy, do what you can to make it their job to resolve the problem. Ask them to work these things out before bringing them to you. They should speak to you with a single voice. Fortunately, this does not come up very often. Most productions are relatively simple, with little if any of the backbiting, scamming, or other potential dilemmas. But at the same time there are virtually always problems and issues that do arise that require you to be strong and aware.

Conflicting views do come up as to why a cue isn't working. A director may say "it needs to be faster" while the producer says "it's much too frenetic." Logic would say they can't both be right. But it could be very beneficial to listen to them both and see if there isn't a problem that they cannot describe in musical terms. Perhaps the cue needs to be faster, but with less percussion. Become a musical translator and you can dig down to find what the client actually wants.

The people you work for are not musicians. They will use the only language they can to describe something that is by nature very difficult to put into words. You cannot dismiss their opinions, and in fact a good producer or director can be very helpful to you and your score.

Another issue that unfortunately rears its head from time to time is honesty. For the most part, I've found the people I have worked with to be honorable and reliable. But I've run up against the occasional snake in the grass. Why would a person already in a position of power and authority need to lie to a lowly composer? In the long run, I don't have a clue.

I only care about dishonesty when it affects me directly. I don't care much if people lie to each other. I've been lied to about money (promised a certain amount until the contract shows up), about my chances at a particular gig (people love to make job offers even when they don't have the authority to do so), about what is expected of me (I've frequently been asked to write additional songs or other pieces after I've made an agreement to not be responsible for those parts of the score) and about the budget for recording the score.

Someone to Watch Over You: The Lawyer

With those occasional problem projects, there are times when having someone to watch over your interests is invaluable. If you feel like you are getting shafted in any way and you aren't certain you can deal with it without a fight, it is best to get someone to protect and fight for you. This is what a composer's agent does. They sweat the details and watch out for you. If you don't have an agent, then consider getting an entertainment-savvy lawyer to help out. Just be careful and clear about what you want. I once had a situation in which I was forced to decide whether I was willing to walk off a film if the film's executives would not make good on some of the initial promises they made and were now starting to break. I was pushed into having to make compromises that would have potentially ruined the score, and no amount of convincing was making this particular producer budge from his misguided stance. I said I was willing to quit, my agent relayed that information to the producers, and, lo and behold, within an hour or two the problem was miraculously solved. It wasn't pleasant, but I was not interested in being stepped on or having the quality of my work threatened. You don't want to be in a position of turning in a score that doesn't, due to problems out of your control, represent your best work. It's not fun being a tough guy, but every so often you may need to stand up for yourself, and your only real bargaining chip is your work or your recording. Don't make idle threats. Be careful, and don't bluff. Most of us are replaceable.

Also, I find that a composer should never discuss money, contracts, complaints, or problems directly. It is best to always do these things through an agent or lawyer representing you. You must remain an artist, and not a business person in the eyes of the director.

Next to talent, one of the most important things any producer will look for in a composer is trustworthiness. The question they ask themselves is "can this person get the job done, done right, done on time, and done with the budget we've provided?" Your job is to let them know that you can deliver. They must trust you, depend on you, and go to sleep at night not worried about their choice of composer. How can you put someone's mind at rest? By delivering the goods without excuse, delay, or misstep. That's not so hard, is it?

Anyway, remember: It takes two to tango, but three or more requires some creativity.

In Which I Say "YES" To Sundance

Scoring *The House of Yes*

This is not a pretty story, but it is one worth telling, as it was one of the more educational experiences of my own career up until that point. It illustrates some of the ideas mentioned in the above sections. During one December of a busy season of scoring television shows, my schedule was beginning to lighten up prior to the holiday break. I was in the midst of making some holiday travel plans when I got a call about a film. The producers had just lost their composer, had only a short time until the film had to be finished, and someone had recommended me for the job. It seemed to be my musical karma at the time to always be called in at the last possible moment to score something that really requires more time. I'm not the faster writer around, but I'm willing to devote every waking moment (and even some sleeping ones) to completing a task. Thus I became, with only nine or ten days left until completion, the composer for a small film called *The House Of Yes*, an independent feature which was already accepted into the prestigious Sundance Film Festival (details of that to follow).

The timing was very fortunate: Two weeks earlier or later and my other projects would have prevented me from being able to accept, and it looked like a very enjoyable film. More difficult was the notion of being able to write enough music in such a short time and still retain musical quality. An even more problematic aspect of the project was that the film's director and producers were in real conflict about the style and approach for the score. In fact, the film's original composer ran into trouble for this very reason. He worked closely with the director for quite some time, which is normal. But the producers rejected most of his music, since it didn't fit with the approach they wanted. It turned into a battlefield until the composer simply couldn't deal with it any more. Taking sides in a situation like this is treacherous. I stepped very lightly until I got a sense of what would work for everybody. I told them that I wanted a single voice who would speak on everyone's behalf, so that all conflicts would be resolved prior to my efforts. I explained to them that with so little remaining time, there was no time to guess and rework major parts of the score. We had to agree on what we wanted, and then they needed to let me do it. We also agreed that while I would use some live musicians for the score, they would not get the fully acoustic score as they wanted. With all that in mind, I began.

The film was a dark comedy about a rather dysfunctional family. It was directed by a first-time director, who adapted a successful play for the script. The film was a coproduction of two production companies here in Los Angeles. It looked to be a good film, which made the prospect of working on it, regardless of how daunting the schedule, exciting.

After looking at the original spotting notes I made the request to respot the film, that is, to reconsider all the places where music would go. Movie scores, more so than TV, tend not to sound so good with too many very short cues. They tend to draw attention to themselves much of the time. There were quite a number of these in the film, and I strongly disagreed with their presence in this particular case. This was a source of contention, because the director had strong feelings about some of these little five second transition-type cues. We compromised on this, but while the film became much better spotted, there were still several tiny cues whose brevity concerned me.

Composing the Score

I started by writing the film's main title music. This would become a major theme for the rest of the score. Because the title music played over nearly continuous dialogue, it had to remain very simple. The producers explained what they wanted very concisely by explaining that, while the film was a comedy they didn't want music that would make people laugh outright, but would let them know that "laughter was allowed." You tread a fine line with scoring comedies.

Sometimes what is happening on the screen isn't ostensibly humorous, but in the context of the story or characters is indeed quite funny. Writing music with lightness helps comedy along; however, it is important to remember that *you should never tell a joke twice*. If someone slips on a banana peel on screen, there is little need to play something slapstick and silly in the music too—the audience is already (hopefully) laughing. Keep the mood light, and if you want to hit the comedic action with the music, just keep in mind that less is usually more unless you are doing cartoons where you hit everything.

As described earlier, the key to starting any film score is to find the essential elements that will run throughout your music. This applies to both themes and colors. It can also be conceptual as well as musical. Writing a tango for a murder scene is a musical concept that might be exactly right for the right movie. In this particular case I wanted something to go with one highly manic main character. The character was perpetually on edge emotionally, and it was an opportunity to find a fun key element for the score. I came up with a bottleneck slide acoustic guitar playing these odd out-of-tune, quasi-microtonal melodies that were loony and a bit kinky. Instead of doing it on the standard electric or steel string acoustic, I used a nylon string guitar, which makes it more melodic since it produces fewer of the overt overtones you usually get with a bottleneck. I doubled the guitar with a soprano sax and flute for the main title melody, playing a main theme that was a sort of twisted chromatic tango. I also featured vibraphone a lot for its quirky lounge-jazz appeal.

✪ An excerpt from this theme can be found at www. reelworld-online.com

I had the producers and the director over to my studio during the entire time I was writing. Because of the compressed schedule I had them over every other day to approve cues and give notes. Fortunately, things were going well so far, and I started to get a number of cues signed off, meaning everyone agreed that they were accepted and finished. After cues are signed off, they are ready to record and mix. As cues were signed off, I gave MIDI Files and DAT tapes of my demos to my orchestrator, who began preparing parts for the small ensemble of players I was using. Some cues had to go through two or three revisions before I came up with the goods that they would accept, but some cues got nailed on the first or second shot, so I was keeping up with the deadline, more or less.

A few days later I was told that the film's dub was moved back by a couple of days, giving me a little unexpected breathing room. I had a conversation with the film's sound mixer, and we agreed on how the music would be delivered to the dub stage.

A Disappointing Mix

I had to keep writing as they began the dub, but I was able to attend a playback screening of the entire film. This screening was for the producers to give their approval of the mix, or to give notes for changes and fixes they wanted. There would be another few days of mixing to accommodate their requests. I knew that if I had any comments or suggestions about the music (which is the only thing I could really comment about to these producers) this would be my only chance to make them. I happened to be as sick as a dog that day, I could barely stand up, let alone drive across town and sit through a screening without coughing my lungs out. But I hauled myself out of bed and went. I was pretty disappointed with the way the music sounded, but I had to be careful with what I said because the producers were all very pleased with the mix. To my clogged but sensitive ears, the music sounded pretty bad. It seemed far too soft and far too dull. All the sparkle and sheen were gone, along with most of the percussion. Apparently this was due to a carelessly done transfer made between two analogue machines for the music. But because the producers seemed genuinely happy with nearly all of the music levels, I mostly bit my tongue and said little or nothing. I did speak up on a couple of specific spots where I felt the problem was the worst, and I got them to agree with raising the levels there and do a little brightening.

Mixing the music overly quiet can siphon off most of the music's emotional quality, as many details vanish into the background. It takes a skilled mixer to get music to lay into a scene gently without it becoming wimpy sonic wallpaper. This particular film, as with many other non-action oriented films, centres around the dialogue. But if there is to be music in a scene, why not let the audience really hear it? This is why underscore needs to remain very simple and carefully mixed. If you can barely hear the lead parts, you are guaranteed to lose all the little interesting elements in the background. I realized that some of my musical mixes needed rethinking, both to rebalance some elements, and to increase some of the brightness of the music in order to make it stand out better at low volume.

Fortunately, some last minute music fixes were requested that would need me to remix a few cues for the following day's mix session. Back at my studio I made it a point to do all the remixes extremely bright. It sounded overly bright in my studio, but I knew that by the time they made it into the film, they would probably be just about right.

My illness kept me from the dub on the fix day. But I got several calls from the producers and the director, and everyone was very pleased with the final cue revisions and mixes. It was done. Ten days earlier I hadn't even heard of this film. Little did I know what was in store for me.

And so the film was "in the can" as they say, meaning finished, and was scheduled for its premiere at the Sundance Film Festival, in Park City, Utah. Being somewhat of a film junkie, I'd wanted to go to the prestigious festival for a long time, but wanted a film of mine to be shown there to give me a real reason to go.

Attending the Sundance Festival: Mecca for Independent Films

The independent film world is one based more on creativity than finance. These are films made outside of the big studios, whose size and clout makes it possible to bankroll and produce larger feature projects all the way from scripting to final distribution. The producers of independent films use these festivals to sell their wares to distributors—companies that are able to take a finished film and get it into theatres both in the US and abroad and handle the film's marketing. Sometimes these rights are sold to multiple distributors, each having an exclusive deal for some part of the world. In addition, the rights for distribution on video are sometimes sold. Films that get a "buzz" at Sundance become the subject of bidding wars between multiple buyers. Others screen, get their applause, and never make it to theatres. Independent film making is risky—a very small minority of films make it to distribution. *House of Yes* was entered and accepted (still with the temp score from before I began) into the Sundance Film Festival before I was ever involved. It just made the stakes that much higher for me because the expectations for the film were now very, very high.

I was busy completing the score for the dub, which came only two weeks before the festival began. I was eager to go and see the film's premiere and see some of the other films being presented at Sundance. That turned out to be a very daunting logistical task. Everyone else connected with the film had booked their plane tickets and accommodations and had reserved tickets for films at the festival months in advance. In fact, Sundance usually sells out weeks before it begins. With just under two weeks before the festival, I didn't seem to stand a chance of getting in to see anything.

I politely asked the director and producers if they had any info on getting a room or tickets to the festival. Unfortunately that was a dead end since they had made their own reservations well before. Calling the festival office directly was of little use also. They told me to call back a few days later when more blocks of tickets went on sale, but the phones were permanently busy that day. I was about ready to give it up when, during a conversation with a producer's assistant, I mentioned my plight; I've learned, by the way, that the keys to the kingdom of Hollywood are often kept with these hard working executive assistants—always be kind to them. She knew of a recent cancellation and gave me the number of a fellow in Park City who could "take care of things." Within a day I had a room right in town. This was a lucky break.

I still wanted tickets for the films (including my own) at the festival. Here's where some ingenuity came in. While many screenings were already sold out, a block of tickets reserved for Utah residents only (Park City is in Utah) was about to be released. I got ahold of a festival program via fax from a friend, selected a number of films that seemed interesting, and then faxed that list to the man in Park City handling my accommodations. He then paid a local ski bum, who lives by odd jobs just to make enough money to eat and ski, to wait in line at the festival box office for four hours. I got a great bunch of tickets. All was set.

Park City is a small, lovely, ski resort town with old buildings, beautiful mountains, and a single main street with shops and restaurants, and yes, a park. Everything becomes a Sundance-oriented orgy for the two weeks of the festival. After flying into Salt Lake City, I took a shuttle bus into the main part of town to see what was there and get my bearings. The first thing I noticed after getting off the bus was that when walking down the street you had to be careful not to poke your eye on the abundance of cell phone antennae that sprang from every other head. The Sundance festival is overrun with film company executives and scouts looking for the Next Big Thing. It was almost funny to see what a media frenzy there was of photographers, TV cameras, interviewers, celebrities and their entourages, studio heads, actors and actresses. The aura of glamour and finance was pervasive. What Robert Redford had started years before as a small forum for young film talent had turned into a major film market.

But I was there to see movies, and that is what I did. Thirteen films in four days. I must say that I was rarely disappointed. There were documentaries, short films, dramatic, and comedic features. The best part of it all for me was that the music in these small films was uniformly excellent—and I hadn't heard of a single composer for any of them. Unlike so much of the standard Hollywood orchestral fare, these scores were stylish, interesting, adventuresome, experimental, and clever. When you don't have a budget, you learn to find the most direct way to express your musical ideas.

Some of the films are presented as part of the festival's competition. The rest are premieres and special screenings of noteworthy films. *The House Of Yes* was there as part of the competition. The cast and crew of the film met for a pre-celebratory dinner prior to the film's first screening. It was fun to finally meet the people who made and appeared in the film. I had been so rushed to score it that I never met anyone other than the director and two producers. I sat with the writer and a few of the actors in the film and had a nice chat. Then we carpooled over to the theatre. It appeared that the movie had a "buzz," and there was a massive crowd trying to get into the screening. It was a big theatre, but hundreds were turned away. The cast, crew, and I sat in the back of the theatre and watched the film. This was the first time I was seeing it with the final mix. How did it sound? To be honest, I had a hard time hearing the music in many of the spots where I hoped the music would be loud and clear. It was a disappointment. I enjoyed the film, but felt that had I been up to attending the mix the music would possibly have sounded much better. There was no music editor on the film, so no one really familiar with the music was at the mix. This was an important lesson—don't assume that other people know how you want the music to sound in a mix. You must be there, or see that someone very familiar with the score is. This is one important role of a music editor.

There are some other fun things about Sundance in addition to seeing good new films. At most every screening the filmmakers are on hand to introduce the film and answer questions afterward. It's great to be able to interact with them while the film is still fresh in your head. Sundance also hosts seminars in a variety of film making topics, with one on film scoring that BMI sponsors. There are some lounges where snacks and drinks as well as reading materials are available, including the scripts to many of the films screened.

House Of Yes was purchased for distribution by Miramax and won a festival award for one of its stars. I met some wonderful people, saw some great films, met a couple of composers, had a couple of excellent meals and got the chance to relax and have fun. I even skied. Then time to get back home. I was back to work the next day.

Return to L.A. (and Some Bad News)

As I mentioned before, while I was working on the film, there was considerable contention between the producers and director as to the musical tone of the film. I had ended up following the direction given me by one producer, who had emerged as the one claiming to be in charge of the music. I finished the score with his final approval. The director of the film, though involved throughout, had no final say, and it was obvious that he was very frustrated by this. After Miramax purchased the film, they did a test screening in New York. It did not test well. Certain changes were needed by Miramax before they would release the film. The director was called in to discuss this. One of the changes discussed was to take the film's score in a different direction. This is one of the less expensive things you can do to a film in order to attempt improvements. They wanted a completely fresh take, so I would not be in the running for the job. A Miramax executive called to tell me the bad news. He was very nice about it, even apologetic. Some composers don't find out about their scores being replaced until the film is released and they see the credits. I was devastated by the news at first. We discussed how the score had been so poorly mixed, making it impossible to hear the music that was there. But an executive decision had already been made to support the director's wishes to rescore the film. This was a far more political move than a creative one. The director felt slighted and excluded by the original producers, and now he had the chance to get what he wanted. It was a lousy feeling,and I did my best to be philosophical about it. Virtually every composer I know has had this happen to them at one time or another, but it never feels good. I stared at the wall for a long while. Then I buried myself back into my work. Time to let it go and move on.

There are big lessons here. One is to be ever vigilant about watching over the dubbing of your film scores. You are responsible for insuring the quality of your music, including the final dub. There are too many opportunities to have the music lose its power and become lost in the mix of dialogue and sound effects. This can be due simply to the fact that no one at the dub knows your music as well as you do, even the director. You must remain an advocate for what your music can do for each scene of the film. You can bet that the dialogue and sound effects editors will be on hand to be sure nothing of theirs is missed.

The other lesson is more political, but no less true. When disagreements between producers and directors come up, you should be siding with your director, if sides must be taken. Directors are the ones most likely to hire you again. It's a difficult situation that requires the greatest amount of diplomacy you can muster. You want everyone to be happy with you and your work. Choose your battles wisely, but your allegiance should be with your director.

The movie came and went, with little critical acclaim or box office success. A blip on the movie industry screen. It's not something to gloat over, but it would have been a much worse experience had the movie been a hit. I learned my lesson, and things have gone much better for me since then. I think of that whole mess from time to time and feel a bit wiser. It had no long term effect on my career except, I'll never work for that director again. A tough lesson.

Getting to Know...Who?

Determining Your Suitability for a Project

Most every film composer wants a range of projects to showcase their musical breadth and capabilities. Some composers get, for one reason or another, pigeonholed into specific types of scores. Sort of the musical equivalent of type-casting in the acting world. Some composers do horror film after horror film while others are offered nothing but comedies. And perhaps it's not always best to go after every project that may come along. Taking on a project and not being able to deliver a first-rate score in the requested style is a very dangerous proposition. When do you know you're the right person for a project, or if a particular project is right for you?

If the desired style of music for a film isn't one from your preexisting repertoire, you should hopefully be able to do it perfectly, adding range to your musical resumé. In the golden era of Hollywood film scores, composers were employees of the studios they wrote for. They were expected to be fluent in virtually any musical style that might be required. While it is still important to have the versatility that allows you to take on an extensive range of projects, the emphasis on being a musical jack-of-all-trades has diminished. Now, a composer's personal, unique style and approach is more often an essential part of what gets them considered for work. It's not just about compositional technique. In fact, more and more non-trained composers are finding a comfortable niche in the film scoring world. Musical ability, previous credits, personal compatibility, musical taste, experience, and style all go into making you the right person for a job. It's the whole you—your vibe. Don't seek out or accept a job if you aren't certain you can do a great job.

Conversely, there are times in most composers' careers when a film will come along that is either of such artistic quality, or will call for a score that allows a composer to write something unique and special, but pays very little money. Is it good career sense to accept a project that pays less than you have typically gotten in the past? The concise answer is yes, absolutely. High-quality projects are few and far between and are good long-term career builders regardless of the financial rewards. Occasionally, a project may come up that is more lucrative

ON THE OTHER HAND

One composer I know had scored a film for a young new director. The pay was lousy, just enough to cover expenses and maybe break even. The film was crappy and didn't look like it had much chance at commercial success. Even with all of that, the composer really wanted another film credit and did a good job with the score. The film never got released theatrically, but it did get picked up by HBO as a cable television movie—a decent credit. As a result the director went on to get another deal to do a bigger film, with a decent budget and a good cast. He was moving up the professional ladder. Did he return to the composer who helped him get his start to score his next film? Unfortunately, no. Why? Two reasons. First, the director could afford a more experienced (and expensive) composer on his next feature. The composer who did the first film set a precedent of being "available for nothing." In the world of marketing it's called "perceived value." Charge too little and people will think you are only worth that much. But the more important reason was that the composer and the director did not develop a strong personal relationship. As far as the director was concerned, he was starting from scratch to find his next composer. Less experienced and successful directors also are put under greater pressure from producers and studio executives to work with composers of their liking and preference.

It is essential to really get to know all the people you work with. Understanding the artistic temperaments and tastes of directors and producers is as important as them knowing about yours. Then you can really know if you are the right person for the next job. You may want to stay in touch with them, even when you are not working together. People's memories are short, especially in film and television. You should also get to know the editors, mixers, studio or production company executives and everyone else you work with. You owe them your appreciation.

than normal for you, and you get to make a better profit. So these things can balance each other out. Careers are built on things other than money.

Consider each potential project carefully. Naturally, a credit is a credit, and you want them, as they add to your marketability as a composer. Is a credit on a bad film better than no credit? Scoring a successful film is of tremendous value to a composer. If a project goes straight to video or cable, as many low-budget films do, it will probably do little to enhance your resumé. If you have nothing on it yet, then they are much better than nothing.

Next, look at the people making the film. Do the director or producer look like someone who has a shot at bigger things in the future? Maybe scoring a film for an up-and-coming artist will pay off in the long run. Danny Elfman scored Tim Burton's student film, and they went on to collaborate on several hugely successful films afterward. It paved the way for Elfman's entire career. However, this is not always a business known for loyalty. Doing favours, such as working for little or no money for people doesn't necessarily promise future work. Some directors and producers do work with the same people again and again, and others do not. Regardless, developing relationships is always important.

A New Director, a New Relationship

When you begin a project with someone new, you owe it to yourself to get to know them on a personal level and find out what they like and don't like, musically and otherwise. This can help you a great deal in the long run. I had been involved in an interesting project—a six part dramatic anthology series for television produced by Robert Altman. Since I shared a studio with five other composers, I suggested that each of us do one of the episodes. We all submitted demos of our music and got the job as a group. Several of the episodes had been edited using temp scores which included pieces of our music. One of the other executive producers on the project was in charge of music. The first episode was to be scored by another of the composers on the project. He got started and wrote several cues and sent a demo on video tape to the producer. The demo was not well received.

After having each version of every cue he wrote tossed out several times, it became clear that there was a deeper underlying problem. The music was very good. But everything got rejected. The deadline loomed and not a single cue was approved. There was a lot of nervousness. The composer was nervous, and I think the producer felt his growing lack of musical confidence, like a dog smelling fear. In response, the producer couldn't feel confident about any of the music that was being written, regardless of what it really sounded like. Every time another revision went to him, he would turn it down and then wonder if the entire musical direction of the episode should change. He wasn't polite about it either. He was sharp, direct, and very difficult to understand. We banded together to try and help fix the situation, but no one really knew what this guy wanted, only that he didn't like what he was hearing. The score careened from style to style, necessitating massive rewrites. It is a producer's or director's perogative to change their mind as they wish, but when the communication is good, these things can resolve more quickly. It's a normal part of the process. How do you get a score finished and approved when things are not going so well? Talk. Play CDs of any music that seems to work for a scene and figure out what they like about it. Find out some of their favourite movies or composers. Do what it takes to get through to them and connect with their musical tastes and esthetics. Eventually we got a sense of what the producer wasn't liking by asking him what scores and albums he most liked and thought would fit into this project. He had a number of suggestions, some that made more sense than others, but some that the composer used to guide his score better, and in the end he nailed it.

When it was my turn with that producer I was apprehensive, but I had the benefit of my friend's misfortune. I was able to connect more quickly, even though this producer did not have a good musical vocabulary; very few do, actually. But your job is always the same. Get the score done, and do a great job. Learn what a director means when he says "make it more nervous" or "it lacks emotion" or "I want something more heroic here." Know your audience, which starts with the producers and directors you are working with and then extends to the target audience of the film. You can't do that by yourself. You can only do it with a director and producer who understand and enjoy what you are doing musically and personally.

From a career perspective, there are three main reasons to do any particular project. One is the quality of the film as a credit on your resumé. Another is for the development of a relationship that may take you on to better and better projects. And the final one is simply to take on a project because it pays well, even if it is not a particularly enjoyable prospect. There's no shame in making a profit from time to time—it helps pay for the other two reasons.

CHAPTER TEN

⊘ Making A Living

Dollars and Sense

So let's talk about money. Learning to take care of money is an important part of life. Ultimately you want to be in a position where you don't have to worry about it or even think about it too much. There is much truth to the notion that you are as rich as your satisfaction with the things you already have. With that in mind, let's focus on how to use your scores to make money.

There are composers who make gobs of it, mountains of it, more than some of us would know what to do with (though we all would like the opportunity to find out). There are other composers who are no less busy in their careers, but whose income is far more modest. As with many other professions, there is a curve of success, both in terms of work load and income. Each of us has the opportunity to succeed at our own pace. It is important to remember this—the opportunity to do something you truly love to do, and on your own terms, is worth far more than any amount of money can give you. On the other hand, there is nothing wrong with making money, and we should all be compensated fairly for the services we give to others, and for the value of our efforts.

Money flows. You have a much better chance of making it if you first learn how to spend it. I'm not advocating overspending, because being smart about spending money is of critical importance, but in order to be attractive and desirable to the people who will be giving us money we need to have some things in place. A professional composer needs to have the right tools for the job. It takes certain amounts of musical and audio gear to be taken seriously as a pro, and it's not insignificant. The competition is fierce. There are composers vying for the same jobs you are who have invested lavishly in their personal studios, or have found ways to record large ensembles of musicians for their demos. It seems that the stakes are always rising as to just how good people's demos sound. If you want to get into the race, you need a car that can keep up with the pace, or, as one successful composer (with a mammoth MIDI setup) is fond of saying, "A house can't buy you a sampler, but a sampler can buy you a house." Your demos need to sound and look good, and you must do whatever it takes to accomplish this, though it can be done slowly over time. Any business trying to succeed invests in itself, and it is no different with you. You need to be able to present yourself in a professional manner, which requires an investment.

How Composers Make Money

Composers make money in a few different ways, and from different sources. Some of this depends on your level of success and desirability as a composer. In most cases, more experienced and in demand composers charge a fee for their services, negotiated on a film by film basis by their agent, and the production company that hired them foots the bill for all expenses related to delivering the score within a specific agreed upon budget. In other words there are no expenses taken out of the composer's fee—it is all profit. In other cases, a composer, through his agent, will negotiate something called a *score package* that includes all expenses related to recording and mixing the score. They are responsible for all costs incurred in delivering the final master tape to the production. The profit is what ever is left at the end of the project. If you are inexperienced at "packaging" a score, you should get help in estimating and budgeting your costs. You can do this by contacting the people you plan to work with, such as an orchestrator, copyist, musical contractor (see below), engineer, and recording studio. These people can give you a very good sense of your costs. You can make a number of choices that will affect your costs up or down, such as doing a mostly or all synth score, recording at home instead of a studio, doing your own orchestration and copying (via computer probably), using a less expensive engineer, etc. No producer expects you to lose money on a package. If the budget for a project is too small for a live group, then you make sure they know that they will get an all-electronic score and maybe a few soloists. If they insist on a certain number of live players, then you must renegotiate the package to make hiring musicians and recording them financially feasible.

Budgeting examples can be found on the website at www. reelworld-online.com

Once you've really gotten the hang of how to put a score budget together, a package can often be as lucrative as a fee. If a score is all electronic, a package is much less risky than when recording musicians in a studio. Until you have a bit of clout as a composer you will probably not be paid a fee. More and more productions function almost exclusively with packages because they work in the producer's best interests.

Calculating Expenses

What are the expenses that a composer is expected to incur within a package? They include everything it takes to deliver a master tape to the production. This can include: musicians fees (often having to handle all musician's union fees as well); a musical contractor to handle all the union contracts; a payroll company to help get all the musicians paid; orchestrators and copyists (if needed); all studio time and engineering fees; all tape costs including dubs and transfers; singers (including all AFTRA (American Federation of Television and Radio Artists) and SAG (Screen Actors Guild) contract fees; music editor; gear rental; messenger services; and any other cost associated with getting your score on tape.

If you will be working with live players, you may need to know about union musician rates before hiring anyone to determine just how big of a group you can afford for a project. You need to also determine about how long it will take to record your score, as you may need each player to come to several recording sessions to get everything done. With a full orchestra, most recording sessions average between five and ten minutes of score per hour of recording. Doing overdubs with only one or two players typically goes faster. Working with union players on soundtracks requires a three hour minimum.

If you determine that the sessions can be nonunion, usually not the case on bigger projects, then you can have some say in how much you want to pay players. The best players usually don't work on nonunion sessions in large metropolitan areas, but those who do expect to be paid about the same amount. You can contact your local musician's union and get a list of rates and fees.

Some composers who have worked for package deals ended up losing money by the completion of the project simply because they didn't work out their musician budgets.

Packages make it far more attractive for a composer to go mostly or all synthesized, since that cuts down significantly on costs. Frequently, producers will request some sort of minimum number of live players to avoid a composer taking money intended for musicians and recording costs and pocketing it. Since everything is negotiable in any contract, you have the ability to put *exclusions* into a package. Items you don't want to be responsible for in a package can be made the responsibility of the production company. For example, vocalists, who are paid through the SAG and AFTRA unions, are a frequent package exclusion. If you are concerned that a cost will cut too significantly into what you hoped to earn on the project, then attempting to make them exclusions is a good idea. Exclusions are part of the negotiation that is best handled by your agent or lawyer.

Joining the Union

It's a good idea to join your local musicians union. In America there is the AFM—American Federation of Musicians. Elsewhere, there are other unions which are the equivalent. There are some tangible benefits to union membership for a composer if you are doing regular film or TV work. There are repayments paid to union players when your work is released on video or shown on TV. Sometimes it is small, but it can grow to significant amounts over time, especially if you are one of a small number of musicians on a larger, more successful film. If you are doing regular work and appearing on union contracts as a musician, you can also be entitled to a superior health insurance plan. Some productions will not allow you to use union musicians, or at least not file any union contracts. There are financial incentives for them not to, because union musicians do receive extra compensations later. On occasion this point can be argued and won. The difference for the producers is actually very small, and the potential gains for you and your players can be significant over time.

Royalties and Collection Agencies (the Good Kind)

There is no composers union to protect the interests of composers like there is for musicians and singers. There are performing rights societies to assist composers (and music publishers) in collecting royalties for the use of their music around the world. In the US there is ASCAP and BMI, for Europe there is SACEM (France), GEMA (Germany), SOCAN (Canada), SESAC, and PRS (England). They all function more or less the same. You join for a nominal fee. Every time you compose a score for a film or TV show, you (or your music editor) must file a cue sheet with your performing rights society. The cue sheet lists every piece you wrote for the score and its running length. Cues that you compose, but do not end up in the film, do not go on the cue sheet. Cues used over again in the soundtrack count as separate compositions. Cue sheets can be prepared for you by the production company, but you should always get a copy and confirm that the information is correct and complete. Your performing rights society will then oversee the collection of all royalties you are owed for the use and reuse of that music forever. They will also monitor its use in foreign countries as well. The amount collected is determined by the number of minutes of music performed, the use of that music (underscore is paid differently than songs or main themes), and under what circumstances the performance takes place. Network, syndicated, and cable television all pay different rates for the use of music. Currently, performances in movie theatres in Europe pay a royalty to the composer, but not elsewhere. When you have music performed in films and television, you will receive a check from your performing rights society along with a statement showing when and where your music is being performed.

The royalties collected by a performing rights society are divided 50/50 to the music's composer and publisher. Who is the publisher? Usually it's the production company that made the project you scored. So for every dollar you make for your music, the producers or studio that made the film are getting the same amount. On smaller projects that have very small music budgets, composers may sometimes be able to negotiate to keep some or all of the publishing rights in lieu of a better fee or package. This is only worthwhile if the project gets shown on television. Film cue sheets have both the composer's and the publisher's name. They are sent to the performing rights society at the conclusion of the dub. If you have made arrangements to retain the publisher's share of your music you will need to set up a publishing company. This is very simple. Contact the same performing rights organization you joined as a composer and tell them you want to be a publisher, and you become one. You simply need to come up with some clever name for your new "company," and pay the same nominal fee to join, plus a small fee to check that the name of your company isn't already in use by another publisher. Once you've gotten confirmation of your company's name, you are a publishing company. While you cannot join more than one per-

Figure 3.2a-b Two cue
sheets in slightly different formats. Both list
title, duration, com-
poser, publisher, usage,
and royalty affiliation.

```
                          MUSIC CUE SHEET

TITLE: "Double Jeopardy"
DESCRIPTION: Feature Film
PRODUCTION COMPANY: Paramount
RECORDED AT: Paramount, Stage M
MUSIC EDITOR: Craig Pettigrew



CUE: 1M1           TITLE: "Still Waters"
                   COMPOSER: Normand Corbeil (SOCAN)

                   PUBLISHER: Ensign Music Corp.

                   LENGTH: 1:22        USAGE: Underscore

CUE: 1M2           TITLE: "Juicy Lucy"
                   COMPOSER: Horace Silver (ASCAP)

                   PUBLISHER: Ecaroh Music, Inc.

                   LENGTH: 1:31        USAGE: Non-Vis Source

CUE: 1M3           TITLE: "The Morningstar"
                   COMPOSER: Normand Corbeil (SOCAN)

                   PUBLISHER: Ensign Music Corp.

                   LENGTH: 2:13        USAGE: Underscore

CUE: 1M4           TITLE: "A Little Knife Music"
                   COMPOSER: Normand Corbeil (SOCAN)

                   PUBLISHER: Ensign Music Corp.

                   LENGTH: 1:42        USAGE: Underscore

CUE: 1M5           TITLE: "Charged With His Murder"
                   COMPOSER: Normand Corbeil (SOCAN)

                   PUBLISHER: Ensign Music Corp.

                   LENGTH: 1:05        USAGE: Underscore

CUE: 2M6           TITLE: "Matty Loves You"
                   COMPOSER: Normand Corbeil (SOCAN)

                   PUBLISHER: Ensign Music Corp.

                   LENGTH: 1:37        USAGE: Underscore
```

DOUBLE JEOPARDY

No. 33315

May 10, 1999

PARAMOUNT PICTURES CORPORATION

REELS 1 & 2

#	Title	Time		Composer	PRO	Publisher	Usage
1.	OPENING CREDITS (1M1)	1:14	inst bkg	Normand Corbeil (SOCAN)	BMI	Ensign Music Corporation	IN during Paramount Pictures logo. Continues through first part of Main Title. OUT as Ashley Judd (Libby Parsons) instructs her son as they fish, "Slowly... slowly..."
2.	JUICY LUCY (P)	1:31	inst bkg	Horace Silver	ASCAP	Ecaroh Music, Inc.	IN just before cut to party in progress on deck of house, as main title card reading "Bruce Greenwood" appears. Continues through party as Bruce Greenwood (Nick) discusses business and guest discusses painting. OUT on cut to Greenwood about to make speech.
3.	THE MORNINGSTAR (1M3)	2:11	inst bkg	Normand Corbeil (SOCAN)	BMI	Ensign Music Corporation	IN after Greenwood tells Judd, "Close your eyes... close 'em." Continues as they go sailing. OUT after slow dissolve to Judd and Greenwood making love.
4.	A LITTLE KNIFE MUSIC (1M4)	1:36	inst bkg	Normand Corbeil (SOCAN)	BMI	Ensign Music Corporation	IN after Judd awakens the next morning and calls "Nick?" Continues as she follows trail of blood out onto deck where she finds bloody knife. OUT on cut to crowded dock as raft is pulled in.
5.	CHARGED WITH HIS MURDER (1M5)	1:02	inst bkg	Normand Corbeil (SOCAN)	BMI	Ensign Music Corporation	IN as Jay Brazeau (Bobby Long) tells Judd, "I'm here to advise you, make no statements whatsoever..." Continues as Brazeau tells Judd that bail is denied. OUT as Brazeau asks Judd, "Can Angie keep looking after Matty?"

forming rights organization at a time, you can join one society as a publisher and another as a composer, though there is no advantage to this. There are certain time commitments that the societies require, after which you can change affiliation if you so desire.

In addition to retaining your music's publishing rights (which also gives you the right to reuse or license the music), there are other ways to make small budget films more lucrative. Some composers can negotiate some forms of profit sharing in a film in lieu of a significant up front fee. This is risky because you only make money if the film does, and most smaller films do not. Profit sharing can be done in two ways. One is to be given "points" on the film. This is a percentage of any and all profits the film makes. It is usually a piece of the producer's or director's profit share. The other way is to ask for "bumps." A bump is an additional amount of money based on the gross profits of the film. You can request bumps at specific box office receipts, usually as reported in one of the film industry trade papers such as Variety. For example, you can request bumps like this:

- If box office on the film exceeds $5,000,000, composer is paid an additional $5,000.
- If box office on the film exceeds $8,000,000, composer is paid an additional $5,000 again.
- If box office on the film exceeds $10,000,000, composer is paid an additional $10,000.

You negotiate the bumps and the amounts to be paid at each bump. It needs to be scaled to the size of the film and the expectations of the film's success. This is a bit more appealing to some producers because they pay nothing extra until the movie is doing well.

Who Signs the Composer's Check?

Composers are paid by the production company making the film. Sometimes that will be a major studio, such as Paramount or Warner Brothers. Usually, though, it will be a smaller production company either working independently or contracted by a major studio in order to make that film. You make your deal with that entity, whichever it is. Although it's not good business sense, formal contracts are often not completed until your work is well under way, or even nearly done, and sometimes not until after a job is completed. The first step then, is to create a "deal memo" which is a simple one or two page legal document that outlines the basic points of your agreement including the fee you will be paid, payment schedule (e.g. half now and half upon handing in the final mixes), what expenses may be excluded from your package (musicians, tape transfer costs, music editor, etc.), whether or not you will keep any part of the publishing of your composition, your share of royalties from any potential soundtrack album deal, and any other basic points of your deal. A composer should not begin work without at least a deal memo in place, if not a complete contract. Again, if you do not have an agent, then having an attorney experienced in entertainment law to look over a deal memo is important. If you are doing a small project with a client who does not offer you a deal memo, or a fully prepared contract, then you may wish to have one put together, though generally it should be up to the producers to provide the deal.

So now the big question: How much should you be charging for your work? The easy answer is: as much as you can! The more complex answer is that it depends on the nature of the project, its overall budget, how much they want you, and how much you made for your last project of similar scope. Everything is negotiable. Even if you consider yourself to be a great negotiator, you will always want someone to do the negotiating for you. As mentioned earlier, an artist should not be the deal maker. On very small projects, it may not be worth the expense of an agent or attorney. Agents charge a percentage of your fee to do the negotiating, create a deal memo and handle all critical contract details. Usually agents charge 10 percent of the composer's fee, though many charge less on a package. Episodic TV is often charged at a slightly lower amount. Beware of anyone wanting to charge significantly more. Attorneys typically work at an hourly fee for their services, though some will work on a percentage basis as well.

There is no set music budget for scores. Music budgets are based on a number of factors including the overall cost of the production, how much music is anticipated for the film, and how much money is needed for licensing songs and other source music. Movies may set aside anywhere from less than one to more than three percent of their total budget for music. Based on that, a $5,000,000 film may have between $50,000 and $150,000 for music, more or less. After buying songs and other music, what money remains must pay for the composer and all the recording costs. There is enormous variability in low-budget films, depending on the savvy of the producers (often making their first film) and how important they consider music to be. Many films spend next to nothing on music. Don't be surprised to find some amount of unprofessionality on very low-budget films. You may already be far more experienced then the people hiring you. Be patient, but firm in your demands. A small film may only have a couple of thousand dollars for music, and sometimes they just look for favours. Since music comes at the very end of a film's production, they are usually already over budget and may have dipped into the music budget to fix other problems and oversights. We suffer for their art. These numbers scale upwards. Your previous fees will have an effect on your next fees. Some composers will lower their fee for a certain project they want to do for other reasons than money, and can request a clause in their contract that makes that fee secret. Normally a producer will call the producer of your last film and ask what you were paid.

Remember that no one, especially a producer, will come to you with their best offer first. If you are offered a small fee or package for a score, just realize that there is probably more where that came from. Maybe not a lot, but there is almost always a bit more, and you should try to get some of it through negotiation. When a producer says "there isn't any more money," that really means "there isn't any more money that I want to give you."

A film's overall budget is naturally a factor in determining the film's music budget. Composers of larger films can make anywhere from tens to hundreds of thousands of dollars for their services. Top composers can make better than $1,000,000 per film, and that is often just their fee, not counting expenses. This is the current stratosphere of the composing world. Regardless of how much you are making currently, your fee should hopefully rise between 10 percent and 20 percent on each film of similar budget. There will always be an occasional project that will pay less than one you've already done, which is fine as long as it is a project you consider worthwhile for your time and efforts. It's always better to work than not, but it is not worth it to throw your time away on projects that bring you neither money nor professional nor artistic opportunity. It pays to be picky at times.

Television Music Fees and Budgets

Things are a little different in the world of episodic television. The fees are more modest than most films, but there are lucrative royalties for television that help compensate for that. TV series pay almost exclusively as a package, unless there is an orchestra involved. On the low end are shows for cable or syndication as well as local programming. Above those are national network programs. Half hour comedies pay much less than hour long dramatic series. Television series usually produce between twelve and twenty five episodes per season. Composers are paid per episode. A series composer can make less than $3,000 for a smaller project, to over $20,000 or more for an established composer on a top primetime show. These fees seem to move up and down every few years, so you might find things very different now. Some composers are able to get commitments for doing an entire season of a TV show while others, in fact most, work on a show by show basis.

Some types of television programs, such as soap operas, news magazines or sports programs will often buy *library music*. These are collections of music not written for specific projects, but licensed from library music companies on CDs for use in any program. Producers who use library music pay a smaller up front fee, with royalties paid by the minute of music used. The drawback is that the music is generic and not composed to the picture used.

Occasionally there are projects that are done as a "buy out," meaning you will see no further money. If the project is used in broadcast, this practice is unethical and possibly illegal. Someone is usually collecting the writer's royalty. You should always be able to keep all of your writer's share of the royalties. It is yours. There are several books on the business aspects of music, and some have sections on film and television deals. You may want to look through some to learn more about these negotiations.

For a list of books on music business, go to www.reelworld-online.com

Remember, everything is negotiable and deals will rarely start at the point at which they will end. While hiring a lawyer may be seen as aggressive, it is always better to let someone else be the bad guy (as well as the smart guy) so you can be the artist. On very, very small projects your legal fees could be more than your creative fee. There might be situations where you need to hash things out yourself. You'll find example contracts in some music business books. A well designed deal will make for a smooth relationship between you and your client, who may also be the person offering you your next job. Don't be a pushover, don't be a chump, and don't be a target—some producers will want to see just how far they can push you in a deal. Most get paid based on how much money they don't spend (meaning on you). Make your deal, then set it aside and do your work. Ultimately it will be the quality of your work, and the quality of your working relationship that will determine how you do on your next job.

Contracting Music (Don't Worry, You'll Live)

An Interview with David Low, Music Contractor

It's obvious just how much music is enhanced from using live musicians. Sometimes, due to budget, time, or both, it simply isn't possible. But when it is in the budget, you need to do things right. Sure, you know how to write for any musical ensemble, but you also need to know how to put a group together. And if the project requires you to use union musicians, things are a bit more complicated. A *music contractor* is the person that handles the hiring of musicians for recording sessions. Putting together a group of any size can be complex and time consuming, and it's important to have someone to help you.

David Low is a music contractor and cellist in Los Angeles (Hollywood, Baby!). His work is heard on a majority of the major films scored in Los Angeles—and that's a lot of films. We chatted poolside between gigs during his hectic schedule.

JR: How does a composer go about getting musicians for a score?

DL: The first thing is to pick up the phone and call! Seriously, the process is pretty simple. When recording in Los Angeles, something called an *Assumption Agreement* needs to be in place before a score gets recorded. It basically connects the project to all the necessary union contracts. The music contractor hiring the musicians needs to have this prior to calling in players. The contractor will contact the production company on behalf of the composer. The Assumption Agreement is created between the producers and a payroll company, not the composer.

JR: Explain the role of a payroll company.

DL: They pay the musicians, taking care of their union benefits, taxes, etc. Lots of paperwork.

JR: Does the composer write the check to the musicians, the contractor, or the payroll service?

DL: In package deals, where the composer is responsible for all the expenses incurred for a recording, the composer will write a single check to the payroll service, which then takes care of paying all the players. The payroll service sends a bill to the composer after the session.

JR: What would happen if the composer doesn't get paid for their services for some time, is there a time limit and penalties?

DL: Yes, usually 15 working days. After that the union can add penalty fees to the contract.

JR: What about those projects where the producers refuse to deal with union musicians and won't sign an Assumption Agreement?

DL: The composer should first find out why they won't sign. Many times the producers don't understand what is entailed with the agreement. They think that it will cost them a great deal of money later on, but in fact in television there is virtually no difference. In films there are some additional responsibilities for the producers to pay players, but not nearly as much as many of them think, and it's based on how well the film does at the box office.

JR: Should a composer try to sway a producer who is set on a non-union score, or does that cause too much friction?

DL: A composer's main concern should be about the quality of musicians hired to play on the score. I don't think that a composer should wear too many hats. Everybody has their own job for a film score; the music contractor, the engineer, the orchestrator, etc. A contractor will help out by making these arrangements and taking that pressure off the composer's shoulders.

JR: If a composer only needs a small handful of players, say one to five musicians, is there still a need for a contractor's services?

DL: That's up to the composer. Union contracts don't require a contractor below a certain number of players. I think it's around 11. However, the smaller the size of the group, the more important each player's role is in the quality of the recording. With a small group, it's like every player is a soloist. Plus, a composer may not want to deal with all the contract paperwork.

JR: If a composer wants a specific musician on a score, say a friend who is a fantastic guitar player but who isn't in a musician's union, what should he or she do?

DL: Every musician who is not a member of a union is allowed to perform on one project under what's called the Taft-Hartley Law. After that initial project, the player needs to join a union in order to do more union sessions. Joining is very easy and inexpensive. Composers can always contact a friend directly and just record their score, but should try and find out how to file proper paperwork for the project.

JR: What about all-electronic scores? Can a composer be on a union contract alone, and is there any advantages to it?

DL: Yes. If there is an Assumption Agreement in place, there are advantages to a composer putting him or herself on a union contract, even for an all-electronic score. Health insurance, pension, and reuse payments on motion picture scores are available to union players only. Obviously that means the composer must be a member of the union themselves.

JR: What is a reuse payment, and who pays it?

DL: Any secondary use of a score recording must pay all the participating musicians a "reuse fee." Records, commercials, use on other film or TV scores must repay all the original musicians whose names are on the session contracts. It can pay up to 100% of what each player would have made on the new recording, if it were actually rerecorded.

The reuse fees are paid by the companies reusing the music. For example, if a score appears on a soundtrack album, the musicians get a repayment from the record company. There is another type of residual payment made to union musicians when a film score is subsequently shown on network or cable television, is released on video, or shown on an airplane (but only on east-bound flights—on west-bound flights the musicians have to give the money back)! This is called the Special Payments Fund, and is paid by the film's producers or distributors into a general fund that is split up among all the players of that score. For those players who do a lot of scores, it really adds up after a while, especially if those films are successful at the boxoffice.

JR: What do composers who live outside of major urban areas do when putting together a score with live musicians?

DL: Outside of New York, Los Angeles, Chicago, or Nashville—where there are long traditions of recording and studio work—a composer should call either the personnel manager of the largest local orchestra, or call the local musicians union and ask for a list of reputable music contractors (which I hope doesn't sound like an oxymoron, now that I think about it). The best thing would be to try recording in one of those major cities, if there is the budget for it. Los Angeles is the centre of the film scoring universe right now. No place else has as many top-quality players as here. But a score can be recorded in most any city a composer lives in or near.

JR: Are there problems with recording scores using non-union players, or without union contracts? How about on television, or very low-budget films where there is just barely enough money for the composer?

DL: The obvious problems are the level of the players that a composer can get, and those players' expertise in recording filmscores. Sure, there are lots of scores recorded without union players, either with small groups of local musicians or with one of the nonunion orchestras that are available for recording scores for cash (both in the US and abroad). But every composer that comes to me to put together a recording session for them after they've been to one of those orchestras is usually shocked at how much better their music sounds and how much smoother and faster the sessions go. Sometimes it ends up costing more to try and save money with those groups, in my humble opinion.

I rarely hear about the little projects that only use a musician or two. There are certain production companies, such as the major film studios or TV networks, which do not allow music recorded without union contracts on file. A composer always needs to be sure that they do not get caught with non-union sessions or players on one of those projects. It can lead to trouble.

The bigger problem comes when a composer tries to put together a non-union session with union players. The players are the ones at risk here, and can be penalized in a number of ways. The really good players are never going to put themselves in that kind of situation and will simply not do those recordings. The best thing is always to seek out the best players possible, either through personal referrals or through a good contractor, and make it possible for those players to appear on your score.

JR: How much does it cost to put together a session with an orchestral group? How does a composer put together a budget to decide how many players he or she can afford?

DL: I will help do a budget for the composers I work with—it's part of my job. There are different pay scales for different types of projects. There are scales for low-budget films (which are films made for under $13 million), low-budget TV movies, motion pictures and television, records, jingles and commercials, and several other categories. Anyone interesting in knowing exactly how much it costs per musician can go to the musicians union website at www.promusic47.org/Contract.htm. They can also just contact any union local and request a scale chart. But remember, these wage scales do not include benefits, taxes, or handling fees that can add another 31 percent to 35 percent per player. There are also overscales paid to certain key players, such as the concert master and certain section principles, and cartage fees for the bigger instruments such as harp and percussion. Again, a contractor will gladly help a composer put together a reasonably accurate budget for almost any size group.

JR: How do you go about choosing which musicians will play on a score?

DL: The most interesting part of my job is being like a casting director for musicians. Matching players with a composer or a style of score is the fascinating part of contracting. With bigger ensembles, I will work very hard to match players within each section by how well they play together. Over the years I've been doing this, and because of my experience as a session musician, I've come to know every player's personal style and how it meshes within a section, with a style of score, and ultimately with the composers I work with. I've been fortunate to work under one of the best contractors in the world, Sandy DeCrescent. You will see her name in the end credits of tons of major motion pictures. She's helped to create the sound that exists in the studios of LA.

JR: What do you think of samplers?

DL: I think they are a great tool for composers creating demos and temp scores! Synthesizers have changed the nature of music today, especially in television music. There's far less work in television and jingle recording. There are only a couple of TV series using live orchestras anymore, the rest are done by composers using their electronic instruments and only a handful of live players. On the other hand, orchestras for motion pictures have actually boomed. Film producers want to distance themselves from what they consider to be the "TV sound" of small groups and samples. They want the "big sound" that only live players can provide. I can always tell when a score is using samples. Live players offer both a richness and warmth in the sound, and obvious versatility that composers really need in showcasing their music to its fullest level.

The quality of studio players has never been higher. Yes, there's been some loss of work for studio players from samplers and other electronic technology. It's just the reality of the situation.

JR: Before you finish your drink and head back to the studio, any final thoughts for our readers out there?

DL: I'm not a composer, in any way (when I was in music school, I paid someone to finish my composition assignment!), but I can imagine that hearing your music played by great musicians is one of the greatest thrills a composer can have. That's what we do here. For a composer new to orchestral scoring, one of the keys to a successful session is developing a full support team with a contractor, copyist, orchestrators, engineer, and musicians that are there for her or him. It is the single most important aspect of successful recording sessions for newer composers, and seasoned pros as well. Then a composer can focus on what's really important—shmoozing their next gig with the director!

Agents of Change
An Interview with Cheryl Tiano, Composer's Agent

A career in music is made up of many things. There's learning your craft, developing a style, making contacts in your field, producing work that is well received, and finding projects that will bring you closer to your artistic and financial goals. Along the way, there are people that you connect with who will help you in some way. In fact, these people can be vital to your career's growth. There are teachers, mentors, collaborators, employers, and even critics.

Perhaps one of the most important people that works to help a composer's career is an agent. They do not typically start a career. A good, ethical, and effective agent usually does not take on a composer with no credits, regardless of how good a composer they are. Most composers get an agent after they have already gotten a few projects under their belt. I got my agent when I was offered a large project and went to the agency to negotiate the deal. So they got a commission for doing almost no work. But that was OK. They did a good job on the deal, and they started to put me up for better projects shortly thereafter.

I had a conversation with film music agent Cheryl Tiano from the Gorfaine/Schwartz Agency, one of the largest and most successful of the film music agencies. During our talk she touched on a number of the most critical elements of a composer's career.

JR: What exactly is a composer's agent?

CT: In film and TV music, we work for our clients to get them work! We pursue projects, we make deals, and troubleshoot problems, certainly an ongoing activity in this business. I talk with producers, directors, music supervisors, editors, and anyone else working on a project that will need music composed. Our agency is also involved in career development—giving advice to our composers on which projects to take or not—depending on where he or she is in their career at the time.

We get involved in our clients' projects whenever they get into a problem with a producer, director, or whomever. We help with soundtrack album deals. We hook composers up with publicists, attorneys, music editors, orchestrators, contractors, and any other service they might need to get their work done the best way possible. Our goal is to make our clients as successful as possible.

JR: How do you market a composer?

CT: It depends who you talk to. There are music executives at the major film studios, production executives, studio presidents, department heads—all who might have a say in who will score their upcoming films. On bigger feature films we will pitch certain composers that we think are the right choice for the project. We go straight to the decision makers and offer to send them demos on CD (we haven't sent a cassette tape for over a year now!), bios, and we even take them to lunch and tell them why a certain composer is the best for that job. We threaten their lives (um, just kidding!). We do whatever we can to get them to listen and consider our clients. Our goal is to get a meeting between the composer and the person or people who will make the final decision. While composers get hired based on the quality and appropriateness of their music, the meeting is just as important. It's like an interview of sorts, and if it goes poorly, even very gifted composers will be overlooked. Some composers know how to give "good meeting."

We also take politics into account. On some projects the producer will decide on a composer, on others it's the director, or a studio executive. We will try to determine who the right person is and then track them down. We ask a lot of questions and we deal with a lot of egos. It's all highly political.

In television, it's a little different. The networks have in-house music executives who have some say. Producers also have a lot of say as well, but the studio often will make the final choice, even against the wishes of directors and everyone else. As cable stations grow in popularity there are a whole new set of players in the market. They are producing a lot more series, movies, and miniseries. We stay on top of that world now as well.

JR: When is a composer ready to get an agent, and what do they do until then?

CT: Assuming they have talent and technique (meaning the ability to score to picture in a number of styles), they are ready for an agent. Our agency, GSA, doesn't take on composers without some solid credits already on their resume. Not huge credits, but established credits. We also need to believe in them musically. Other agencies may be more willing to take a chance on a new composer with fewer credits.

JR: If you are fresh out of music school or a film scoring program, where would you go to find an agent?

CT: The *Hollywood Reporter* puts out an annual film music guide which lists over 30 agencies that handle film and television composers. The vast majority are based, like ourselves, here in Los Angeles. Another way to find an agent is by referral. If one of our current composers whom we trust recommends a new composer to us, we will definitely listen and see if we want to take them on.

Composers without an agent can also look into getting small films on their own to start building a resume. Again, the *Hollywood Reporter* publishes weekly production charts. These list most of the current films in preproduction, production, and post production. A composer can look through the lists and call the numbers listed to find out the right person to speak to about music. You might have to talk to dozens of people before you find the right person, but it can be done, at least on some of the smaller independent films. There are people, even at the big studios, who are interested in taking chances with a lesser known or unknown composer, but it's a long shot. There are also resources on the Internet that might help to track down film productions.

There are also composers organizations that are worth joining, like the Society of Composers and Lyricists (SCL). For emerging composers, it's a chance to meet other composers and attend events that can be very informative. It's a chance to learn more about the politics of the business.

JR: If a composer finds an address for a film's production office, like those in the *Hollywood Reporter*, is sending a "cold" unsolicited demo all right?

CT: Yes. There are people who will take chances. It's always worth it.

JR: When a composer without an agent gets connected with a project, do they need a lawyer, or can they handle the dealmaking on their own?

CT: I would never suggest that a composer handle their own deal negotiations, even if they were an attorney! If I was going to go and score a film tomorrow, I wouldn't make my own deal—and I'm an agent! You can't be that close to it. It's too personal. Even if you are going to score a project for a good friend, it's best to get someone else to handle things. A composer should be a creative entity and no more. You shouldn't be involved in any arguments. And if you don't get into an argument, you probably won't get the best deal you could.

Producers expect agents to be adversarial. I have screaming matches with people that I'll go to lunch with the next day. That's just the nature of the business. No one thinks anything of it. But it would be wrong for a composer to be that way, they must stay creative. A composer can still be a good businessperson and discuss those things with their agent or attorney to get the best deal they know, but it should stay there.

JR: What do you think goes into making a successful demo?

CT: It depends. People scoring films today come from a lot of different places. Some from the concert music world, some are rock 'n' rollers turned film composers. There's such a wide range, and their demos are just as diverse. A rock composer's demos will reflect their rock roots until they've built up a catalog of actual scores.

For a producer or director who doesn't know you, and especially if it's not for a specific project, a demo should be as concise and varied as possible. Realize that these people probably won't get past the second cut. You want those first couple of cues to be blockbusters. Don't make them too long, maybe between thirty seconds and up to two minutes. Don't make them too short or it doesn't sound like music.

These people are nonmusicians—they judge a demo on a much more emotional, gut level. Most relate to melody. They relate to primitive musical elements such as percussion and voice. That's probably why rock and pop music are so successful in the film world. People relate to singing as much or more than instrumental sounds.

JR: Do you think having academic credentials helps (or hurts) a composer looking for film work?

CT: It could go either way. Say a film is looking for a very contemporary vibe, heavy on electric guitars and drums and the like. So I submit a composer who does just that. But his bio shows that he studied at the Paris Conservatory. They may look at that and think, "Well, he's not the right guy." We like to tailor both the CD as well as the bio to the specific project whenever possible. We don't lie, but we carefully select those aspects of the composer's work that most suits what the film is looking for.

And speaking of credits, I have to stress how important it is not to lie about them. I've seen bios of composers not with our agency who have padded their credits with the names of films on which they maybe helped on a small cue or two, but list the film as theirs. People do check these things out, and those kinds of exaggerations usually get caught. It's a small world.

But in terms of academic credits, a more classically oriented score or a period piece might want a more formally trained composer. Most of today's composers have very little formal training, but it doesn't mean they won't be very successful. I think that composers with more training are often more "detailed" composers, but it doesn't mean they are better "film" composers. There's a big difference. I came from the concert musical world, and most of the composers there could not cross over into film. Most rock composers couldn't cross over either. Film is such a different ball game. In the concert music world a composer may spend the better part of a year writing a piece, but in film they may get barely a week or two. Academic training may give someone strong musical techniques, but it doesn't necessarily give them a strong dramatic sense, or the political sense to deal with producers and directors.

JR: What makes for a good first impression between a composer and a director or producer? What goes into "giving good meeting"?

CT: A lot of how you act depends on who you're meeting with. The first thing you need to notice when you go into a meeting is the body language and the personality types of the people you're meeting with. This applies to any job interview. Sensing how to fit in with the people you are meeting with is very instinctual. It can't be taught, it comes from experience and a certain intuition. You need to get the sense of whether they want you to listen to their musical opinions, or that they have no opinions and really want you to take over and give yours. Knowing when to give your opinion, or just keep quiet and listen is very important. The egos in this business are very strong, and the people that a composer meets with about work may think they know a lot more about music than they actually do. So it's a matter of accepting that and making them feel important. Tune into that, try to learn what it is they want, and then make them feel they will get it. Even if you disagree with them.

Now there may also be times when you might feel that it is OK to disagree with prospective clients' musical opinions. But it's more about how to go about it. There are little ways of making a point in a way that doesn't make them feel they are wrong. It's a bit manipulative. I do it with my spouse all the time (laughs)! But seriously, keep in mind that many times these people are very scared because they don't know how to describe what they want in a musical language. It's the one aspect of the film making process that they can't communicate about the way they wish they could. Because of that they are very dependent on the composer drawing them into the process and making them feel that will get what they want.

JR: Let's talk about money.

CT: OK. Ten percent! Hand it over! (laughs)

JR: So by that, you're saying that an agent charges by commission and not by the hour or some other way?

CT: That's right. We charge a standard 10 percent agent's commission on the projects we do. Managers can take more depending on the situation. We do some managing of a few composer's concert careers, and we charge differently for that. There are some agencies that call themselves management companies who aren't really doing management. They say it so they can take more than the standard agent's fee. Agents are required to have an agent's license in order to actually make the deals. Managers don't make deals like we do. They handle other kinds of details.

Most ethical agents charge between 10 and 15 percent of the creative fee the composer gets to write a score. There are also "package deals" in which a composer is given a lump sum to both compose and produce a score, including musicians and all recording costs. We charge 7 percent on package deals. Other agencies may charge somewhat differently.

JR: How does a composer know if they are getting a good deal?

CT: It varies, but most bigger movies pay between 1 percent and 2 percent of the film's budget. Sometimes it's less, but sometimes it can be a lot more. That applies to TV movies as well. On smaller indie films, made for around a million, the composer may only get about $10,000, which is still around 1 percent. But on small films there are sometimes ways to get "backend" money that isn't available on the bigger ones, such as publishing (the royalty usually paid to the film's producers), distribution bonus deals, and record royalties from soundtrack albums. So there are ways to be creative about deals that don't have a lot of up-front cash. Will you ever see any backend money on these small films? It's a big question mark. But at least you set precedents which are important for future deals.

So a composer (or their agent or attorney) can ask what the overall budget of a film is to determine what the ballpark music budget should be. Some small films just lay it on the line, "This is how much we have for music on the film. Take it or leave it." Then the composer has to decide. If a composer doesn't have a lot of credits they should probably just do it and not worry about the money. Build some experience and credits.

Ultimately, I think there are three reasons to do a film. One is money. Two is for artistic reasons, and three is relationships, new or old. If you get the chance to do a crappy to mediocre but well paying film and you need money, then do it. If it's a great artistic opportunity and it's something you've never gotten to do before in a film, then do it. If you have the opportunity to work with a talented up-and-coming director but it pays nothing, do it. It all depends on where you are in your life and your career. Agents sometimes can be helpful in making some of these kinds of decisions.

One of my more successful clients has a space in his schedule and is doing a very small film that pays much less than his standard fee. But they are allowing him full artistic control, which is quite rare. It's a favour for a very successful producer, and so it's building a relationship as well. Relationships are so important. If a big name producer, director, or what you believe might be a rising star, calls you, do it. Build relationships with people who are going somewhere. I can't emphasize it enough.

JR: Are student films helpful for resumes?

CT: If you're just starting out and trying to get with an agent, it helps if you've done something. I wouldn't put student films on a resume for a bigger project. It makes it look like you aren't ready.

JR: What would be your advice for someone just getting started? Any pearls of wisdom?

CT: Be incredibly persistent. Put together a great CD, even if you haven't done a film. Get to know other film composers. Get to know lots of new people. Try to meet two new people a week. Find people in the industry as much as possible. It can happen. Your first film could be a big hit and you're set, or it can take years and years. Typically it's somewhere in between. Don't give up. Anyone who quits will never succeed.

At the same time be realistic. Just because you get a few breaks doesn't mean you've caught the big brass ring. People pay dues for a long time. Be patient, persistent, and good.

And with that, Cheryl Tiano leapt from her desk to run off to another three-hour lunch meeting. From my experience, agents each have a different way of working. Some are more aggressive than others. Some are more careful to build careers slowly and solidly. Composers all have unique relationships with their agents. Some form close bonds while others will change agents several times. There are composers who leave their agents only to return later.

An agent, even a top-notch agent, doesn't take the place of personal efforts toward achieving your goals. They work with you, not for you. An agent might arrange a meeting between you and a prospective client or submit a demo of yours to someone looking for a composer. They can't, however, help you build lasting relationships and friendships among the people who will continue to hire you, recommend you and work with you throughout your career. That's up to each of us. (Agents do make excellent scapegoats when things aren't going as well as you might wish.)

Had I asked the same questions to other film music agents, most would no doubt answer with more or less the same concepts, even though their approaches might be somewhat different. Some agents are better than others, though an agent that is right for one composer may be wrong for another. Some agents specialize in certain types of films or certain types of composers. If you have a few films on your resume, you would be well advised to do some shopping to find the person that feels like they will do things the way you want them done.

I Pick the Songs
An Interview with Chris Douridas, Music Supervisor

Discussions of film scores, especially modern film soundtracks, would be incomplete without learning some of the aspects of song usage. Songs have always been an important and integral part of film music, it's true, but never more so than with contemporary film.

As a composer, you are usually not part of the song selection or production process, though there are exceptions to that. But as a composer you may be asked to arrange a song that is used elsewhere in a film, to base a theme on a theme from a song used in the film, or create a score that integrates carefully with songs.

Film music budgets are often broken into two parts, one for score and the other for the licensing of songs. When a song is acquired for a film, the producers must approach the song's publisher and negotiate a deal for that song. It continues to get more political when the need for an entire soundtrack album comes into play. As a composer you are not immune from this, but you can coexist peacefully.

The chore of song placement falls upon someone called a *music supervisor*. I had the opportunity to sit with Chris Douridas, an emerging talent in the world of film soundtrack supervision, having worked on projects such as *Austin Powers* 1 and 2, *American Beauty, 187, Grace of My Heart*, and many others. Here's some of what Chris had to say about it.

JR: Is choosing songs for films experimental, or is it a more planned-out process?

CD: I'm sure everybody has their own system. For me, I just start. You know, you can talk about music all day long, but until you're actually hearing ideas and getting on the same page creatively with the people you're working with, you're not really going to get anywhere. So the first thing I do is start feeding the director tapes—tapes of things that have come to me or have occurred to me as being possible ideas that fit within the world of this movie. I'll try to do a broad range of things so I can outline the parameters of where I understand this world to live. So the first tape might contain ten songs that really stake out the parameters of this film's world, its story, and characters. I ask the director not to think of specific scenes but to come back with feedback as to whether or not these pieces fit the film's world as he understands it to be as well. Then I'll take that feedback and keep the ideas that were good, discard the ideas that didn't fit, and then on the next tape hone it further so that by the fourth or fifth tape we're starting to really define the musical world of this movie. We're still not talking about specific scenes or characters, just the world of the movie. Usually by the third or fourth tape the director will already have hit on some of those songs or choices being right for a certain scene or character, so without knowing it, we're starting to get the job done.

JR: Do any of the directors you've worked with come to you with specific songs in mind?

CD: Sure. I think it's great when a director has some musical ideas at the start. Often they'll have that from their own reading of the script. If they wrote the script then they often have songs or musical ideas in their head that may still be undeveloped, but important to the essence of what the film is going to be. I use those as launching points to build a musical world around me and the film.

JR: Do you ever find yourself in disagreement with the director?

CD: I don't think any creative participant in a film project should be shy about challenging the director's preconceived notions. Film is a collaborative medium, so that's part of what I'm there for. Every creative contributor to a film has to speak out and be prepared to challenge the ideas if they feel they are inappropriate or in the wrong direction.

JR: How did you get started doing music supervision in film?

CD: My story is unique—as I'm sure most are. Music supervisor is not something you study in school. In my particular case I was a radio DJ for about 15 years. The last 8 or 9 years in Los Angeles gave me a great forum. I did a daily morning music show that presented new music from all around the world. It was only natural that a lot of that great music might find its way into film projects. So I started getting called upon because of the variety of music with which I was familiar.

JR: What was the first film you worked on as a supervisor?

CD: As a supervisor I worked on a film with Kevin Reynolds called *187* starring Samuel L. Jackson. Prior to that I began as a consultant first on the TV show *Northern Exposure*, and then Michael Mann's film *Heat*. In both cases the directors of these shows were fans of my radio show.

JR: Can you explain the difference between a supervisor and a consultant?

CD: A consultant will usually be brought in as a contributing element to the musical vision of the film. They work with the music supervisor to contribute ideas in the preproduction, production, or the postproduction of the film. It is a more limited role, and may be focused on a single aspect of the soundtrack.

JR: Tell me a little bit about the interaction between you, as a music supervisor, and a composer who's writing the underscore for a film There are certainly situations where it's a toss-up whether a scene will be scored with underscore or a song. Who makes those decisions? How do you get involved, and what sorts of interactions do you have with a film's composer?

CD: Again, because the medium of film is so collaborative it's always a diplomatic process, especially with regard to relationship between the film composer and the music supervisor. Both roles are essentially to provide the necessary musical ingredients for the film. There's a limited amount of space available, and the film composer will want to have the opportunity to get his vision across with the score in as many moments as possible. The music supervisor might have other ideas for the same reasons, but initially it's the director's decision. The film composer is usually brought in late in the process, unfortunately, which can make the process even more difficult, since decisions get made before they are even on the job.

JR: As supervisor, you come in sooner?

CD: Yes. The supervisor tends to come in toward the beginning of the process. I'll earmark scenes for score or for songs, but that may change. When the composer comes in he'll have ideas.

JR: Have you ever been involved in putting together temp music on films, or have influence over the choice of composer?

CD: It's a different story with every film. Sometimes the composer will be already in place when the supervisor's hired. There are a lot of composers who work with directors consistently, they have a history together. If a director sees eye to eye with the composer and they have a great working relationship then that may continue over the course of that director's career.

One of the biggest difficulties in the process of film music is the temp score. Often the director will fall in love with a temp score and sometimes it will be nearly impossible to sway him from using the temp. Composers are routinely asked to emulate temp scores, sometimes even to do a blatant rip-off; this can often be a thorn in the side of both the composer and music supervisor. These can, however, also be very helpful in getting an idea across to a composer or director where words fail.

A music supervisor should help guide the director to the options that are available to him. Ultimately it is the director's choice as to who will compose the score. It's incumbent upon the music supervisor to work closely with the composer to establish the musical personality of the film. The songs and musical element aside from the score should enhance the score.

JR: From time to time it seems that there are film scores that have a preponderance of songs simply to justify a successful soundtrack album and not necessarily geared specifically to what a director might want for the film just for the films' sake. Do you specifically get asked to try to ensure a hit record?

CD: I've been really lucky. I haven't had to work on many films that demand that of me. But, yes, it has come up. On the films *Austin Powers*, *Austin Powers 2*, and *Forces of Nature* I was involved as an A&R person. *Austin Powers 2* was building on a franchise that had huge expectations and they were a little burned by the lack of commercial success of the first soundtrack album. So, from the very beginning on the second soundtrack album, it was clear that it was important to sell records. I was a consultant in preproduction to help build on the musical personality that I helped develop for the first film. It was my role to come up with the theme of the film, that Quincy Jones soul bossa nova thing, as well as all the kitchy sixties pop stuff such as the Bacharach and Sergio Mendes stuff. So I staked out that part of the job and left the hit making part of the job to the music supervisor on the second film, Danny Bramson. He was working on behalf of Warner Brothers Records as their film person.

All that said, sometimes there can be a conflict between the musical needs of the film and the needs of the soundtrack album. That's just a symptom of the fact that film is at the heart of our pop culture, and by being there stands to generate a tremendous amount of cash.

JR: Do you not see it at the detriment of some films?

CD: Absolutely. It gives films a disposable quality. Look at the Giorgio Moroder version of *Metropolis*, with his new soundtrack. It became a very dated version of the original, which was heralded at the time as being cutting edge. But the new version is like a piece of candy compared to the original. I think it's very shortsighted of the film makers because over time the songs aren't going to remain current.

JR: You're saying the pop status of the film can last a lot longer than the pop status of some of these songs?

CD: In the case of Dreamworks' *American Beauty* we were very conscious not to date the film with a slew of contemporary bands, so I think if you watch the film it doesn't sound like 1999.

JR: What's the budgeting process on a film score with songs, and how involved do you get with that? Are you given a budget which you have to work within?

CD: Usually when I get a script the writer has peppered it with song choices with no regard to the potential budget limitations. I'll read scripts that have Beatle songs, or Rolling Stones, or Led Zeppelin only to come to the budgeting point and realize that's prohibitive. Even in *American Beauty*, the original script had "Fixing A Hole" by the Beatles at the front of the film. There were also Pink Floyd and Led Zeppelin references. While they were helpful to the film makers to help build that cinematic world, when it came time to lay out the song budget we were dealing with a relatively small independent film with a total budget of around $15 million dollars. A sliver of that is earmarked for music. When we started American Beauty the music budget was about $200,000. As a project gets rolling it starts to build momentum. The director jumps on board, there are stars attached and you have the filmmaking crew put together. Then the film studio producing the film can get a sense of where the picture is headed. As the dailies (the scenes as they come out of the camera, prior to editing) start coming in we see the performances that the director is getting, and a buzz starts to build around the film. People start to see there is something serious happening here, that it's a real film in the making. Then I can make a case for more money with regard to the budget. And they're more likely to go along with it. When we were done we got (film composer) Tom Newman to come in for a fraction of his normal cost. It's because the script was so attractive to all the creative people involved, so everyone took lesser fees because they wanted to be associated with a "golden" project. All of these money savings tactics go a long way to getting more funds from the studio. It's about timing and seeing what the market can bear.

JR: Do you get involved in the negotiation of song fees?

CD: If it's a studio project they'll have an in-house department that handles those negotiations. I'm happy to push it off to whoever wants to take it. Like me, I think most supervisors prefer to stick to the creative side of it, because it's your relationships with these artists and these record labels that helps grease the wheels of your career. If you get too involved with the negotiations it hinders your relationships with the musical creative people you want to work with in the future.

JR: What if it's an independent film? Do you find a lawyer to do it or do you do it?

CD: You can always find someone who will do clearances outright for set fees—there are clearance specialists. I would advise any supervisor to extricate themselves from the process of clearances if possible. It's easy to find somebody to come on board on a consultant or freelance basis to do clearances for somewhere around $1000 per track.

JR: Do you have a vague sense going in of what a song is going to cost? Do you have a sense of what a Beatles song would cost and how flexible are those prices?

CD: You go to publishers to get a ball park figure when you're budgeting the film. If you have songs that the script calls for you have to allow for those or be prepared to make changes later on. In the case of *American Beauty* we ended up with a Beatles song. But we didn't use "Fixing A Hole" as the script called for, but for the end credit song we used a Beatles song covered by Elliot Smith.

JR: It's cheaper to use somebody else's recording of a song than the original?

CD: Sometimes. There are no rules. In the case of this one, the Beatles committee was fond of the script and the idea and the project. While it was still very expensive, they did come down in price for us. This is where people pull out whatever relationships they have. We had a Who track that we wouldn't have been able to afford had the director not been a friend of Pete Townsend. That's why I like to work on great scripts. A great script can change a lot of people's minds and help you tremendously in the negotiation process. If you're working on a crappy film, nobody wants to be a part of it unless you pay full price. But if you're working on a great project, everybody wants to be a part of it, and the rules change.

The Executive Suite
An Interview with Robert Kraft,
Film Studio Music Executive

Major Hollywood film studios serve a number of functions in order to get movies made. For instance, they function as a bank that finances film projects. They are a think tank that helps to conceive of projects and figure out how to put all the elements into place. They are a focal point that works to attract the best talent in every creative area of film making from actors to directors, writers, and producers. They are also marketers who sell a product: entertainment.

Each major studio has a number of executives that help run some aspect of the overall function of the studio, and that is true of music as well. A music executive oversees the day to day running of a group of people whose job it is to combine music with the films and television shows they produce. Every working film composer who is scoring a studio-based film must be approved by, and then work alongside, the music executives of the studio. A music executive is responsible to the studio to be sure that nothing goes wrong in the process of the film's scoring process.

20th Century Fox is synonymous with great film scores and great film composers. For many years it was run by a musical dynasty of brilliant film composers the likes of Alfred and Lionel Newman, who not only ran the operation of the music department, but continued to compose and conduct for their pictures as well. Today, the Fox music department is run by another composer/songwriter, Robert Kraft. Kraft is an ex-New Yorker, a Harvard-trained musician, who wrote and had various rock and pop bands until he, by accident, had some of his music picked for a highly successful TV series produced in Los Angeles. He packed his bags, moved to the West Coast and started a successful writing career that got him better known in the Hollywood film music circles. He scored a number of successful TV series and films. His abilities to handle problems and find solutions eventually led him into the position he's held for the past several years, as head of music for 20th Century Fox.

I paid Robert a visit at his offices on the Fox lot. His walls are covered in gold and platinum soundtrack records for the films he's worked on, along with photos, signed scores, and other memorabilia of the composers he's hired and worked with. You can tell immediately that he is not only a composer and musician, but a real film score fan as well.

JR: Tell me what it is exactly that you do?

RK: I am responsible for ensuring that every Fox feature and TV show has first class music as part of the final product. I make sure that, by working together with the director, the producers, the studio, my staff, the composer, and frequently the record label, that we both fiscally and creatively decorate and support this filmed entertainment—from a two hour film to a half hour TV show—with underscore and songs to enhance, support, and market it. Whatever the priority is. How do I do it? By listening to the director, seeing what he wants, seeing what he can afford, then taking a horrible meeting and letting him know he's completely crazy and can't afford anything he's asking for. I listen to a lot of people's points of view and do responsibly what I think is best for the picture, accommodating everybody's ideas. I'm a consensus guy until I need to do what's best for everyone concerned.

JR: How do composers get connected with films?

RK: Composers get connected with films two or three ways. My favourite scenario is when a director is about to start a picture at 20th Century Fox; in my first meeting with him (I have an initial meeting with every director who does a project here), he tells me he has a favourite composer he's worked with before and would like to work with again. I usually get down on my knees and praise him and Allah for making my job so easy, unless it's a terrible choice he's made, which is rare with a big-time director making a big-time movie. For example, Robert Zemekis likes Alan Silvestri. They did pretty well on *Forrest Gump*, and he wants to work together again on the next picture we're doing, then all I say is, "Where do I sign?"

If they don't know exactly who they want, then we go through lots of listening. I send them CDs, I recommend other movies they should see, and I start calling music agents. I tell them we have a picture here that needs a composer, and then it becomes a big derby. The agents all chuck in their best composers, or at least the ones we can afford for that project. There are about a half dozen in Hollywood I'll speak to, and just three or four that represent the bulk of the composers. If you are not represented by one of them, you are really, really out of luck. It's as if you wanted to play in a major league ball game, but you're not on any of the name teams. You're really in bad shape in terms of getting to me. Because there is no way I have access to your abilities and talent, because there's no one advertising you.

JR: Do people ever send you demos directly?

RK: They do and it never gets to me. There's this box right outside my office door that they all go into. When it's full we go and get another box. People call and ask if I've listened to their CD; I tell them that not only have I not listened, I won't. My time is completely used up just listening to the music we actually are using in our films.

JR: What do you think are the elements of a good film score? What excites you about film music?

RK: One of the most wonderful things I was taught about film scoring is that the composer is the last writer on the film. I've always loved hearing that and feeling that the composer comes in to support dramatically, tragically, romantically, comedically, a film. A great film score first and foremost is a successful elevation of what's happening in the movie. An enhancement of the drama, gearing up of the suspense. So it's not musical attributes that you first look towards. Did he succeed in what he was asked to do? He was asked to make the film better. In a scene where the action or dialogue wasn't as cool as it could have been, the composer can make it cool. I've seen situations where the composer makes the movie a lot cooler than it was. So, did the composer write film music, which is a very special kind of music?

What excites me? I'm lucky. I get to be next to the greatest composers. Not only film composers, I just get to be with great composers. What excites me is going to a Hans Zimmer recording session, a James Newton Howard date, a Danny Elfman date. These guys are writing great music and working with great players. It's cool. You're hearing great music, which is always exciting.

JR: What do directors and producers look for in a composer?

RK: The flippant answer is: a mirror. They want someone who says yes and agrees with them and makes them look more famous. That's the greater bulk of directors. The more wonderful directors look for great sensibilities that make their pictures better. What the director should be looking for is a guy that has a big dial in his hand who can dial up all these wonderful kinds of emotions musically; tension, romance, lust, uncertainty, sadness. So a director should be looking for a guy who can put those into the score, like a quiver on his back of arrows of all those emotions that he can shoot at the screen.

One of the ways that film composers wipe out is when you get guys who are just rock musicians, who have never scored a film before, and they can't do it because they don't have all those different chops. They can write their own type of music, but when it needs to be a different kind of music, they say "I don't do that, man, that's not me." Great film composers can do it. They can write anything from boogie-woogie to orchestral, 19th century symphonic music, often in the same score. Those are the good guys. Directors look for someone who is complete.

JR: What mistakes do you see less experienced composers make?

RK: The first mistake they make is showing up for the job unprepared. The thing about being a film composer is you need to continually watch movies and learn about different musical solutions, because a film composer is a problem solver. The big mistake is when they say, "I've never really liked movie music, I haven't listened to a lot of movie music, but I'm ready to score a film." That occasionally happens. Even with some big rock stars I've had in here.

The other thing that I see is a composer more involved in their own musical expression than in expressing the film. It's a big error. They are hired by the director to express the film, not to say, "Hey a Hammond B3 is a cool instrument, I've always wanted to use one." Yeah, but it's a Western! You have to be egoless in a wonderful way to be a film composer. You're a musician, but you've got to support the film first.

JR: Do you listen along with the director to the demos that come from the agencies?

RK: Never. I'm aware of why I'm sending a particular guy's stuff and sometimes even know the scores myself. So I hope to God that what gets sent is appropriate. I get so much music there's just no way for me to keep up with it and still get my job done.

When the director gets real serious about the final two guys, then I listen to the CDs. But when we're submitting 15 CDs to a director, I don't really listen to any of them. It's a frustrating part of this job because it's so hard to actually find any time to listen to any music other than the hysterical topic that's in front of me that day.

JR: What do you think makes a composer successful?

RK: Attitude would be Number One. After that somewhere down the list is talent. The attitude of the composer is essential because he has to be political, strategic, flexible, amenable, humble, because he has a lot of idiots telling him what to do, all day long. He's the best musician in the room, and everybody's telling him how to work. But if he can survive a situation where the director is saying he doesn't like a cue, or a producer is saying, "Gee, I wouldn't put a snare drum on that," and someone from the studio says, "You know what, this should be much faster. I don't know why, but it feels like it should be faster," when the composer has created, as I've often seen, the exact right cue, then he's on the right track. The composer says to everybody, "Don't worry about it, I'll fix it!" Then I see I can work with this guy again, because I just saw him do exactly what he has to do to get the next job. After you see someone's got a great attitude, if they have great aptitude, the other component of attitude, then you know you've got a really successful composer on your hands. Because not only does he say he'll fix it, he fixes it. That's a wonderful combination. Attitude is essential, both for film composers and cab drivers.

JR: How has technology such as samplers, synthesizers, and home studios influenced the way movies are scored and the scores themselves?

RK: Great question. It's affected the way movies are scored 100%. You don't have to know how to read or write music to score films, something you had to know before, unless you were Charlie Chaplin and could hum a melody to a composer. You'd be what was called a "hummer." Now you can just put a video tape into a VCR, lock it up to your MIDI sequencer and score a film. You can score the entire film without anybody else in the room. I see it done all day long. You can lock up SMPTE, MIDI, variable clicks and make a lot of noise. And you don't need any real music education at all. You don't need to know how to write for timpani because you can sample timpani. You don't need to know how to write for a string orchestra because you can just dial it up on your Proteus.

The good news, in some ways, is that the technology has brought a very special skill, scoring motion pictures, to a much larger community. However, like many other aspects of music, technology has denigrated the quality of the music, because things that should be more difficult (snaps fingers) are done too rapidly and easily. Sequence it, loop it! The machine does a lot of work that a composer would otherwise need to dig in and do. With very few exceptions I can hear it in film scores—a lack of originality, a lack of development. I hear the loops, even if they're being played by an orchestra. I know when someone wrote the cue, cut and paste those four measures, transposed it up an octave, and they just play the same frigging notes again. And you think, "I wonder what sequencer they wrote that with—Logic or Performer?" I think it might remove an aspect of emotion to a very wonderful art.

JR: Do you think there are more good composers, now that there are more composers capable of scoring pictures?

RK: I think there are a lot of wonderful composers right now. I don't think there are ever that many really great composers, just like there aren't that many great writers or directors or actors. There are a few that are really good, and there are a lot that are OK. One thing I've started to realize is that people who are really successful and working all the time are usually really, really good. Funny thing! There's a reason that guys like Hans Zimmer are doing a lot of movies. He's a really good composer. He doesn't read or write. He's one example of somebody for whom technology has simply been there as a tool. He has uniquely not let it degenerate his originality. Getting Duane Eddy to play twang guitar on an action movie like *Broken Arrow!* He arrives at unique solutions—he does not let the technology control him.

I'm so relieved when somebody's good. It's not always the composer's fault when a score isn't the best. I feel badly for composers who are good but scoring projects that aren't so great. Hey, here's a word to all budding composers: try your best to get on a really great film. It'll make you look much better. When you end up on a mediocre film, you sound mediocre, whether you did a good job or not. Music just tends to sound about the way the picture looks. It's hard to have a great score on a bad movie. It happens occasionally, but try to get on a good picture. People might even think you're better than you really are!

JR: What do you think the chances are for a composer who is a good musician, but who doesn't use technology, to get into the world of film scoring?

RK: I would say it was like it was showing up at Wimbleton with a wooden racket. You can probably play, and be a hell of a tennis player, but everyone out there has Wilson titanium, and you've got to be Superman to compete. There's no reason in this day and age not to have music technology in your arsenal because of how much your sonic palette is increased.

JR: How do the film and television music worlds differ?

RK: Hugely. It's a very difficult thing to explain to people. It's a bit like film and television actors. If you are in one world, you will have trouble crossing over into the other one. Bruce Willis and George Clooney are a couple of the rare actors who have managed to go from TV to film. It's not dissimilar with television composers, of which there are many wonderful ones. But when you bring their name up for a film, directors most often say, "Can you get me a film guy?" I'll say wait a minute, this is a good composer—he just did some TV shows. "Yeah, but I want a film guy." Composers face this when starting out. They're offered TV work and they've got to take it because they've got to work. But sometimes it's difficult. Film and television music is different because TV music, with some exceptions, is episodic music. Stings, play-ons, play-offs, short cues. With film music you have the luxury of bigger budgets and longer cues you would rarely get in a TV show. The budgets are quite different, making it a different kind of assignment.

JR: How do the film score world and the pop music world influence each other?

RK: Before I answer that, I just want to say that the grass is never greener—and everyone thinks it is. Film guys really want to write pop songs, make pop records, sell records as pop artists, and be pop stars. And lots of pop guys want to write for films. To the pop writers out there, I say film music is a really, really special area that, unless you know what you're doing, don't come near it. I for one will eat you alive. If you show up with A A B A song structure for every cue, if you don't know how to write anything if it isn't to a click, and you think of the cues all as little songs, because that's what pop guys so often do, there will be a big problem. It's a completely different approach. My favourite pitch is, "Hey man, I've written a song for my record, but I'm not going to put lyrics on it 'cause it sounds like MOVIE MUSIC to me. Do you think you could put it in a movie? Or maybe you could put me in line for scoring a film, because it sounds like I'm writing MOVIE MUSIC." What is movie music? What does movie music sound like?

Film and pop music influence each other mostly in commercial ways. Soundtrack records with pop music on them sell far more than albums of just score. Do they influence each other musically? I don't think so. Except for some trends now in film scores that try to be ersatz hip-hop or techno. More of a pop soundtrack vibe in the score itself. Beach movies in the sixties did the same thing with their scores, trying to be as much like the current style of pop music as possible.

JR: How do you think film scores have changed in the last few years?

RK: I wish I could tell you they've gotten more interesting. Film scores have changed by getting relegated to the wrong end of the bus as songs have taken more and more precedence. As the head of music for a motion picture studio I should be doing what Alfred and Lionel Newman, my fabulous, brilliant ancestors in this gig did—concentrate on film music. Great film scores, great underscores, great arrangements for scenes, that's what these guys did all day. They sat in this very office during the day, and at night went to the Fox scoring stage and conducted or wrote some great film music. It's an incredible concept to me. I spend most of my time making sure that Jewel, Leann Rimes, or the Smashing Pumpkins are happy with where their song is, how much money they're being paid, or whether their song is going to be used?

So the song portion of film scores is taking precedence over the film scoring part, which is where we've come to at present. Why? Because everyone's so concerned with getting a song onto VH-1 and MTV for their movie. So film scores have shrunk in importance.

JR: Is the film score dying?

RK: No, it's too important an art form. It'll roar back when a big score comes out. John Williams and James Horner do a lot for film scoring when they write big film scores that people go out and buy. I spend a lot of time being sure that film composers and film scores don't get overlooked. And yet, it's hard to do. They say, "Oh yeah, the score." Thirty-eight minutes of underscore between the sixteen songs they've stuffed in. I'm actually in a place where, after making about 28 soundtrack records in just four years, I'm trying to make very specific soundtrack records for specific films, and make *score* movies again. I think the soundtrack market is glutted. And films just need great underscores. It's not about some hip band's song in the film.

JR: You don't think people go to see a movie that has a song by a major pop artist?

RK: Once in a while they do, but it's very rare. They'll do it if a Whitney Houston is in the movie, and a big hit song shows up eight weeks before the film opens. They've seen the video, heard the song, and now want to complete the whole media experience. Same with *Romeo & Juliet*. Did people go to see *Matrix* because of a Korn song in there? I don't know. They may have bought the record after they saw it, but it's just part of the whole mix of the film's appeal. Do people go and see the movie just because they heard a song they liked? That's the fantasy of every film marketing person.

Waiting To Exhale is an interesting example. The timing of everything worked out, and yes, the song "Exhale Shoop Shoop" sung by Whitney Houston, the number one diva at that moment, was the number one single in the country on the Friday that the movie came out. Did that help the movie? Everyone here seemed to think so. I got a lot of pats on the back. Boy, was I a lucky guy. The movie's release date had been moved back four weeks which let it work out perfectly with the song's radio play.

JR: I've noticed how much influence techno music is having on film scores at the moment. And there also seems to be a trend to work with European DJs with little or no film score experience as opposed to using film composers to work in that style.

RK: I have very specific opinions on that. We're doing a picture now with a fellow named Pete Tong, probably the number one DJ in England right now. He's putting together the entire soundtrack for the film. Not actually scoring the film, but working on the soundtrack as a whole, including working with one or more composers. This sort of thing is showing up all around me on a number of projects. And it's given me some perspective.

Those musical approaches have certain limits for me. They are all sequenced, and at one tempo. In most film music there is a flow to the scenes where the music can change in any way it wants to. When I was a song writer, I had a hard time thinking in terms of music that could change so much—have themes go away for a while, speed up or slow down. I always thought "songically." I see these guys with their sequencers writing cues that are always one tempo, or the electronic and techno stuff that stays at one tempo throughout the scene and I think, "Hey, get me out of this tempo! The scene has changed!" So there is a limit to what techno music can do in film, and I think it will play itself out only because after a while those kind of cues don't wrap themselves around a film. They just lay there. In a fight scene, like in *Matrix,* it's cool. But in other more emotional scenes with the need for underscore, it doesn't hold up.

At the same time, there are projects we are doing at the moment that I am absolutely loving musically. We are doing a film right now with the Dust Brothers that is fantastic. It's amazing how well it is working in so much of the film. However, I am still drawn to the fact that the tempos never change. But it works in a cool, contrapuntal way. With the DJ I mentioned, I don't know that it works as well. There are beats going all the time, and sometimes I just wish they'd shut off the drum machine for a minute! But he doesn't know how to do that, and the director wanted to explore that, so it's fine to give it a shot. With the Dust Brothers, it works so well because it's so appropriate to the movie. We'll see. It'll all change.

JR: Let me ask you something a bit more mundane. How are film score budgets made?

RK: They're created at the very end of budgeting of the entire motion picture, and they think, "Oh, we have to throw something in for music," and they throw in an inappropriately low amount. Then I have to go in and say, "Wrong!" That's how they are created. They are not thought out at all. They are thrown in as an afterthought. Even on more musical pictures. If a picture costs $12 million, they ask, "Can we do the music for $400,000?" If a movie has a $60 million dollar budget, they ask, "Can we do the music for $750,000?" And that's just how many people go about it.

1.5 percent to 2 percent of the film's overall budget used to be the rule for music budgets. Now it's just these little numbers that have no relationship to the film's budget, and I am expected to sign off on these. So I end up having to get into some arguments with the guys in production or the executive producers on these films and say, "What are you thinking?" I had one this morning about a beautiful, wonderful new Fox film. I was asked to sign off on its music budget, and I had to say I wouldn't do it because the music couldn't be done for that amount of money.

I sign off on every budget for every film. I basically have to guarantee that for each film, the score can and will be delivered as promised with top quality music and production. If a film has musical scenes where people are singing or dancing on screen, or someone is singing "Love Me Tender" in the shower, or calls for a big orchestral score, and the budget is $200,000, then I have to say, "On which planet are you planning to score this film?"! That doesn't even come close. It barely covers the fees of most of the better composers, and then you have to add all the expenses of recording, licensing, and musicians. And the producers will almost always say to me, "But all the people on this film are so passionate about it and are cutting their prices." And I say, "All the other people are not composers!" For the kinds of composers they want, cutting their price might mean going from $900,000 down to $750,000 because they love you and they'll take it out of my hide down the road somewhere!"

So budgets are not created scientifically. They are just tossed out there. Aren't sausages made from all the scraps and bits that are left over? Well, that's pretty close to the state of film budgets right now. There is always the hope that sound track album deals with the various record labels will make up for the deficiencies of the budgets. I keep having to say that we can't do that any more. It's too risky. Budgets have gone down lately, in direct proportion to how movie stars' fees are rising. This is not a coincidence. People go to the movies to see Leonardo DiCaprio, Tom Cruise, and Jim Carey. They are not going, unfortunately, because it features a wonderful score by Ennio Morricone. So there isn't the budget to hire someone like Morricone a lot of times.

JR: What advice do you give to a talented composer who goes to the movies and says, "That's what I want to do!"

RK: The flippant answer I give to people is somewhat of a riddle. I say, "Give up." I figure that since everyone always told me to give up when I wanted to be a songwriter, that if you really want it, you'll ignore me. I say it with all due respect. You have to be incredibly passionate. You can't just want to do it, you *have* to do it. You can't live without it.

The other advice I give is that, unlike other types of music, in film scoring you must be proficient both musically and technically. So study is not out of the question. In pop music you can get off the bus with five strings out of six working on your guitar, strum away, write a couple of cool songs, and get a shot at a record deal. People do it without necessarily playing an instrument all that well with just a lot of personality, charisma, and sex appeal. That doesn't go very far in the very specific arena of film composing, which is a technical as well as musical and artistic skill.

I had to hunt down someone to teach me about click tracks. Now there are a lot of schools all around the country teaching film music. You need to study, watch movies, stand next to composers, apprentice to composers, and learn as much as you can so when the day comes when you get the big call you have a clue what to do. It happened to me. I was studying at UCLA and I got a call to have a meeting with Francis Ford Coppola. And I could say in the meeting, "When's the spotting session?" Because I had a class where they taught me what a spotting session was. I felt so important! So you've got to learn all that stuff, because you'll need it. The competition is fierce! And there'll be a lot of other composers standing right next to you who have studied hard.

And continue the therapy, because you need a good attitude when you get there.

The Day The Earth Didn't Stand Still

T his book is based on columns which I've written for *Keyboard* magazine about my professional experiences as a musician here in the City of Angels. I came across one column that didn't fit into the topics here, but that I felt needed to be included. It concerned an experience so overwhelming as to defy comparison with anything I've done before or since. It is about my experience of the "Northridge" earthquake here in Los Angeles in 1994. At the time I lived only a few miles from the epicenter of the quake, which was one of the strongest to hit the area in decades. It left a lasting impression, to say the least. I included it to add an important perspective to everything in the Reel World.

It started with a sound. A low, visceral noise like a train both distant and right in your face. Then came the shaking. It began very small and then crescendoed to unbelievable proportions. There is no other feeling like it. The real terror of the earth shaking is in that crescendo. Will it continue to grow, or is this the apex of its violence? I heard the sounds of glass shattering throughout my house, of objects hitting the floor and breaking. It was like someone holding a half-empty matchbox in their hands and shaking it as hard as possible. The sound of the house and its holdings mixed with the thundering sound of the earth itself.

If it grows more, when will the house come crashing down on me? For a few brief moments at 4:31 AM on January 17th, I was asking myself this question. I'm still alive now, but how much more will there be? I waited a second more and asked the questions again. In the meantime, there was a need for action. I ran through the pitch dark (all the lights went off in a brief blue flash) with my wife to get to our infant daughter, who had no protection or recourse from the shaking. When we got to her in the next room, the sound and the shaking begin to subside. We were still standing. In all of that, our girl never awakened until we picked her up. She must have wondered what the whole commotion was; she just wanted to go back to sleep.

Then silence and darkness. I put on shoes, got a flashlight and walked around the house. It looked as though everything that could fall had fallen. There was broken glass everywhere from pictures that had leaped from the walls. Bookshelves had emptied onto the floor. Along with the books were candlesticks, and other small glass and ceramic mementos. I found some of my collection of rare, handmade ceramic flutes on the floor. The only one that had broken was one my late grandmother brought me from Czechoslovakia. It was the last material thing of hers I still had. Now she is just in my memory.

A few aftershocks hit, and each time my heart would leap into my throat and every muscle in my body would tense. I would run back to my wife to be sure she was coping all right, but it made me feel better to see her as well. After the shocks subsided, I wanted to get to my music studio to see the bad news. I knew there would be problems. On the way, I went into the kitchen to find that at least some of our dishes and glasses decided to stay on their shelves. There were broken glasses on the floor along with all our spices and other pantry items.

I gritted my teeth and walked into my studio. The first thing I could see was that my big speakers were gone. I tried to get to where they would be behind my mixer, but piles of DATs, videos and CDs blocked the path. I peered over my mixer to see that my speakers had toppled to the floor, pulling several other wires with them. I scanned the rest of the room with the flashlight, and couldn't believe it. Except for books, tapes, and disks heaped onto the floor, everything looked OK. I pulled all of the plugs out of the wall sockets. Whenever power would get restored to my neighborhood (and who knows how long that could take), it could be erratic and potentially damaging to any electronic equipment plugged in at the time.

Another aftershock. I made my way through the mess back to the bedroom to see that everything was still alright. The aftershocks were still very intense, so I took down the few remaining pictures that were still on the walls. I went outside for the first time to get a portable radio from my car. I saw beams of light coming from the other flashlights of my neighbors. We quietly stood together in the street, then asking each other if everyone was unharmed, and what damage each has taken to our houses and things. Fortunately, everyone made it through unhurt, but with varying amounts of damage to their property.

I was not prepared for what I saw when I looked up into the sky. In LA, because of the bright city lights, you can't see too many stars. On this night, there were more stars than I had ever seen in my life. It was breathtakingly beautiful, all thanks to the fact that the electricity was gone for miles in every direction. The city was completely dark. Were I in a better frame of mind, I would have stayed and stared at the sky for a long, long time.

With flashlight and radio, I scanned around the outside of my house, but found no cracks, broken glass or other outward signs of damage. Then I noticed that the long cement block wall between a neighbor and me had mostly toppled. Most radio stations were off the air, but one all-news AM station was already discussing the event. It was a big quake centered in the area of Los Angeles where I lived at the time. Later announcements calculated the center of the quake to be less than ten miles from my house. It was strong enough that it had awakened people hundreds of miles away. Freeways had collapsed, buildings had fallen or were no longer safe for inhabitants. Most of the area was without water, gas or electricity. People were missing. There were fires. This was serious.

I went back inside and tried to call some members of my family. At first there was no phone service. But within an hour, my phone rang. I was able to contact my family and a few friends. Thankfully, everyone was shaken (pun intended), but all right.

By 7AM the sun started coming up. I have never been so glad to see the dawn in my life. In the light of day, the mess that now was my house didn't seem quite so bad. Though we were asked to not drive if not essential, I checked in with a few other friends who lived near the epicenter of the quake. Most of the phone lines were still down. With no electricity, our options were simple and limited. We went for a walk in our neighborhood to see how all our other neighbors were doing. Most people were out in front of their homes or in the street talking with other neighbors. People we had never met would come up to us and ask how we were, and how our baby and house fared. I realized that unlike anything else I had experienced, this was a common shared event in the lives of every single person I saw that day. This quake hit us all, regardless of income, profession, religion, or lifestyle. We were all in this together, we all made it, and now we all were facing the prospects of recovering from the damage. But the surprising theme of the day was "Well, at least WE are all OK." There was compassion and pathos like I had never seen in a big city, and not just in my immediate neighborhood. I drove to check on some friends I couldn't reach, and while stopping in those neighborhoods it was the same thing. Strangers walking up to strangers to say hello, to ask how they got through it, to share their story and to express "at least we're here to talk about it!".

To my surprise, by the end of that day most of us had our electricity back. We saw the amazing amount of damage on the TV news. For several days we had to boil water intended for drinking or washing food, due to damage in the water treatment plants nearby. It took several more days for electricity, water and gas to be restored to the rest of the area, but the speed at which the healing had begun was astonishing. We HAD made it. Some of our friends lost their houses, their job places or both, but they were all fine. However, not everyone made it. Over 50 people lost their lives to this disaster, which lasted all of about 15 seconds.

Why write about all of this? Priorities. Not just mine, but all of ours. The musical world that I've written about is of great importance to you and me. This world holds the tools, techniques and opportunities with which we express ourselves. But if you lost everything you owned in the next 15 seconds, what would be important then? It is the same as what is important right now—that you're here to read this and I'm here to write it. That's important. That's who we are. The rest is simply what we *do*, and what tools we might use to do it. After the event, the local papers were filled with information on how to be prepared for the next big quake.

How do you prepare for an earthquake or any other kind of natural disaster? You protect those things that are most valuable in your life; make sure that your friends and loved ones know how you feel about them, and get a good insurance policy for your music gear. Think of such disasters as God's way of telling you that you own too much stuff!

Finally, I'll add that while this book by no means represents an exhaustive look at making film music or developing a film music career, I hope you'll take at least some of it to heart and apply it toward your own personal goals. Good luck out there. Frankly, now that I've written all this, I think I need to go over some of it myself and do better. See you there.

⊘ Thinking in Reel Time

Computer sequencers able to display and synchronize to SMPTE or EBU timecode can be used to calculate certain timecode problems. For example, if you need to start a cue a bit earlier, you may choose to add a measure to the beginning of your sequence. It should be simple to slide your music over one measure and add something into measure 1. But you also need to figure out the new start time of your cue so that everything stays in sync with the picture. Most sequencers will display the corresponding timecode for any measure and beat entered into the sequencer's locator. By entering a bar number of "0," the sequencer will display the new start time for the sequence.

But reel changes are a more complex matter that may require you to make a quick calculation if your music must run across two reels. When a film is edited in shorter, non-"tied" reels, it is possible to have music cross between reels when going from an odd numbered reel to an even numbered one. Music should not cross between reels going from an even numbered reel to an odd numbered one. All of this has to do with editing and projection issues not yet solved by digital technology. Each reel's number is also used as the hour value for the timecode on that reel, thus the timecode on reel 1 begins at 01:00:00:00 and the timecode on reel 7 begins at 07:00:00:00 (though a few editors skip the first six or eight seconds of each reel).

So when your music must cross the boundary from one reel to another, the timecode makes a numeric leap which no timecode synchronizer can track. The solution is to have two copies of the cue: one that will play over the end of the first reel, and one that plays over the top of the second reel. The only difference will be the SMPTE start time of the sequences. Here is an example of how to calculate an offset that will allow both sequences to be in sync.

Sequence Start: 03:09:11:04

Last Frame of Reel: 03:11:04:25

Subtract "sequence start" from last frame of the reel. Keep in mind that frames are numbered 0 to 29. To make the above calculation you need to "borrow" thirty frames from the "seconds" column, making the frames calculation 34-25=09. The rest of the calculation is pretty simple:

03:11:04:25

- 03:09:11:04

= 00:01:52:09

Finally, the result of this calculation (which is the amount of time of the cue in the first reel) is subtracted from the First Frame of Action of the second reel. Assuming the reel starts right at 04:00:00:00, you do the following:

04:00:00:00

- 00:01:52:09

= 03:58:07:21

Copy the sequence, enter this new start time, and the sequence will synchronize with the rest of the picture exactly as it will when the reels are joined in the final film.

Orchestral Instrument Ranges
and Transpositions of Popular Instruments

*(Transposing instruments are marked *)*

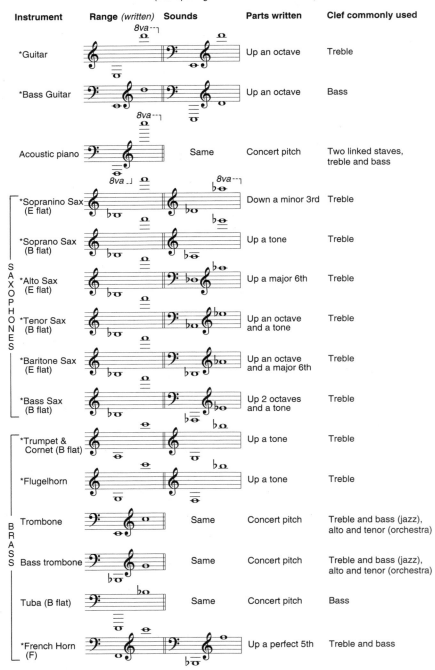

Instrument	Range *(written)*	Sounds	Parts written	Clef commonly used
*Guitar			Up an octave	Treble
*Bass Guitar			Up an octave	Bass
Acoustic piano		Same	Concert pitch	Two linked staves, treble and bass
*Sopranino Sax (E flat)			Down a minor 3rd	Treble
*Soprano Sax (B flat)			Up a tone	Treble
*Alto Sax (E flat)			Up a major 6th	Treble
*Tenor Sax (B flat)			Up an octave and a tone	Treble
*Baritone Sax (E flat)			Up an octave and a major 6th	Treble
*Bass Sax (B flat)			Up 2 octaves and a tone	Treble
*Trumpet & Cornet (B flat)			Up a tone	Treble
*Flugelhorn			Up a tone	Treble
Trombone		Same	Concert pitch	Treble and bass (jazz), alto and tenor (orchestra)
Bass trombone		Same	Concert pitch	Treble and bass (jazz), alto and tenor (orchestra)
Tuba (B flat)		Same	Concert pitch	Bass
*French Horn (F)			Up a perfect 5th	Treble and bass

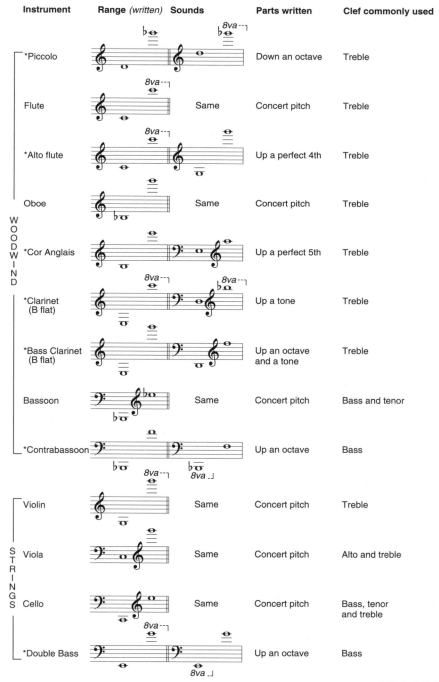

Instrument	Range *(written)*	Sounds	Parts written	Clef commonly used
*Piccolo			Down an octave	Treble
Flute		Same	Concert pitch	Treble
*Alto flute			Up a perfect 4th	Treble
Oboe		Same	Concert pitch	Treble
*Cor Anglais			Up a perfect 5th	Treble
*Clarinet (B flat)			Up a tone	Treble
*Bass Clarinet (B flat)			Up an octave and a tone	Treble
Bassoon		Same	Concert pitch	Bass and tenor
*Contrabassoon			Up an octave	Bass
Violin		Same	Concert pitch	Treble
Viola		Same	Concert pitch	Alto and treble
Cello		Same	Concert pitch	Bass, tenor and treble
*Double Bass			Up an octave	Bass

WOODWIND

STRINGS

Instrument	Range (written)	Sounds	Parts written	Clef commonly used
*Celeste			Down an octave	Treble
*Glockenspiel			Down 2 octaves	Treble
*Xylophone			Down an octave	Treble
Marimba		Same	Concert pitch	Bass and treble
Bass Marimba		Same	Concert pitch	Bass and treble
Vibraphone		Same	Concert pitch	Treble
Tubular Bells		Same	Concert pitch	Treble
Timpani		Same	Concert pitch	Bass
Harp		Same	Concert pitch	Two linked staves, treble and bass
Harpsichord		Same	Concert pitch	Two linked staves, treble and bass
*Chapman Stick (10 string)			Up an octave	Treble and bass

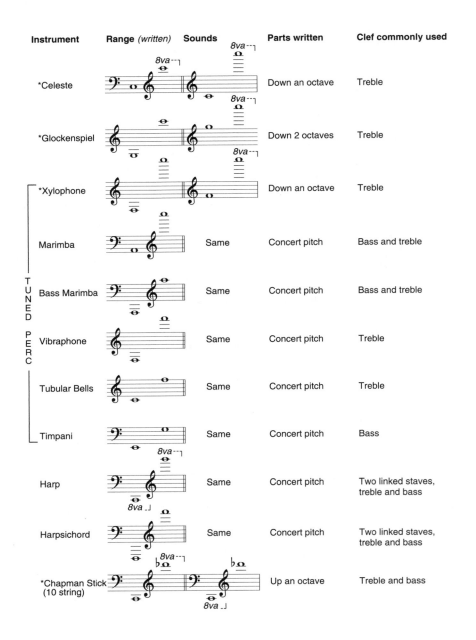

Excerpted from *Inside the Music* by Dave Stewart, © 1999 Dave Stewart. Published by Miller Freeman Books. ISBN 0-87930-571-1.

For More Information: www.backbeatbooks.com.

Resources

The Hollywood Reporter
Subscribe: (323) 525-2000
www.hollywoodreporter.com

Daily Variety
Subscribe (818) 487-4554
www.dailyvariety.com

Both of the above entertainment industry trade journals have annual special film and television music issues, which include names and contact information of leading music recourses such as agencies, music supervisors, studio executives and more. They also list current films in production on a weekly basis.

Lone Eagle Press
http://www.loneeagle.com/
a number of useful resource books for the film community

http://www.filmmusic.net/
the film music network—an excellent resource for all things related to film music

ASMAC (American Society Of Musicians and Composers) is a service, educational and fraternal organization of professional arrangers and composers working in commercial music, primarily for films, television, recordings and theater. ASMAC has a long history in Hollywood, beginning with its founding in 1938.

Membership information:
(818) 994-4661, email: info@asmac.org

The Guild of Canadian Film Composers
Box 291, 275 King Street East, Toronto, ON M5A 1K2
Tel (416) 484-4091; Fax (416) 484-7409
e-mail: gcfc@gcfc.ca
URL: www.gcfc.ca

The Guild of Canadian Film Composers is a national association of professional composers and music producers for film, television, and new media. The Guild's purpose is to further the interests of its members with respect to Canada's cultural industries and agencies, film producers and music publishers.

IFP
Information: (310/475-4379, ext. 53)

The Independent Feature Project is a not-for-profit service organization dedicated to providing resources, information and avenues of communication for its members: independent filmmakers, industry professionals and independent film enthusiasts. It is committed to the idea that independent film is an important art form and a powerful voice in our society.

The IFP provides services to independent filmmakers with varying levels of experience, assisting them in expressing their unique points of view. It facilitates a connection between the creative and business communities. Other goals of the organization are to expand and educate the audience for independent film, and to encourage the diversity and quality of independent production.

SCL (www.filmscore.org)

The Society of Composers & Lyricists is committed to advancing the interests of the film and television music community. Toward this end, the SCL:

1. Disseminates information concerning the creative and business aspects of writing music and lyrics for film and television;

2. Presents educational seminars to provide the SCL membership with the latest technological information affecting our industry;

3. Seeks to enhance the workplace and working conditions in order to maintain the highest level of quality in our crafts;

4. Encourages a sense of community and the sharing of experience and knowledge among our membership and related organizations worldwide;

5. Provides opportunities for dialog and the exchange of information between our membership and filmmakers;

6. Establishes forums where issues confronting the film music industry can be openly examined and debated.

The creation of scores and songs for motion pictures, television, and other media involves unique skills and presents special challenges. The SCL assumes a central role in helping composers and lyricists achieve their full career potential in a demanding and ever-changing field.

ASCAP

Information:
ASCAP Building,
One Lincoln Plaza,
New York, New York 10023
800-95-ASCAP
www.ascap.com

ASCAP is the American Society of Composers, Authors and Publishers, a membership association of over 100,000 composers, songwriters, lyricists and music publishers. ASCAP's function is to protect the rights of its members by licensing and paying royalties for the public performances of their copyrighted works.

ASCAP is the only American performing rights organization whose Board of Directors consists solely of member composers, songwriters and music publishers elected by the membership. The 24-member Board meets regularly to set policy and actively guide all aspects of the society's business. In addition, there are 18 Board committees providing oversight and direction to management in various areas of ASCAP's operation.

BMI

Information:

320 West 57th Street

New York, NY 10019-3790

(212) 586-2000

8730 Sunset Blvd.

3rd Flr West

West Hollywood, CA 90069-2211

(310) 659-9109

10 Music Square East

Nashville, TN 37203-4399

(615) 401-2000

www.bmi.com

BMI is an American performing rights organization that represents more than 250,000 songwriters, composers and music publishers. The company collects license fees on behalf of those American creators it represents, as well as for the thousands of creators from around the world who have chosen BMI for U.S. representation. The fees for the "public performances" of its repertoire of more than 4.5 million compositions—including radio airplay, broadcast and cable television carriage, Internet and live and recorded performances by all other users of music—are then distributed as royalties to the writers and copyright holders it represents.

INDEX

FROM THE PUBLISHER OF VIDEOGRAPHY

From the studios of Hollywood to the lofts of Manhattan, filmmakers at every level are discovering the creative power and economic advantages of **DIGITAL CINEMA**.

New camera, recording, postproduction, distribution, and projection technologies are making **DIGITAL CINEMA** the choice of filmmakers, studios, and theater owners around the world.

DIGITAL CINEMA is also the name of a new magazine to serve this dynamic new market.

DIGITAL CINEMA is for every digital moviemaker, from the highest-end Hollywood producers, directors, and DP's to the smallest independents.

DIGITAL CINEMA is for every postproduction and computer graphics facility working in electronic cinema, HD, and digital effects for theatrical and television movies.

DIGITAL CINEMA is the professional journal of the new age of moviemaking, chronicling the multifaceted transition of film from an analog medium to the most powerful and compelling form of high-resolution digital communication.

DIGITAL CINEMA is written by professionals for professionals, and provides leading-edge advertisers with a unique vehicle with which to reach an expanding new industry.

For more information about **DIGITAL CINEMA** contact Brian McKernan at (212) 378-0414 or bmckernan@uemedia.com. To advertise in **DIGITAL CINEMA** contact Joe Palombo at (212) 378-0496 or jpalombo@uemedia.com.

DIGITAL CINEMA is a product of UNITED ENTERTAINMENT MEDIA, publishers of VIDEOGRAPHY, SURROUND SOUND PROFESSIONAL, and other magazines for digital content creation professionals.

Editorial Contact: Brian McKernan, Editorial Director (Video Division) Tel: 212-378-0414, Email: bmckernan@uemedia.com

Sales Contacts: Joe Palombo, Group Publisher: Tel: 212-378-0496 Email: jpalombo@uemedia.com

East Coast and Midwest: 212-378-0400 • Northern California: 530-893-0217 • Southern California: 310-396-9554 • Facility Ads: 818-886-7586

460 Park Avenue South, Ninth Floor, New York, NY 10016
voice: 212-378-0400 • fax: 212-378-2160